Cheats at Work

Cheats at Work

An Anthropology of Workplace Crime

GERALD MARS

London
GEORGE ALLEN & UNWIN
Boston   Sydney

George Allen & Unwin (Publishers) Ltd,
40 Museum Street, London WC1A 1LU, UK

George Allen & Unwin (Publishers) Ltd,
Park Lane, Hemel Hempstead, Herts HP2 4TE, UK

Allen & Unwin, Inc.,
9 Winchester Terrace, Winchester, Mass 01890, USA

George Allen & Unwin Australia Pty Ltd,
8 Napier Street, North Sydney, NSW 2060, Australia

First published in 1982

British Library Cataloguing in Publication Data

Mars, Gerald
   Cheats at work.
1. Commercial crimes—Social aspects—Great Britain
I. Title
364.1'62   HV6771.G7
ISBN 0-04-301151-9

Library of Congress Cataloging in Publication Data

Mars, Gerald.
   Cheats at work.
1. White collar crimes.   I. Title.
HV6768.M26 1982   364.1'68   82-11666
ISBN 0-04-301151-9

Set in 11 on 13 point Garamond by Computape (Pickering) Ltd, North Yorkshire
and printed in Great Britain by Mackays of Chatham

Foreword

The hidden, shadow, secret, irregular, or black economy is a subject of perennial fascination and a rich vein of anecdote. It is also becoming a focus of official concern and serious research. Wild estimates of its extent and growth are giving way to systematic, discriminating and so far frustrated attempts to measure what is necessarily elusive and concealed. Though personal impressions and the experience of revenue officials point towards a significant growth, there is no firm statistical evidence and professional economists remain sceptical as to its importance. As one put it: 'So everybody knows a plumber.'

It is at this point that one has to turn to the work of sociologists, anthropologists and historians. Their message is that the practices of the hidden economy are nothing new; that they are not exceptional but endemic; that they are not marginal but integral to the organisation and rewards of work; that they involve serious moral ambiguities; and that they have industrial, social and political implications of which anyone who wants to control or discourage them ought to be aware.

Gerald Mars has spent many years investigating a variety of industrial milieux from docklands to hotels, and has demonstrated the importance of paying close attention to the ways in which work and rewards are handled in different settings. In this book he brings together both the fruits of his own studies and those of his fellow pioneers, particularly Stuart Henry and Jason Ditton, in a general framework which provides a neat and helpful means to understanding the motives, opportunities and consequences of fiddling in different occupations. As he argues in the second part of the book, his analysis of the moral economy of fiddling and of the total reward system is of direct practical relevance to those concerned with industrial relations and with the character of our economic institutions more generally. The more speculative conclusions of his final chapters challenge those who condemn fiddling to consider how the energy, ingenuity and initiative which it reveals can be harnessed or released in respectable ways.

At a time when social science comes in for much abuse, it is well to be reminded how much hard-headed practical men of business may learn from a detached, alert and empathetic observer about the world through which they blunder, the slaves of some defunct economist.

James Cornford

Contents

Acknowledgements

If too many cooks do indeed spoil the broth, I hope that this cannot be said of books. In any case there have been a lot of helpers who, I believe, have added to the flavour of this particular broth, though the final responsibility for its taste must be mine.

First, the Nuffield Foundation generously and riskily funded my early ventures into this area with a two-year fellowship that took me to the Cambridge University Institute of Criminology. Professor Richard Sparkes not only arranged my entry to the Institute, but also supported and encouraged early ventures into what was then a relatively strange field for an anthropologist. Professor Nigel Walker and his staff at the Institute were highly supportive during the tenure of my fellowship and it is a pleasure to record my thanks.

Robyn Wallis of BBC–TV early saw the media possibilities of fiddling and in devising and arranging a *Man Alive* programme, 'On the Fiddle', first projected my ideas to a wider audience. One result was a commission by Jill Norman, then an editor at Penguin Books, to write a book about them. This book, albeit with a different publisher, directly follows from that sequence.

As in cooking, so in authorship – different ingredients come from different sources. My agent, Frances Kelly, has proved invaluable in sorting out the various administrative and organisational quagmires into which an author can fall. The same role of creative administrator has been taken up at Middlesex Polytechnic by Alf Holt, the Dean of Social Sciences, whose ingenious, unorthodox and unflagging attempts to further social science research at Middlesex are now bearing fruit.

Many of the ideas in this book derive from others. The overall intellectual debt that I owe Professor Mary Douglas will be obvious to fellow anthropologists but working through her ideas on grid group analysis when applied to occupations has been helped by the time and ideas of many others – too many, alas, to mention.

Mention must be made, however, of colleagues and friends at the Centre for Occupational and Community Research at the Middlesex Polytechnic and particularly of David Binns, Michael Nicod, Ronald Stansfield, Steve Rayner, Ken Saunders and Nigel South, whose help and continuously available criticisms and support have been highly valued. My special thanks must, however, go to Stuart Henry who as colleague, friend and collaborator over several years has contributed not only to the form and style of this book but also to its ideas. Much of Chapter 7 derives directly from his work and it was he who suggested the names of the animal categories I use. The book would have been less easy to read as well as less worth reading without his enthusiastic advice.

As well as ideas, a book like this needs data – and though the fiddlers who so readily told me their reasons, motives and methods, would prefer to be anonymous, they after all provided the raw material with which I worked. I am extremely grateful, therefore, for the generous responses of so many people who had little reason to help a prying stranger.

At different times and in different places, Jason Ditton, Peter Mitchell, Richard Jenkins, Roger Venables, Harold Bridger, J. S. Grimshaw, James Cornford and David White have all made inputs of different kinds. Some of these have involved the continuous retyping of drafts and this has been carried out by Daphne Clench and Shirley Webb, whose almost inexhaustible patience has been much appreciated.

Finally, my wife, Valerie Mars, has provided the most constant support. In this venture she has not only advised, discussed and argued about aspects of the book, but has been assiduous in collecting cases and talking them through. Like everything I do, this is a shared work.

Introduction: Cheats at Work

What This Book Is About

This is a book about crime at work. It is not, however, about crime in the normal sense. First, most of the 'criminals' do not regard what they are doing as remotely blameworthy and secondly, they appear in all respects to be no different from other people. And nor are they – since self-report studies show that between 75 and 92 per cent of us regularly add to our incomes in ways that are technically against the law (Cort, 1959; Horning, 1970; Laird, 1950; Zeitlin, 1971).

More recent studies have argued that occupational crime is characteristic of a whole range of occupations (Henry, 1978, 1981), while intensive studies of particular occupations (e.g. Ditton, 1977a) have confirmed the findings of earlier self-reports. What has yet to be done, however, is to distinguish *types* of occupational crime and to link these to *types* of occupation. That is the principal purpose of this volume.

This book, then, is about the normal crimes of normal people in the normal circumstance of their work – what has been called 'part-time crime' (Ditton, 1977a) – and its implications. It is not concerned with the spectacular or the one-off crime, but with activities that are an accepted part of everyday jobs.

None the less, the extent and variety of these activities are astonishing. The range of description alone indicates their extent. In England one speaks of 'pilfering' and 'the fiddle', in the USA it is called 'skimming' or 'gypping', in France *le travail noir* and in the Soviet Union it is known as *rabotat nalyevo*, which means 'on the left'. These terms are not exact synonyms. Indeed, the complexity of these activities is such that no one word or phrase can convey the scope and ingenuity they involve. In English there are also words such as 'moonlighting', 'tax evasion' and 'perks'. Although almost everyone is aware of them, and although the majority of us fiddle

1

in one way or another, fiddling is still considered a trivial activity without serious implications. This view needs to be challenged.

My main emphasis will be on the study of occupations and on the hidden benefits normally obtainable in them – what I have called elsewhere their 'covert reward systems' (Mars and Mitchell, 1976). These aspects of occupations are discussed in Part One, where I have divided all jobs into four categories: hawks, donkeys, wolves and vultures. The jobs placed in each category will be found to possess structural characteristics in common and to exhibit broadly similar arrangements to rob, cheat, short-change, pilfer and fiddle customers, employers, subordinates and the state.

Hawks, like their feathered counterparts, are individualists. They perch unhappily in organisations; when in them they tend to bend the rules to suit themselves. These are the entrepreneurs, the innovative professionals and the small businessmen. Their aim is 'to make it'.

Donkeys are people highly constrained by rules who are also isolated from each other. Some transport workers are donkeys – their jobs isolate them and they are dominated by rules governing safety; so are supermarket cashiers and machine-minders, both highly constrained and isolated. The response of donkeys is to resist often by breaking the rules – to sabotage the systems that constrain them – or to fiddle. When they do the effects can be highly disruptive.

Wolves, on the other hand, work – and steal – in packs. Dockwork gangs are good examples: they have hierarchy, order and internal controls. When they pilfer they do so according to agreed rules and through a well-defined division of labour. Like real-life wolves, they know who is their leader and who are the led – and they penalise their own deviants.

Vultures need the support of a group but act on their own when at the feast. Travelling salesmen are vultures – so too are waiters – linked and supported as they are from a common base, depending on information and support from colleagues, but competitive and acting in isolation for much of their work. Because vultures show a paradoxical combination of competition and the need for co-

2

operation, their groupings, as might be expected, are unstable and sometimes turbulent.

The fiddled benefits obtained within these groupings (unlisted in audits and unmentioned in official statistics on incomes), far from being the exceptional activity of the minority, are an integral aspect of all the occupations they include. They are indeed the shadow side of conventional economic transactions. It is because *regular* fiddling affects the incomes and life-styles of so many people that it has to be studied, discussed and understood by anyone trying to set out a description of an economy, to establish a policy for assessing industrial performance, or to institute economic, technical, or organisational change.

This is why the implications of covert rewards go well beyond the study of occupations. We find that some occupations are so fiddle-prone, for instance, that the workings of whole sectors of the economy cannot be understood unless these aspects of reward are taken into account. It is impossible to explain industrial relations in much of the personal services sector, for example, or to understand the real reasons behind some strikes, or why technical changes are blocked, or why some trade unions make no headway, when orthodox theories of strike-proneness or of trade union growth are all we have to depend upon. Part Two of the book therefore moves from micro case studies emphasising occupations to macro concern with fiddle-prone sectors of the economy, with industrial relations and with the political and economic implications of these activities.

Cool appraisal of fiddling is difficult because it is hard to view the evidence objectively. If we fiddle in our own jobs we tend to view this as an entitlement – as a 'perk'; whereas if we are victims of the fiddles of others we become morally indignant. In these circumstances the suspension of moral judgement is far from easy.

Then and Now: the Past in the Present

The existence of invisible wages – of tips, fiddles, perks and pilfering – is of long standing. Their extent and history are well documented (Ditton, 1977b; Henry, 1978) and extensive. There are Egyptian *papyri* that record vulture and wolfpack fiddles of over three thousand years ago which are highly reminiscent of modern storehouse theft. Theft from storehouses in 1160 BC, for example, depended – then as now – on the presence of inside access men linked to outside and mobile 'disposal' men. The outside man in a typical case was a ship's captain who colluded with temple scribes and priests to dispose of fabrics and grain from the temple stores (as reported in Peet, 1924). There is no account of how the stock records were altered in this case – as they must have been to allay suspicion. A contemporary warehouseman, however, explains how the same kind of systematic collusion permits timber to be spirited from the timber store at his worksite:

> Once a week – when the [colluding] security guard is on duty at the gate – the driver will call with his lorry at the wood store and load up ... He'll drive through the gate – then go round to the carpenters down town and flog the lot. This has gone on for a couple of years that I know of. They have a good thing going because they're a service store – it's easy to get vouchers for timber on a big site – it's being used up all the time. And there's always a ready market for timber. They never go mad though – never too much.

As we shall see, collusion between levels and the co-ordination of self-policed limits is common to much of occupational pilferage, especially among vultures and hawks. So too is a degree of ambiguity – so that by removing ambiguity we can often stop fiddles. It is said that Archimedes owed the discovery of the principle that bears his name to the presence of fiddling among the royal goldsmiths. By realising, as he bathed, that the displacement of a liquid is equal to the volume of the solid causing its displacement, Archimedes was able to calculate the amount of gold abstracted during the manufacture of a king's crown. The problem then, as now, was to devise a way of removing ambiguity over quantity – which is likely to prove particularly expensive where precious metals are involved.

Again, it is not difficult to find contemporary parallels. A hospital dentist, dealing with hawks whose work is also involved with gold, explains how he was able to resolve his ambiguity problem:

> We order a large number of [dental] bridges at the hospital. These are made of gold and then they're covered with porcelain which is really for cosmetic purposes. The technical companies always insist that they charge us for the gold they use at cost. But normally there's no way of checking on this because the gold's covered over by the time we get it. Well, I decided to try fitting bridges for size *before* the porcelain went on to be sure they really did fit well. And while I was doing this I thought that it would do no harm to weigh them. Then I waited for the bills and checked these with my weighings. I found a consistent twenty-five per cent overcharge on the gold component. There is always some loss in manufacture but ten per cent is ample enough to cover this – twenty-five per cent, though, is well over the top. This was constant for all the companies and there were four of them. When I complained they all settled up without argument – said it was a mistake in calculation! We got back several thousand pounds.

I shall show in Chapter 6 that ambiguity over quantity is only one kind of ambiguity which is developed and exploited by fiddlers – though one particularly common when amounts taken are relatively small compared with the amounts stored or transacted. In 'The Manciple's Prologue', for instance, Chaucer shows that boring a fine hole in a barrel and inserting a straw – called a monkey's straw – through which its contents could be sucked was well known in the fourteenth century:

> You'd think he had been drinking monkey-wine,
> And that's when one goes playing with a straw.
> (Chaucer, 1951 edn, p. 500)

This practice later came to be known as 'tapping the admiral' because it was flourishing in 1805 when Nelson was killed at Trafalgar. To preserve his body for the voyage home, it was placed in a rum barrel. When the admiral's flagship docked and the barrel was opened it was found that the monkey's straw had been used to good effect – the admiral was high and dry. Gilding (1971) gives this account and then recalls that tapping the admiral was common among coopers in the London docks as late as the 1950s. The use of metal barrels has now put an end to this practice. We shall see that though technical change can block particular fiddles, the systems and principles on which they are based stay constant.

Henry (1978, p. 8), in giving an account of Colquhoun's description of dock pilferage in London at the end of the eighteenth century, shows that, like warehouse theft, it too depended upon a system – people with access to goods needing to link with others who could provide necessary support: in this case, look the other way, clear documents and dispose of and sell the cargo they obtained from ships. But since more roles have to be articulated to further dock theft than for warehouse theft the system in docks has necessarily to be more complex. In Chapter 4 I describe just such a complex system operated by wolfpacks in the port of St John's in Newfoundland. When I discussed these findings with a London magistrate who had tried many dock workers for pilferage, he confirmed that the same methods I found in Newfoundland (see Mars, 1972), and which were described by Colquhoun (1800) as existing in London in the 1790s, were still in use in the mid-twentieth century. Even the technical means that men used had hardly changed – they were still, for instance, wearing cloth pockets under their outdoor clothes which they filled with tea. The introduction of containers has reduced these opportunities, but it has increased others – not least because of what can be concealed in containers.

Informal Work and Total Reward Systems

A concern with the informal working of occupations, therefore, is not new. What is new is a growing understanding that the whole range of social institutions in our society, from the family, through education, to the social services and health care, can only be understood if they are examined from a 'warts and all' perspective. There is growing acceptance that, first, we cannot understand how our society operates unless we consider the informal side of our social institutions, and secondly, this can only be accomplished if they are treated comparatively. In a book dedicated to this approach Henry asks (1981, p. 1):

> How can we look at marriage and the family, for example, and ignore extra-marital affairs which may maintain the very existence of many families? How can we estimate the real economic activity of a country when as much as one fifth of its work force may have unregistered second jobs or be involved in informal trading networks? How can we judge the effectiveness of our health care services when the bulk of health care takes place in the family and local community? We need to know how these informal institutions operate, and also how they relate to their formal counterparts.

Henry has created a typology of informal institutions that neatly differentiates them according to the degree to which their transactions and relationships are integral or alternative to their formal counterparts. These are then further divided according to their legal standing. This typology not only allows for informal institutions to be seen together and to be related to each other, but also for their components to be systematically identified and compared.

Henry's concerns are wider than the concerns of this book but his approach can be adapted to work equally well for us. The central feature of occupations from the standpoint of our interests lies in the way *rewards* are allocated within them − particularly in the nature and source of the informal rewards which a job normally allows to its *average* worker (see Table 1).

Formal and criminal rewards are separated on the basis of the recognition granted them − both being officially recognised and both, therefore, having official status. Because of this both sets of rewards are found in official statistics; the difference between them depends upon their legal standing.

Table 1   *A Typology of Work and its Rewards*

	Official	*Unofficial*	*Alternative*
	(1) *Formal Rewards*	(3) *Informal Rewards*	(5) *Social Economy Rewards*
Legal	Wages, salaries, commissions, overtime	Perks, tips, extra work, consultancy	Domestic production, barter, exchange, 'do-it-yourself'
	(2) *Criminal Rewards*	(4) *Hidden Economy Rewards*	(6) *Black Economy Rewards*
Extra-legal or illegal	Returns from professional crime, prostitution, etc.	Pilfering, short-changing, overcharged expenses, overloading and underdropping	Unregistered production and service organisations, moonlighting

Unofficial rewards form a continuum from legal informal rewards to the illegal hidden economy rewards that are derived from official work. Both these areas of reward are therefore linked with formal rewards and together contribute to the *total rewards* that an individual receives from work. If we look at the hotel and catering industry, for instance (Mars, 1973; Mars and Mitchell, 1976, 1977), we see that a waiter will receive basic and formal pay from Box 1 in the form of wages and overtime payments and that this will be supplemented by informal rewards from Box 3 — the tips he receives and the perks of 'free' meals and perhaps also of 'free' accommodation. From Box 4 he may well be allowed to indulge in colluded access to pilfered food or be afforded a winked-at facility to short-change or short-deal customers. The contents of Box 4 are usually allocated on an individual basis through an *individual contract* with a specific contract-maker — usually a first-line supervisor. It is the receipts from Boxes 1, 3 and 4 which, in their entirety, comprise a person's *total rewards* from work.

It is therefore not only meaningless to compute an individual's income entirely from Boxes 1 and 3, let alone exclusively from Box 1 – it is also grossly misleading. It distorts policy-making – for instance, by directing attention from the concerns of the really low paid towards those whose claims are not as well justified.

Boxes 5 and 6, though not the central concerns of this book, distinguish the rewards that derive from alternative economic activity; they are distinct from official rewards, are allocated outside the official system and do not appear in official returns. They often involve a higher degree of social satisfaction than is derived from the same activities carried out for formal rewards and located in Box 1 – a point central to many of Henry's concerns (Henry, 1978). At the same time, the economic component of this reward is often less than would be expected from work derived from Box 1. When people obtain rewards from Box 5 it is likely to involve an element of reciprocity – a doing of favours, a swapping of services – so that high expense or scarcities or bureaucratic complexities inherent in obtaining official provision can be overcome by mutual co-operation. It may also be characterised by an exchange of obligation or increased prestige in return for economic benefit (Chiaramonte, 1971; Henry and Mars, 1978). It is this area that is increasing as Gershuny (1977a, 1977b, 1978) and Gershuny and Pahl (1980) have noted. They attribute this to the growing inadequacy of official provision particularly of services utilising cheap capital goods such as hand tools. This reflects a shift in formal production towards high technology at high wages and a reduction in services provided formally which, being labour-intensive, cannot compete. Box 5 covers much of the small-scale alternative technology and alternative food production that has flourished in recent years as well as reciprocal neighbourly exchange such as when a neighbour fixes my car in return for my decorating his bedroom (Henry, 1981).

Box 6 is concerned with rewards from the black economy. As with the two pairs already described, this box also represents the extra-legal or illegal end of a continuum – the social rewards of Box 5 blending into the unregistered production of Box 6. A group of co-operating artisans might well decide, for instance, to build themselves houses by working for each other at cost. If, however, they then extend their activities on a business basis by working for cash, not paying taxes and employing unregistered non-union or moonlighting labour, then they will have gravitated to the black economy. It is Box 6 that is expanding, as we shall see, and the building industry that regularly provides a sizeable constituent of this increasing total. It is estimated, for instance, that a quarter to a third of Italy's total production is now black and that a consistent 100,000 houses a year are built by this method, which has amounted to over a million illegal houses produced in the last ten years (Deaglio, 1979).

Some Definitions

It should be apparent that the boxes in Table 1 are not as distinct as might at first appear: fiddled time or goods might well, for instance, be allocated as a 'perk' from Box 4 by a manager to a worker and then be used for moonlighting work in Box 6. In a similar way an employed hawk in Box 1 may consistently carry out extra work on his employer's premises for his own benefit as 'a business within a business' (England, 1980). His activities would then come under Boxes 4 and 6. 'Fiddling', therefore, is wide-ranging and covers a variety of activities. It can now be defined as:

> the movement of resources to individual private use that do not appear in official accounts – or that appear in official accounts under different headings and which are acquired by individuals through their relationship to a job. These resources may derive directly from the job itself or be allocated from an outside source that relates to the job.

It is, of course, the totality of *all* rewards from work that is important – not only to those who receive them, but to those concerned with industrial relations and especially with the fixing of wages and salaries. This *totality* of reward in a particular location, the regular though covert arrangements that govern its distribution and the values and attitudes that sustain them are what I term a *total reward system*. And it is the regular presence of total reward systems and of the networks of work-based social relationships through which total rewards are differentially allocated to individuals by what I term *individual contracts* that are the 'covert institutions' of occupational life. It is precisely because such covert institutions have been largely ignored that we need to spotlight their presence and assess their implications.

Estimates of the Extent and Implications of the Concealed Economies

It is, of course, difficult to calculate the extent of any of our 'boxes' except for Box 1 and to a lesser extent Box 2, since the contents of the rest are largely concealed. It is also misleading to attempt to compare the concealed components of different national economies since attempts at measurement often measure different things, take data out of different boxes and are likely to derive from different statistical methods. Finally, there are problems that arise from variations between the efficiency of data collection and modes of analysis which differ from one country to another.

When these problems and provisos are taken into account we find that three main methods of assessment have been tried, sometimes separately sometimes in combination (O'Higgins, 1980). Most of these are concerned to assess the size of the black economy – Box 6 (and some of the undeclared components of Box 3). Most of them extrapolate from a small sample. The British Revenue in its annual report for 1980, for instance, estimated that in that year about $7\frac{1}{2}$ per cent of British GNP was black. This figure had been derived by assessing the proportion of cases in which taxpayers had been found cheating. The Revenue estimated that its loss could be between 3 and $3\frac{1}{2}$ billion pounds a year. The report makes it clear that the black economy is by no means a single phenomenon and that it includes many different types of tax evasion by various types of people. It considers, however, that moonlighting is the single biggest component but one especially difficult to deal with because of the relatively small amounts involved in each case.

Using similar methods, the US Internal Revenue estimates that in the US in 1976 what they call the underground economy amounted to between 5·9 and 9·0 per cent of gross national product and that between 15 and 20 million people failed to declare income to the Revenue, including $4\frac{1}{2}$ million who live entirely on earnings from unofficial jobs (US Department of the Treasury, 1979).

A second way of calculating the concealed aspects of a country's economy is to look at differences between the expenditures people admit to making, compared with the declared incomes of groups of similar people. This is a method that attempts to calculate the contents of Boxes 2, 3, 4 and 6. Dilmot and Morris (1981) in using it found, for instance, that between 2 and 3 per cent of the UK national income was black, though even this low figure implies that the average British household spent £300 a year on the black economy in 1980. Most observers in this field, however, believe that 2–3 per cent is rather low for the UK. After assessing all the evidence, O'Higgins (1980) finds it 'difficult to believe in a figure of less than 5 per cent' and finds $7\frac{1}{2}$ per cent 'not implausible'.

Some estimates of the US black economy have been based upon a third method of assessment. This has been to calculate the increase in the amount of currency in circulation and particularly the number of large-denomination notes, which it is believed are used to fund black economy transactions. An exponent of this method is Gutmann (1977), whose calculations led him to suggest that the size of the American black economy was approximately 10 per cent in 1976 amounting to an average of $381 per head. The figure is higher for the USA than for the UK because of the greater number of small businesses which are well-placed to practise taxation deception. It is the relatively small number of such businesses in the UK that projects the greater component of its black economy on to moonlighting (Alden, 1981).

These figures are in line with those from Europe. According to the International Labour Organisation, between 3 and 5 per cent of workers in the Organisation for Economic Co-operation and Development (OECD) are unregistered workers. Unregistered work probably reaches its peak in Italy where an estimated 3–5 million workers operate its black economy. Franco Ferrarotti of Rome University believes that a third of the active population now have two jobs and that 'We have come to the conclusion that the so called invisible economy is what makes the country as such tick. The invisible economy, the hidden economy is responsible for Italy's survival' (Ferrarotti, 1978). According to an article in *The Times* (Grapin, 1981), Italian government statisticians believe that less than 80 per cent of the true gross national product is reflected by official figures and that:

> almost 30% of exports which struggle to balance the country's heavy imports (of energy products in particular) are made in areas where the black economy thrives. For instance in Prato in Tuscany, 8,650 small businesses out of 9,605 use undeclared labour. Throughout the country there has been a large increase in small firms which declare 4 and 5 employees and have an effective workforce of possibly 50.

It is fascinating to realise that the tradition of not declaring incomes for tax and the methods and subterfuges that are used are consistent and localised through the centuries. Prato is famous among economic historians as the home of 'The Merchant of Prato' who in the fourteenth century built up a flourishing commercial empire that extended beyond Prato through Europe and North Africa. He spent considerable ingenuity during a long, active life in avoiding payment of his taxes and he recorded his methods and techniques in careful detail. He was also careful to ensure that he in his turn was not fiddled by his employees, and he avoided this by offering all of them different degrees of partnership. The documents which itemise all his lifetime's transactions are stored in his house in Prato – now a museum. A statue to the merchant stands in one of the town's main squares (for a fuller account see Origo, 1963).

Trade associations, particularly in Germany, are now beginning to make their own estimates of the extent of moonlighting since they rightly see *schwarzarbeit* as a threat to their interests. According to the report in *The Times* already quoted, '70% of carcass work in [West] Germany is done by illegal butchers and 90% of painting is done on the "lump" (by which workers are allegedly self-employed and do not declare their incomes)'. In the garage business 'more than 2 million brake changes and replacements of shock absorbers and exhaust systems on 4 million vehicles' are similarly now carried out by black economy workers. Many of these are full-time workers in garages who either moonlight or carry on a 'business within a business'. The same article quotes a report from the Bielefeld opinion research organisation in West Germany which estimates that almost 2 million workers now operate in the black economy and that about 8 per cent of employees have a second job and between them account for 2 per cent of West German GNP. They estimate that undeclared income has increased five times in the last five years, while an article in *Intersocial* estimates that loss in tax from these workers amounts to DM 10 billion a year.

Figures from France are not as clear as from elsewhere and tend to be on the low side, though this may well be the result of determined efforts by French officialdom to stamp out *le travail noir*. According to the French Insurance Documentation and Information Centre, only about half a million workers are employed in the black economy, though *The Times* (op. cit.) quotes reports that 10 billion francs or 3 per cent of official salaries and wages are now black.

The extent of these practices raises several questions: the first is concerned with whether they are static as a fixed proportion of their country's GNP or whether they are growing. Linked to this is the question of why, if they are growing, this should be so; and what, if anything, should or indeed could be done, either to stop them growing or to encourage them to flourish.

I have already briefly outlined the arguments put forward by Gershuny (1978) that black work – particularly that found in Box 6 of Table 1 is likely to increase as much of the service sector slides into illegality. This is a topic I shall return to in Chapter 9.

Most commentators, however, also believe that black economies are growing in reaction to the ever-growing controls that derive from government. Certainly black work is increasingly an escape valve for workers who can further their aspirations and achieve greater independence by bypassing administrative systems which are seen to act onerously and without discrimination. As the Report and Recommendations to the Council for the European Communities notes:

> we do not consider it desirable to suppress all forms of marginal work. Marginal employment acts as a valve, it proves that the social system reacts against the inflexibilities which it imposes upon itself . . . the second job, which is generally illegally combined with the main job, is often a type of work which would not be offered or would not be accepted. Usually it is part-time, offers wages which are adequate only as a supplement to the main income, and a worker is likely to be treated as self-employed rather than employed. Most important, 80% of such jobs are in service industries, whereas it is in productive industry that job creation is required.

But inflexibilities do not derive only from governments; they arise too from the growing size and necessarily increasing bureaucratisation of many organisations which operate onerously and without discrimination both to their public and to their own employees. The inflexibility of bureaucratic rules provides both the *motive* for job-holders – frustration at doing a highly con-strained job – and also the *means* to bypass them – as a junior civil servant colleague of mine demonstrated by abusing flexi-time to take a three hours a day part-time job pulling pints in his lunch 'hour'.

Inflexibilities are not just a feature of Western Europe and

America: they are much more pronounced in countries with centralised planning and administrative procedures such as in the totalitarian countries of Eastern Europe. It is well known that what have been called irregular, shadow, or secondary economies are a well-marked feature of socialist societies:

> the rigidity of central planning creates the need for alternative informal arrangements to facilitate production, and the control and rationing of consumer goods encourages unofficial markets. These unofficial markets are more or less tolerated by authorities, and the low official priority given to the service sector and low wages combine to create an extensive Moonlight market for services ranging from plumbing to private tuition. (Outer Circle Policy Unit, 1978, p. 1)

If it is difficult to calculate the extent of black economies in the West, it is even more so for Soviet countries. One observer, however, guessed that the black economy of the Soviet Union amounted to 20 per cent of its total economic activity (Kaiser, 1976, p. 317). This figure is in line with Peter Wiles's estimate based on a more careful assessment of economic statistics for the Soviet Republic of Georgia. He calculates that 25 per cent of personal, disposable incomes are there derived from this source (Wiles, 1981). Among Soviet watchers, Georgia is regarded as the most free-enterprise-oriented of all Soviet republics (Grossman, 1977). These figures however, require care. Any assessment of black economic activity in a Soviet state will necessarily include items not considered illegal elsewhere which makes comparisons between the two systems extremely difficult.

It is also difficult to make valid comparisons between Third World countries and those of the West, since so much Third World economic activity bypasses official figures in any case. None the less, because the need to raise taxation is crucial in Third World countries, the presence of a flourishing black economy can cause considerable disquiet. It is estimated, for instance, that £15 billion is a likely figure for tax evasion in India. The Indian government has, on two occasions, declared certain high-value currency notes as no longer legal tender and it has done this to limit black economy savings. Its latest scheme is to issue bonds cashable ten years after purchase, which are independent of the tax system since purchasers are immune from investigation of the source of the money with which they buy them (Fishlock, 1981).

Black economic activity, therefore, is found throughout the whole range of economic development. In the Third World it exists because the idea of 'the state' is often hardly legitimated at all, its functions tending to be seen as remote from the stronger loyalties due to more traditional, established and smaller-scale groupings. In Soviet systems it flourishes because of the presence of an overcontrolling centre: life becomes impossible *unless* the rules are broken . . .

In the developed world hidden economies grow as a response to hyper development. Here there is a need for central control over fiscal and technical pressures which produce constraints increasingly resented by ordinary people. Add to this the fact that much of the personal service sector and of small-scale manufacture cannot legitimately compete for labour with large-scale, capital-intensive production. We thus see that hyper development supplies both the motive *and* the means in the form of cheap mass-produced machinery, such as hand tools, to bypass the state, its laws, its taxation and its legally backed appendages such as trade unions, with their own constraining regulations, rules, dues and fines. This is a trend that can only gather pace as cheap micro-chip production processes combine the advantages of large-scale production with the flexibility of the small workshop.

This Study and its Development

This study has had a long gestation. It began while I was working in a wide variety of private and state industries during the ten years between leaving school and going to university when I found that in many occupations fiddles were accepted by workers as an everyday part of work-life. Fiddling was, in fact, entrenched; it was woven into the fabric of people's lives. Not only did it provide a regular proportion of incomes but it was essential to the operation of many businesses. There were tasks, even whole careers, and various kinds of organisation that just could not carry on without a fiddle. In the RAF stores it was clear to me that stock records could never balance unless they were bent. Fairground barkers would not shout, badger and cajole for an unbroken fourteen hours a day in good heart and voice unless they were guaranteed a tax-free share of the takings. Waiters would not wait and chefs would not create unless they were similarly assured that part of their total income would come from fiddles.

All this was accepted not only by those engaged in these practices but often by their bosses, especially their foremen and overseers who either winked an eye or even encouraged and colluded with them. And in the nature of many jobs they could not do otherwise. As one fairground worker put it: 'The whole system of wages . . . depends on fiddles.'

Despite the extent and frequency of fiddling, however, it had received little formal acknowledgement. When publicised it was treated as deviant; as the acts of atypical people. In practice the reverse seemed nearer the truth – that in many jobs indeed it was often abnormal *not* to fiddle.

I went to university at 26 to read economics and social anthropology. In my subsequent fieldwork as an anthropologist among North American longshoremen I began to appreciate the value of my earlier occupational experiences. Like dockers around the world, longshoremen fiddled cargo through the dock gates. More important, though, their fiddling penetrated deep into their culture. It influenced their relationships with one another and with their wives, affected their reputation in the town's wider community, and predetermined their reaction to changes in technology and work organisation when these affected access to cargo. Fiddling also coloured longshoremen's perceptions of the prestige involved in assessing different kinds of dockwork and its unspoken presence was often the key factor in appreciating many of the difficulties in industrial relations that existed in the port (Mars, 1972, 1979, 1981).

Through my work among longshoremen I realised that fiddling was not the anarchic behaviour of a lawless rabble, but was subject to rules. People *never* just grabbed what they could from whomsoever they could. There were *always* rules that governed limits and amounts, rules about who could be fiddled and who not; and rules about who could be incorporated and who must be excluded. We may not like such rules or even be prepared to accept that they exist. None the less, they are rules that govern behaviour and are therefore worth examination.

But these are not the rules of a criminal fraternity: this is not crime as most people think of crime. For a start the views of the law and its enforcers seem markedly at variance with the conventional wisdom. The Chief Constable of Manchester, Mr James Anderton, has constantly insisted, for instance, that fiddling at work is crime of the same order as robbing a bank is crime and that if you do not stop an office worker from using her firm's telephone for private calls 'she'll be 'phoning her auntie in Australia next'. In my experience this escalation is much the exception rather than the norm. It ignores the rules that apply to this as to other fiddles and which govern access and limits here as elsewhere. In fact the use of 'phones by staff tends to follow rules of hierarchy: local calls for the lowly; long-distance trunk calls for the middle rankers; and occasional international calls for the elite.

This study, therefore, has developed as a result of a variety of experiences. Its origin is rooted in personal experience: of having worked in a wide variety of jobs and of starting and running a business which involved frequent contact with small businessmen and tradesmen in the building and construction industry. But I have also been able to undertake retrospective analysis from the perspectives of social anthropology, economics and industrial sociology.

These disciplines have formed the analysis of detailed and extensive interviews with over one hundred informants which form the bulk of the data on which this book is based. These were *not* chosen on any rational basis but as they became available – what has been called the 'snowball' method of sampling (Irwin, 1972).

Many interviews were with people I had worked with in the past; some were with current friends, contacts and colleagues; and many were referred to me by people who knew of my interest in the area. A considerable proportion were, however, gained by the simple method of keeping my eyes and ears open and pursuing inquiries as circumstances arose.

Data received from informants was always cross-checked and discussed with others who had been or were working in the same or a similar field, or who had had experience of it. These included managers, management consultants and those professionally concerned with control; security personnel, the police and probation officers, as well as academics.

Part One

Who Gets What, How and from Where?

1

A Classification of Occupations and their Associated Fiddles

In some jobs fiddles are carried on with the collusion of management; yet in others fiddlers are ruthlessly and swiftly punished. In some fiddling is organised and carried out by individuals in isolation from their workmates; in others it requires the co-operation of a group. And while fiddling is seen by some employers as an incentive, almost a part of wages, and therefore tacitly welcomed and even encouraged, some undoubtedly occurs because of resentment . . . it is a way of hitting out at the boss, the company, the system, or the state.

To understand these differences we need to be able to link type of fiddle to type of job. This has not been attempted before because the very variety of occupations appears to defy *useful* classification. Some, like Henry (1981, p. 15) have bypassed the problem altogether, arguing that fiddles occur 'across the board', while others such as Ditton consider occupations and their associated fiddles mainly in terms of social class (1977b).

To date the main bases for classifying occupations have been by income, class, skill, or prestige. But to explain the mechanics of fiddling so that we understand the different ways people are recruited to fiddle, to show how they reconcile their behaviour with other counter-moralities and how they are moulded to operate their fiddles – for these we need to understand the way different work is organised and the occupational processes that people go through. And for this kind of understanding we need a way of classifying occupations that examines comparable aspects of *structure* – of how jobs are organised 'on the ground'. Only when armed with this can we then apply it to emphasise the characteristic features of particular occupations that encourage or inhibit fiddling, determine its methods and form, and affect the attitudes both of employers and of employees.

The classification I propose to use is an application of the work Mary Douglas (1970, 1978) has developed from the anthropological studies of non-industrial societies. Douglas was concerned that anthropologists had carried out a myriad intensive studies of individual cultures but that these could not readily be compared. Her contribution has been to provide a basis of comparison. Her argument is that *all* cultures can be assessed and classified according to two dimensions – the first she calls *grid* and the second *group*.

The grid dimension assesses the extent to which a culture imposes its social categories on its people and therefore fixes their appropriate behaviour and the behaviour of others towards them. The caste systems of India are strong on the grid dimension and so are all cultures where social position is largely determined by 'fixed' factors such as age, sex and birth. On the other hand, cultures such as those of Western Europe and of North America which are based on technology and competition, place a high premium on achievable status, on social mobility, while the fixed factors of age, sex and birth are relatively less important in fixing social position. In the West hindrances to achievement that are not based on merit are increasingly regarded as intolerable, while autonomy and individuality are highly valued. The West is a weak-grid culture.

Group, the second dimension, emphasises collectiveness among people who meet face to face. These are cultures where the survival of the group is more important than the survival of the individual and where the interests of the individual are essentially subordinate to those of the group. Cultures that emphasise lineage and clan organisation are strong on group. On the other hand, some cultures minimise group control over their individuals and these are weak on group. This is not to say that groups are absent in these societies but that they are unlikely to be all-pervasive: individuals in them may belong to several groups but none can exert an *over-riding* control over them. As well as being weak on grid, Western culture, when considered overall and particularly in its urban aspects, is also weak on group.

These two dimensions are not limited in their use to the classification of non-industrial societies, nor to comparisons between whole cultures. My argument is that grid and group extend equally well to the analysis of occupations in Western society. Occupations can, in fact, be treated as cultures and the way a job is actually structured 'on the ground' can be assessed by using the grid and group dimensions. Strong-grid jobs, for instance, are those which are similar in their structure to the caste cultures of India. There the whole range of social roles is pre-set, whilst in Western cultures some jobs are pre-set in precisely the same way. Jobs which limit autonomy – which define both the tasks and the expectations people have of a job-holder – are therefore strong-grid jobs.

On the other hand, weak-grid jobs are those that grant autonomy and allow their people to carry out tasks in ways they can define for themselves. Thus most senior management jobs are weak on grid and so too are the jobs of most independent professionals.

There are four elements to be considered in assessing the strength of the grid dimension: autonomy, insulation, reciprocity and competition. Low autonomy is found in jobs where there are many constraining rules as, for instance, in the case of security patrolmen. Their jobs are strong grid because controlling rules are many. The insulation of people from others is also a feature of strong-grid jobs. A ranking system separates people and pre-determines their response to others as well as the response of others to them. The requirement that uniforms be worn, for instance, especially those that distinguish different ranks, therefore contributes to strong grid; so too does the need to work by oneself in isolation from others.

25

The third element, reciprocity, has to do with how much a job allows its incumbent to offer to others and how much he has to accept in return. Where a job allows its holder to give more than he normally receives – such as a boss who can allow his secretary time off – we have a situation of weak grid. A secretary, on the other hand, normally has discretion to offer less than she receives; her job is therefore of stronger grid.

Good examples of extreme strong-grid jobs without any group influences are all jobs that fix people to a defined place, time and mode of work where they cannot effectively relate to others. Such jobs as a supermarket cashier, an elevator operator, a skivvy in a one-servant family are of this type. All are essentially insulated in a social sense by the constraints of their job; they lack autonomy and there is no scope for competition. But it must be emphasised that not only low-level jobs tend to be strong grid, though these are vastly in the majority. Members of the royal family are as subject and as subordinate to rules – in their case the rules that flow from the insulating influence of rank and the constraints these impose – as any security officer on his timed round or any supermarket cashier fixed to her seat in the store. The constraints that arise from strong grid can come from afar – they need no face-to-face group to maintain them; indeed, such constraints frequently arise from a distant bureaucracy. And, as with high rank, they can come from the expectations of those below.

Weak-grid jobs, on the other hand, are those with an overall absence of constraints and where this is so is found the freedom for people to transact with a wide range of others. These jobs involve considerable autonomy, and since in this sort of fluid climate there is a constant concern to ensure that control over others is greater than controls over oneself, they are jobs that involve the fourth element, competition. The 'freest' jobs are therefore weak-grid jobs. The jobs of independent and highly prestigious medicos are good examples: they have the autonomy to make the rules and they themselves determine how and where they spend their time.

Group – the dimension of collectiveness – is marked at its weakest points by the freedom of people from group controls. In a strong group, however, the individual increasingly comes under the control of others who can exert and impose group claims upon him. Dockers, for instance, can send a deviant to Coventry – that is, they can ignore a colleague and refuse to work with him so that he can no longer work as a member of a dockers' gang. At the same time, as a member of the gang 'in good standing', a docker can readily call for and obtain reciprocal support from the group as a collective when he requires it, a misfortune for one being seen as a misfortune for all. Among the dockers I worked with one gang contributed fourteen pints of blood for an injured workmate.

The group dimension also contains four elements and these together influence collectiveness and the rights and duties which this involves. It should be noted, however, that a collectivity such as 'the Catholic Church' is not, as Douglas points out, a group in the sense used here, since all four elements are derived essentially from face-to-face contact with others – in our examples, with co-workers.

The first of the group elements is the *frequency* with which people interact with others on the same or on complementary tasks. The more face-to-face contacts with the same people, the stronger the group. But frequency is not of itself enough to provide a strong group influence. A shop assistant may well regularly interact with the same customers but this does not make them a group. Frequency must in addition be linked to *mutuality*: repeated contacts must take place within a mutually interconnecting network. Lecturers based on one college for all their work are likely to be stronger on frequency and mutuality than would be the case where a college has all its lecturing supplied by other colleges' staff.

The strength of a group is further increased as the *scope* of its activities becomes wider. Scope here refers to the range of areas of social life which fall under the aegis of the group. A work-group that shares a common residence – as is found, for instance, in hotels which provide accommodation for their staff or among loggers who live in a common camp – will score more highly on the group dimension than a group that does not live together, because of the additional social activity that it can influence. In a similar way groups will be strong among workers who habitually associate together off the job — as is common among longshoremen or miners whose leisure and drinking activities mirror their work-group organisation or among newspaper print workers whose shift work throws them together in leisure times (Kerr and Siegel, 1954).

One further element is evident in strong groups — the presence of a defined *boundary* to the group. This arises when opportunities exist for those who mutually interact to assemble together. The significance of boundary, however, may not always be apparent. It may need external pressures such as decisions by management that affect the way a job is done to create an awareness of common identity and thereby activate a group's boundary that might otherwise be latent (Mars, 1979).

When these two dimensions of grid and group are considered together, as in Figure 1, we can conceive of a fourfold classification of occupations. Before presenting the main characteristics of these occupational types, it has to be noted that they represent 'ideals'. Many occupations straddle more than one type, while others may be between types. Their characteristics are not, therefore, as clearly defined as the schema might suggest. It is the extreme cases that are the most interesting and the most informative.

We are now able to assess the principal characteristics of occupations and, according to the strength of their grid and group constituents, to slot them into their appropriate type.

Type A, characterised by both weak-grid and weak-group dimensions, is appropriate to occupations that emphasise individuality, autonomy, competition and a control that its members have over others that is greater than the controls exercised over them. This is the type that emphasises entrepreneuriality, where the individual's freedom to transact on his own terms is highly valued; where individual flair is at a premium, individual differences make for disproportionate returns and success is indicated by the number of followers a person controls. Rewards here go to those who find new and better ways of doing things and

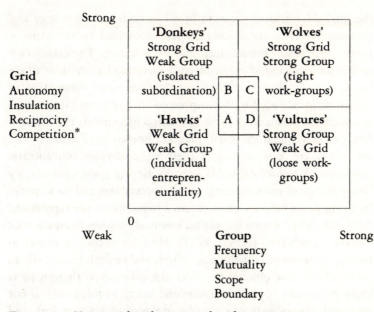

Figure 1   *Using grid and group to classify occupations*

* I am particularly grateful to Steve Rayner for fruitful discussions in this area and particularly for the ideas of reciprocity and scope which he has developed (Rayner, 1979).

where the drive for successful innovation is paramount. I term the kind of people in these occupations 'hawks'.

Hawks are entrepreneurial managers, owner businessmen, successful academics and pundits, the prima donnas among salesmen, the more independent professionals and journalists. But Hawks are not by any means restricted to the upper social levels. Hawkish entrepreneuriality is also inherent in occupations such as waiters (Henderson, 1965), fairground buskers and owner taxi drivers (Davis, 1959). Since competition is a dominant characteristic of this type, and because the group dimension is weak, we find that alliances among hawks tend to shift with expediency and that a climate of suspicion is more common than one of trust.

The need for such innovative, corner-cutting operators on the one hand, and the need to maintain rules on the other, represent

29

the dual dilemmas of societies based on science, technology and innovation. They are dilemmas that often lead to anomalies — particularly where bureaucratic control is strong. The classic case here is probably found in Soviet-style 'command' economies where the basis of their Five-Year Plans depends upon the setting of output targets. Faced with the need to achieve these targets, and because their bonuses are linked to such achievement, the chiefs of factories have men on their payroll, known as *Tolkachi*, who essentially are 'pushers'. It is their job to bypass bureaucratic snarl-ups. A *tolkach* earns his keep by having good contacts: by being skilled at manipulating people, procedures and paperwork; by being powerful enough to obtain a reduction in the targets and by speeding up or even increasing essential supplies to ensure that targets are achieved (Nove, 1977). He is an agent, an expert in beating the system's inherent rigidities, and he deals principally in information. But officially he does not exist, even though he is there specifically to operate fiddles and has to be tolerated — if not nurtured. As an entrepreneur, he organises deals that link and bypass points in the chain of production and distribution ('You supply their furnace and I'll get you some aluminium'). He is vital to the system, though the system tries to ignore him.

In Britain the best-known equivalent to a *tolkach* was probably Sidney Stanley of Lynskey Tribunal fame who flourished in the UK in the immediate postwar atmosphere of what was effectively a command economy. It was Stanley's job to 'fix' licences and permits for scarce building material, and for planning permissions, which he did on a vast scale. His contacts extended to ministerial level. It was as a result of the tribunal's inquiry into this world of government controls and their circumvention that a government minister had to resign and Stanley fled abroad. Stanley protested that his talents should have been rewarded, not punished, and he said: 'If I had been Chancellor of the Exchequer the Americans would now owe Britain money!' This is the voice of a true *tolkach* — the soul-cry of a supreme hawk.

Workers in Type B, whose jobs are defined by strong grid and weak group, are characterised by both isolation and subordination.

A skivvy in a nineteenth-century one-servant family is probably the classic example here (Douglas, 1978). Isolated as she was from social contact with others, unable to relate to fellow servants or the family she served, she was even excluded from contact with 'followers', that is, from male admirers. She was tightly scheduled not only over time and space, but also over work and leisure with a programme of activities which minutely controlled all aspects of her life. Her job was an extreme among 'donkey' jobs.

Donkeys are in the paradoxical position of being either powerless or powerful. They are powerless if they passively accept the constraints they face. They can, however, be extremely powerful – in the sense of being disruptive, at least for a time – if they reject them. Resentment at the impositions caused by such jobs is common and the most typical response is to change jobs. These are, therefore, occupations where high labour turnover is common, but other forms of 'withdrawal from work' such as sickness and absenteeism are also higher than normal (Hill and Trist, 1962, p. 38). At high points of grid, where constraints are at their strongest, sabotage is not infrequent as a response, particularly where constraints are mechanised (Taylor and Walton, 1971).

It is at weaker levels of grid, however, where control is high but where also autonomy is sufficient to allow some elemental control over a job, that resentment fiddling comes into its own. I recall an alienated supermarket cashier whose job, though closely defined by a mass of constraining rules which fixed her time, place and mode of work, was able none the less to consistently extract five times her daily wage in fiddled cash. Her motive was simply that she hated being treated like a programmed robot and fiddling made her job much more interesting; it gave her new targets and a sense of challenge as well as hitting at her boss where it hurt. When she changed jobs to another supermarket she stopped fiddling entirely because she liked the better way they treated her.

Type C, characterised by strong grid and strong group, is the home of those 'traditional' working-class occupations such as miners and longshoremen which are organised into work-groups;

31

but it is not exclusive to them. These are occupations based on groups with interdependent and stratified roles. As well as longshore gangs and teams of miners, it includes garbage collection crews, aeroplane crews and stratified groups who both live and work in 'total institutions' such as prisons, hospitals, oil rigs and some hotels. Where workers do live in or close to the premises in which they work, so that work, residence and leisure then overlap to form a single social field, group activities in one area are reinforced by cohesion in others. Such groups then come to possess considerable control over the resources of their individual members, both material and otherwise, and this includes claims on their time as well as their loyalties. Once they join such groups individuals tend to stay as members and the groups themselves often persist for long periods. Because group boundaries are strongly defined in these occupations, and because their members are stratified and work and fiddle in co-ordination, I have called them 'wolves' and their work-groups 'wolfpacks'.

In traditional docks the longshore work-gang has been shown to adapt all its formal and co-ordinated roles such as stower, signaller and checker to the similarly co-ordinated but illegitimate roles needed to pilfer cargo (Mars, 1974). Here every man's skill is needed to organise pilferage in almost the same way as it is needed to organise legitimate work. And as in legitimate work, there is no place here for the independent individualist: teamwork is vital and highly valued both for success and for security.

Type D is characterised by weak grid but with a strong, though often latent, group dimension. We find here those jobs that offer considerable autonomy and freedom to transact but where this freedom is subject to an overarching bureaucratic control that treats workers collectively, employs them in units and thereby encourages a group collectiveness. Workers in these occupations are, therefore, members of a group of co-workers for some purposes only and they act individualistically and competitively for others. They are not as free-floating nor as free from constraint as are hawks, but neither are they as constrained as donkeys. And though individuals are members of groups, the group is not as intrusive or controlling as are wolfpacks. For these reasons I have termed them 'vultures'. Like vultures, they need the support of a group to exploit their terrain but when they find their opportunity they are on their own.

Vulture jobs include selling jobs, particularly those that allow people to move around and where competitive flair permits the relaxation of rules (but where the rules are always able to be reapplied). Vultures include sales representatives, travellers and roundsmen of various kinds. The classic examples are driver deliverers, linked collectively by their common employer, common workbase and common task, but who have considerable freedom and discretion during their working day. Vultures' skills tend not to be as developed as hawks'; they have relatively less autonomy, and competition between them is weaker.

We find fewer professionals among vultures, more craftsmen and most semi-skilled. Compared to hawks, individuals have less independence and less personal power. Fiddle 'fiefs' are likely to be allocated with normal work – by and through the administrative collusion of management (at least of those at lower levels) – and to be exploited by proven individuals. To prove themselves to their managers brings competition into the vulture group, whereas the articulation of different roles in the wolfpack group ensures that competition is kept out. Problems arise, however, when bureaucratically imposed changes which often come from higher-level management disturb the fiddle earnings of all members of a group rather than involving a single individual. Where all members are affected there is likely to be a collective reaction which focuses on some generally acceptable cause, and which avoids direct reference to the real cause of the trouble (Gouldner, 1954). When, however, a managerial change affects only an individual's access to fiddles, rather than the group's access as a whole, then group reactions are more likely to be absent. This is one of the important distinctions between vultures and wolves. In the latter, an attack on one is seen as an attack on all. In the former, managements find it relatively easy to discipline or scapegoat individual workers and frequently do so to discourage the others.

33

One multinational company that manufactured industrial gases wanted to crack down on a fiddle common among its driver deliverers who – like many in this occupation are 'prone' to 'drop short' and sell the surplus privately. This company's particular product is one in frequent and urgent demand by car thieves who need, and will readily pay extra for, a quick delivery of gases to cut up cars and who cannot spend time or take the risk of going through the bureaucratic procedures necessary to get an order filled. Fiddling, however, was common among these drivers not only because they had a ready market but also because dropping short is normally easy when deliveries are made to large institutional users such as hospitals whose staff often readily sign for less than they receive. In this case the company's security division devised a foolproof system of dating its cylinders by marking them with differently coloured seals which would have stopped the fiddle. But it decided against this when it was pointed out how it would provoke its latently militant drivers to take collective industrial action to protect their common interests. There were no problems for management, however, when the company wanted to discipline an individual driver. In such a case he got less group support than would a longshoreman or a miner in a similar position.

This typology is intended to do more than merely point to the relation between the nature of occupations and their fiddles. It emphasises that there is a link, as we shall see, between the social environment of jobs and what can be called their cosmology (Douglas, 1978, p. 6) – that is, the ideas, values, attitudes and beliefs that are appropriate to them. People at work or elsewhere need a fit between what they do and the justifications, explanations and excuses they can give for doing it. This is not to say that a fit between occupation and cosmology is always achieved, or even possible. But the pressures on people towards making such a fit are socially determined and they cover the processes of selection (and self-selection is important here), training, and the operation of social controls that are exercised when training is over and incorporation in a job is complete.

A lack of fit between job and cosmology can have a number of effects: first, if a person cannot adapt his values, beliefs and attitudes to suit the job's demands, he can resign and withdraw mentally from the conflict; secondly he can suffer breakdown; or thirdly, he may survive incompatibility in that state of tension sometimes called alienation. In such a state he may respond through a higher than usual sickness rate; a greater than usual turnover in the number of his jobs; through sabotage, through absenteeism, or through fiddling. Fiddling as a response to alienation is only one of a possible range of responses and, as we saw, is most often applicable to the donkey jobs in Quadrant B which isolate their incumbents.

When there is a fit between work and a worker's cosmology, however, there is an aspect of 'job satisfaction' which is usually ignored. The worker gets more than just cash benefits from his fiddling. This again can be clearly seen in the overstructured donkey jobs which isolate their incumbents. These jobs offer minimal intrinsic satisfactions to their workers, whereas fiddling can be fun. It can be, and usually is, a pleasurable departure from routine and an implicit challenge to authority. This may take a number of forms. When a worker feels he is 'playing with fire', fiddling is a game of chance played against the risk of detection. Those involved are aware of the risks and the knowledge adds zest to the fiddle. When such a worker feels that by bringing off a fiddle he is beating the system, and is in control of his fate, his rewards are more than monetary. This motive is evident in boring routine occupations in which workers would otherwise be controlled by their jobs. The fiddles appropriate to these jobs are fired by resentment. For donkeys in particular, organising a fiddle allows them some of the individuality and creativity otherwise denied them in their work (see Henry, 1978, ch. 6).

Another non-material reward enjoyed by fiddlers is status in the eyes of contacts and friends. This is particularly evident in clandestine trading networks where members demonstrate that they put themselves out for a friend in pilfering, or risking a fiddle. By getting services or goods cheaply, a network member

35

can demonstrate that he belongs to a group of people 'in the know' who have influence and the ability to get things done – a point well demonstrated by Henry (1978, p. 34) in his discussion of trading networks and amateur fencing. Network members will often get goods for well below market prices and give or sell them to friends without financial profit. Giving away goods to acquire status in this way is not unlike the kind of competitive exchange found in the 'potlatch' rituals of the Haida and Kwakiutl Indians of British Columbia (Codere, 1950), though there is also material advantage from membership of a network dealing in the reciprocal trading exchange of cheap goods.

As well as providing exciting play, allowing self-expression and offering prestige, fiddling, when it involves a group, also encourages the development of alliances among those who participate, and it excludes those who do not. This gives the satisfaction of belonging to participants and incidentally offers uncovenanted advantages to management. These features are well developed among wolves, though they are also found to a lesser degree among vultures.

Fiddling also contributes to the blurring of work and non-work life that is found among hawks and vultures. Here fiddled profit is essentially linked to a self-knowledge of professional success and to the approval of one's peers and superiors. As a journalist explained: 'Everyone knows that "a good story deserves good expenses".' It is also true that a resentful journalist, who is, say, disgruntled by the failure of his editor to publish a story, will 'punish' him by stepping up his expenses claim. In these jobs, particularly among wolves, both social environment and cosmology are congruent and work and non-work lives are blurred. There is no distinction of time or space as allocated between the two, and earnings and fiddled extras are similarly blurred; they are combined to form an appropriate level of overall reward in the perceptions of those who receive them.

But no occupation is static. Some indeed possess a considerable dynamic and their members periodically move from one quadrant to another. This is most obviously seen among vultures where, as we saw in the case of delivery drivers of gases, the boundary element to their groups is latent for most of the time but is always liable to periodic assertion.

We can now perhaps appreciate how this schema allows us to differentiate between the superficial similarities shared by some occupations and how it provides a basis for rational comparison. At first glance a bus conductor's job might well be considered essentially the same as an owner taxi driver's or a selling roundsman's. The three jobs, after all, each involve driving about in a vehicle and meeting different members of the public. But both the grid and the group dimensions of the three are different. On grid, the busman has less potential for competitive entrepreneurial activity than the other two; the nature of his transactions are more limited by his job; his work is dominated by time; he is more controlled by rules concerning space; and he has less autonomy. All of these grid aspects of his job limit his possibilities of unofficial adaption and narrow the range of ways in which he can regularly increase his informal rewards.

If we examine the group dimension of these apparently similar occupations we can see, too, that group is more evident among roundsmen than among the other two, though it is greater among busmen than among owner taxi drivers. Both busmen and roundsmen are subject to the actions of a common unifying employer, being based on the garage and the depot respectively, but only roundsmen typically meet where their rounds cross to exchange goods and services and to share refreshments. In deputising on each other's rounds they must be careful to be supportive of each other's relationships with customers. Both bus conductors and roundsmen share frequent and repetitive relationships but, though latent, their boundary is probably more readily realised by roundsmen than by either of the others. They, for instance, not being shift workers are likely to find it easier to arrange common meetings of co-workers than are the other two and therefore are more readily able to reaffirm their boundary in the face of a common threat. They have therefore a stronger basis of support on which to call if threats or changes arise that can affect unofficial rewards. It is these kinds of consideration that determine the allocation of an occupation to one quadrant rather than another: why, for instance, I would place the owner taxi drivers with the hawks in Quadrant A, the busmen among the donkey jobs in B, and the bread roundsmen as belonging with the vultures in D.

But using this schema as a basis to divide occupations into types is not to suggest that all occupations of a similar type are of the same group and grid strength. The scorings of different strengths both within and between occupations are obviously amenable to greater sophistication than has been used here. One of the big advantages of this schema, however, is that it operates at macro and micro levels with equal validity. It is always possible in effect to slip a more powerful objective lens into any quadrant by simply dividing it into a further 2×2 matrix, and to continue to do so until the analysis applies at the level of the individual (Rayner, 1979).

The question of scale is therefore unimportant: it does not matter what scale is used, provided one uses a classification and states it. Most of the analysis that follows is based at the macro scale of occupational analysis: I am attempting to use the *aggregate* of grid and group constraints that apply within an occupation. To be sure, variations do apply within an occupation, sometimes widely, but the schema as used here attempts to interpret the pressures that apply to the occupation's *average* individual. What follows, therefore, is a classification of occupations – not a classification of individuals – but it is equally relevant at the level of the work-group or of a specific workplace.

There may be reason to dispute the somewhat arbitrary way that the occupations with which I deal have been scored. And there is, of course, the possibility that people may argue, if they wish, about the justifications for putting any specific occupation into a particular slot. But what is of primary importance is that this schema does provide a system of classification into which occupations may be slotted and one offering a basis for comparison between occupations that is, I suggest, more meaningful and fruitful than previous attempts in this field. And it is one, too, that can be used dynamically — that is, as an aid to understanding change and its effects at work.

This basis of classification is, I argue, fruitful because it moves away from class typologies created solely by reference to prestige, ownership and control and allows us to focus on the structural bases of jobs. It is these that facilitate or inhibit fiddling, help to determine its forms and incidence, affect the attitudes and training of workers and influence the complaisance or otherwise of their employers. These are concerns which are examined in the following four chapters.

2

Hawk Jobs

The Small Businessman's Story

Did you read about that speaker at the Labour Party Conference?
He said ninety per cent of small traders are on the fiddle. That's
ridiculous, he's absolutely wrong. It's got to be a hundred per cent!
You just can't survive at all and pay the sort of money out in taxes
that they want. You certainly couldn't keep your labour without
fiddling. Our main fiddle, in fact our only fiddle, is fiddling the
government – they're the only ones we fiddle. We fiddle part of our
workers' wages. All the very small businesses that I know have to
be in on this kind of fiddle. If you employ someone and he earns
below the amount that allows him to get the maximum family
supplement as a low-wage earner – then you make sure he gets the
supplement. You pay him just enough to qualify for the maximum
and you make the rest of his wages up in cash. This is possible
because we've a lot coming through the till.

This way he gets the maximum supplement, which is nine
pounds plus all the other allowances that go with it, like one pound
twenty-five a week for free school dinners and free spectacles and
dental treatment and all the rest of it. This comes to an extra three
pounds a week. And then I give him ten pounds out of the till. And
every week he goes round to the garage where I have my petrol
account and he gets two pounds-worth of free petrol. I pay his
stamp as well. If I paid him the thirty-two pounds a week he gets
from me as a legitimate wage, he'd be taxed on it and he wouldn't
get the supplement and I'd have to pay stamps at a higher rate
because it's linked to level of wages.

I couldn't afford to pay both of them forty-three pounds a week and pay VAT too on all the stuff I sell. With income tax it would mean about forty per cent of the turnover going to the government. I just couldn't do it – I'd have to pack in.

The thing is that Mike now gets in his pocket about forty-three pounds a week. We're not bothered by all these hypothetical figures – what counts is what he gets. Why, I would have to lay out about sixty pounds a week for both employees – I couldn't possibly afford to do that. What I do is give the money to those who use it best. In my experience – with the Department of Trade and Industry and with the Department of Social Security – they certainly don't know how to use their money well. In fact they're bloody hopeless. This way it benefits me no end and it benefits Mike and Rosie as well.

G.M.   Yes – but it doesn't really benefit them in the long run, does it? They can't get a mortgage, for instance, on the low stated wages they're supposed to get?

S.B.   My God, how naive are you? In the first place they can get a mortgage – of course they can. I'm their employer, aren't I? When Mike wanted a mortgage I certified to the building society that he was earning twice what he was supposed to be getting. There was no trouble there at all. And Rosie is in a council house and she gets subsidised rent because her stated wage is so low.

It's obvious when you sell goods that you don't put it all through the books. Not all the wholesale orders that we sell go through the books and some of the retail don't either. So when you're dealing as a wholesaler with a company, they keep no record of it and pay no VAT and you don't either. Do you know, there are many firms now who'll hardly look at you if you want to pay by cheque? It's got to be in cash. And when I deal with any of the other traders in town then it's understood that everything's in cash too.

Even in very large firms it goes on, even in firms where everything is apparently regular. Take a large firm of weavers I know of, for instance. The Inland Revenue knows how much wool makes how much cloth – there's not much chance to fiddle there. But how they *do* manage to fiddle is this: one brother in the firm will, say, sell a car to a brother outside the firm for, say, two hundred pounds. He'll then sell it in his turn for two thousand pounds and they split the difference between them.

Now it's pretty difficult in that kind of a case to prove anything.

But the real trouble with this way of doing things is that you can't expand, because all the agencies that you depend on, like banks, need to have formal statements of correct declared income. It distorts the whole economy, really. For instance, I've got orders this week for seven thousand pounds-worth of stuff for next Easter. Now of course, I don't put it through my books, and the raw materials don't go through my suppliers' books either. And then there are the retailers I sell to. They don't put it through their books. So I can't really go to my bank, can I, and say that I want to finance this seven thousand pound order? It doesn't just involve me, it involves my suppliers and my retailers as well. It's the whole bloody shute from one end of production to the other.

What is developing is a system of barter that completely bypasses the official system. Only this week, for instance, I've spent time shifting Horlicks and tinned tomatoes I exchanged for my stuff. The chap who had the Horlicks is a general dealer and his wife has a market stall. This market stall is very important – it means she can get rid of my stuff without trouble. His problem is that he's accumulating cash all the time and he can't use it legitimately in his business. One way out is for him to finance other people – like me, for instance. So he's supplied me with a couple of lathes that he's got from a supplier he knows who's not put it through his books. In return, I've given him first option on the stuff that I turn out, which his wife can get rid of on her stall. Really, he's turning into a bloody bank.

The nature of fiddling, as we have seen, varies with the nature of occupations. In highly constrained jobs (the strong-grid, isolated donkey jobs in particular), fiddles are by definition disruptive: they break the rules and are the symptoms of a management-designed system going wrong. Hawks, however, are independent; swooping to their opportunities, energetic, adaptable and resourceful. In weak-grid hawk jobs where constraints are few and involvement in any group is low, then everyone is free to make his *own* way. Here fiddles and flexibility are part of the way things actually work, and indeed often the reason *why* things work. Their presence explains why, for example, some successful surgeons remain in the National Health Service where formal pay is relatively low, or why technical brains do not always drain overseas. The fiddles appropriate to hawk occupations cover a wide spectrum extending from straightforward crime through tax evasion and avoidance to perks and fringe benefits, but always and centrally allowing freedom to their practitioners.

In this type of job entrepreneurial, frontier principles make fellow travellers of small businessmen and big fixers, of the more independent professionals and the most successful managers and executives. All share certain attitudes: the most common are a resistance to external constraints and the high value placed on independence. Our small businessman is, therefore, typically and almost by definition, a hawk. His activities take him into but do not submerge him in the black economy. What he describes is the simple archetypal small businessman's fiddle and it is four-pronged. First, because the declared basic wage he pays is so low, his workers can claim from the state the maximum family income supplement for the low paid. Secondly, because he tops up their wages with cash from the till, his workers do not have to declare their real earnings and therefore escape taxation on income. Thirdly, he himself pays less 'payroll' tax than he should because insurance contributions paid to the state on behalf of his workers are based on a lower level of income than they actually receive. Finally, his own income is under-declared for tax purposes. The US Internal Revenue Service identifies two groups – small business-men and farmers – who, it says, understate their incomes by an average but consistent 40 per cent (US Department of the Treasury, 1979).

But the implications of fiddles such as those of the small businessman, quoted above, go further than the mere involvement of himself and his two workers with the revenue: his dealings in cash, as he says, cover connections with both wholesalers and retailers. As he puts it: 'It's [affecting] the whole bloody shute from one end of production to the other.' Dealing in cash in this way not only distorts figures on employment and incomes and therefore negates the intelligence base of government policy-making; it also possesses its own dynamic – once established it grows by feeding on itself and further, it develops into a system of barter that completely bypasses the official system.

These fiddles deal with more than just matters of economics; they are essentially both a defence and an assertion of independence. To function at all, the Revenue must enforce what appear to be arbitrary and inelastic sets of rules. There is little ambiguity about which goods attract VAT, at what point an individual's earnings become liable for higher-level income tax, or when the incidence of corporation or wealth taxes should apply. But such arbitrary trip mechanisms affront the hawk's sense of natural justice — they limit his ability to transact freely. Different kinds of hawk bypass constraints in different ways but their tendency is always to bypass. The small businessman's response, as we saw, is to conceal from his books part of what he deals in. Transactions in cash restore his freedom to operate and compete — sometimes to stay in business at all. The response of employed professionals is to develop their professional links outside the organisation that employs them. Lower down the prestige rating we find collusion between an employer and his key men who together actively declare to the Revenue less than full wage payments, commissions and perks.

Fiddles of this kind, especially those set within the black economy, are therefore not isolated phenomena, nor do they operate in an economic or a social vacuum; they are links in a parallel chain that covers production from initial financing through to final distribution. Like the official economy, the black economy too develops its linked specialists, its bankers who finance deals and stake their capital, and its brokers who bring together different kinds of need. And all of these linked activities are financed by money that flows outside the nation's formal book-keeping system. Such production can also be seen as unfairly competing with legitimate production which pays its full legitimate overheads.

Slipping the Organisation's Yoke

For the employed hawk to operate across the boundaries of the official and hidden economies he needs first to loosen the control of his employing organisation. He can do this by running in parallel 'a business within a business', a practice often found among employed professionals and technicians. As a hospital administrator admitted: 'We couldn't hope to keep dental technicians in the Health Service at the low rates which are all we can pay . . . what we have to do is to wink our eye at their fiddles.' Their fiddles involve the use of hospital time, materials and equipment to service dentists operating formally in their private health practices.

From an employed hawk's standpoint one of the most salient features of all these occupations is the aim for autonomy and a resultant control that allows him to slip off the organisation's yoke: this means freedom to act and transact on his own initiative and the ability to control others rather than be controlled. Together, these create a competitive tension, a dynamic which urges the employed hawk not merely to achieve but to pay himself for his achievement through the strength he can apply in negotiations on his individual contracts. Since in hawk jobs the individual is his own man, his reward is something *he* rather than a group negotiates. Official rewards, therefore, tend to tell only a part of the story: even when the individual is employed it is the extent to which he can earn *un*official rewards that is so often a truer measure of success. The hawk dynamic goes some way towards explaining why the apparently lowest paid are often least interested in trade union representation. Through the tipping system and control of the communal 'tronc' (the pooled tips which are shared out), a head waiter with flair can, for instance, negotiate the level of his own rewards. The chef (with *shaman*-like knowledge of how much food must be ordered, and control of information over how much actually is ordered) can negotiate his own perks, while the fairground worker can arrange how much he is entitled to take from his bag at the end of the day. Such workers stand only to lose by collective wage determination. Here a fairground spieler explains how the level of his earnings is directly linked *by him* to his success as a spieler:

> I take about five pounds a day out in 'the weed' . . . the weed is the amount you can fiddle . . . On a good day you might take out six or seven pounds and on a bad day perhaps only three or four. When I say 'taking out' I mean taking out from the till. It's a kind of commission. You base what you take out on what you've taken in. Your boss is trying to keep the weed as low as he can; you're trying to get it as high as you're able. But the boss knows that if he presses too hard he'll not get a good spieler or he'll get someone who's lazy and his takings will suffer – and you know that if you take out too much you'll get the sack or a split weed [a second worker put with you]. Somewhere in the middle there's a meeting point and both me and the boss are happy to meet on a figure of about six pounds a day for a take of about eighteen.

(N.B. The basic rate of pay was £1 a day at this time.) What is happening here, and it is common throughout the wide range of employed hawk jobs, is that the individual both expects and is expected to reach some tacitly agreed level of reward through stratagems for which the ground has *already been prepared*. Room has been left for manoeuvre. If he does not take advantage of this no one reproaches or praises him, but he has failed. He finds perhaps that he would be happier moving towards higher grid where rewards are more formal and automatic and less competitive. Or he might prefer the security that comes from working in a team where group influence is stronger and isolation less pronounced. But once he can and *does* take advantage of his individual bargaining power he finds that he can personally match his reward to his achievement. And with this discovery he tastes a potent drug.

Thus not only is the idea of a negotiated 'meeting point' within a variable range, crucially important to employed hawks, and closely akin to the limits that vultures and wolfpacks set to pilferage; the possibility of such variation – the chance to overcome rigidities set by organisations and to restore the possibility of face-to-face negotiations – is also appreciated by employers. A tolerance over travelling expenses provides just such a common meeting ground for both parties to an individual contract. It is worth looking more closely at travelling expenses. When an employer allows his employees to submit inflated travel claims or claim first-class travel, but does not oblige them to travel first class, both he and his employees gain room for manoeuvre. At the back of the system there is the idea that the difference can and should reward individual achievement or initiative or at least compensate for a difficult or messy task. The more travelling a salesman does on his company's behalf, for instance, the greater the difference in cash terms between his real and claimed expenses and the greater the unofficial reward. But this must be linked to quality or output, which in the salesman's case means being linked to the level of sales he achieves. A Fleet Street journalist explains how this same kind of individual negotiation works in newspaper offices.

When I say that fiddling is basic to journalism I mean that it's so well understood as a part of total take-home pay that when you take the job on management intimate the fiddle level to you. I was told, for instance: 'You're on the standard but you should be able to make forty-five pounds a week on expenses [about 25 per cent of basic wage]. Mind you, there are limits, and these depend on the quality of your work. In this sense it's a sort of increment paid extra to those who produce better stuff: the better the job, the more the leeway accepted for a fiddle. It's very well known in journalism that 'a good story deserves good expenses', and when I say it's well known, I mean well known by management as well as by staff.

The fiddles, of course, are very basic. You'll always claim first-class travel and go second class, and when you have a meal out you put it in for false entertaining. And then, of course, there's all the entertaining that you don't get vouchers for, particularly beers in hotels and taxis. The most usual fiddle is a conglomerate. For instance, it's not uncommon for you to decide you're dashing up to, say, Bletchley or somewhere after a story. You look up fares plus a few beers for fictitious informants and a taxi or two and bang it in for expenses.

You see it's easy to lose a story on the big dailies. About two out of four are published and two are not.

Mind you, this system of payment, for that's what it is, has its problems. When times are hard, they cut back on fiddling. This of course causes considerable discontent, but as it's not legitimate there's nothing much to be done about it.

Hawk fiddles among the employed often occur as here, when differences in job performances vary widely but basic pay tends to iron out differentials. Journalists provide a good example because they are mostly paid on similar scales ('the standard') but their outputs are particularly and peculiarly personal. This, then, is an ideal situation for the personally negotiated individual contract to flourish. Its likelihood increases if basic pay is low relative to the market value of the services offered, since this fact alone indicates that there is no effective group to exert pressure in its negotiation. Basic pay itself, however, is not an exclusive measure of individual initiative or success – nor is it intended to be. It merely reflects the individual's relative position within a well-structured organisation. In such an organisation, if grid is strong the individual is relatively insulated from all relationships other than those with his immediate superiors or juniors. If the organisation is also strong in group a trade union may negotiate increases in salary. But the individualist hawk tends on the whole to eschew trade unions: he negotiates the most significant parts of his income for himself.

An understanding of motives and pressures at minor levels can give insight into the fiddles of super hawks. These fiddles too aim to bypass constraints, to protect an individual's autonomy. But on a larger scale, they are the assertion of a particular style. Backhanders and slush money (funds with an ambiguous allocation, such as 'entertainment') are an essential part of the freebooting style of big fixers: supranational brokers like Adnam Khashoggi, who was alleged to have netted over 200 million dollars as a go-between in deals between governments and aircraft manufacturers (Boulton, 1978). The hawk fiddle on this scale is what makes freebooting free. How difficult it is to distinguish this kind of fiddling from freebooting is suggested by the ambiguous attitude society has towards the successful entrepreneur. We tend to despise our most successful men precisely because of their success. Admiration for the frontier pattern of success — log cabin to White House — is tempered by a cynicism or contempt for the way it is achieved. And in the UK the price paid for men of flair like T. Dan Smith, who made the north-east of England hold up its head, is the sort of corruption that the Poulson investigation revealed. One problem that all hawks have to face, therefore, is the resentment, envy and occasional outrage that society shows when fiddles become visible. This is because there is only a blurred line between entrepreneuriality and flair on the one hand and sharp practice and fraud on the other. Society needs to admire and reward the first but suspects, and often rightly so, the presence of the second.

Time and its Manipulation

We have seen that a cluster of features characterise hawks, particularly autonomy, the control of others and competition. We can measure the degree of a person's autonomy by the extent to which he is free to make certain choices. Crucial here is the choice of how he disposes of his *time*. Where change is a constant and where, in place of the stability of group, there is a constant milling of individuals jockeying for position, then the ideal of a free market is always in danger of degenerating into a free-for-all. In these circumstances time is seen as a precious resource, to be invested, saved, or spent like money. 'Clocking in' offers the individual a limited choice about how he disposes of his time, while 'flexi-time' offers only a partial choice. But in hawk jobs the individual has, implicitly if not explicitly (that is, by the nature of his job rather than by being given *carte blanche* to draw up his own timetable), a much fuller choice over how he uses his time.

For donkeys and wolves there is no such freedom; an individual's time belongs to the firm or the group. If a donkey does private work in management time it is strong-grid mode of occupational pilferage: a symptom for management of things going wrong. Indeed, the more control exerted over people's time, the more the individual is tempted to squander it. A boss who timed his female staff on their extended visits to the washroom felt he was defrauded as surely as if they had their hand in the till. And among group-based jobs, control by the group over the leisure of its members is often no less onerous. When I worked among Canadian longshoremen I knew men off work through accidents who none the less felt impelled to hobble to their work-gang's tavern at the end of the day. It was vitally important to them that they remained in good standing with their workmates: they had to demonstrate that their time was at the disposal of the group. But in hawk jobs a person's time is his own, or at the very least his discretion over it is wide. He can turn the idea of 'office time' on its head: office time is time the hawk chooses to allot to the office. It is one of a number of options a person of initiative, *hired* for initiative, is expected to have. The justifying phrase is 'I am employed for the *quality* of my work, not the amount of time I put in'.

It is among hawks that the phrase 'time is money' gains real currency. Time can be expanded in the same way that the price for a job can be raised: that is, to the highest level the client can be expected to pay. If a job is taking too much of his time, as an ex-Revenue accountant explained, he can make more time:

> You might wonder sometimes why you get pointless letters from an accountant? Well, if you're very busy and if you have a time-consuming case and need to make time, then you might delay things on a case by sending a pointless letter out [one that asks an unnecessary question] and BF-ing [bringing forward] the file for a fortnight. The Revenue do the same. They often send out pointless letters too – merely to get the files off their backs for a week or so.

Time is also made in other ways. A lawyer will take two weeks to do what can be done in two days. A watchmaker will say 'ten days' for a job he knows will take ten minutes. This juggling with time is rarely questioned. It is accepted, for two reasons: the 'stateless-ness' of hawk occupations which, as we shall see, makes them in effect unaccountable; and the 'status' of hawk occupations, which lifts them above accountability.

Because the time of professionals is valuable, professionals more than most can benefit by selling 'cheap' time at 'dear' prices. They do this by using trainee, unqualified and apprentice labour and charging for it at full professional rates. In doing so they benefit from the ignorance of consumers and the monopoly position that professional status so often confers. Lawyers in the conveyancing of property nearly always use unqualified lay staff. Both types of labour are charged for at prime rates. Lawyers argue that since they bear the responsibility for such work and particularly because they supervise it they are justified in charging the rates they do (which sometimes amount to £50 an hour). Yet it is surely significant that advertisements for unqualified conveyancers in the legal press frequently insist that they must be able to work *without* supervision.

Management consultants in particular benefit from ambiguity over time that derives from constructed ambiguity over status. Since training on the job is the norm, a good job done by a trainee can therefore be charged for at the same rate as that of a fully qualified professional. It is among management consultants, too, though to a degree in all consultant jobs where the rate is charged by daily time, that we find the well-established institution of 'invisible days'. If a job takes five days but the customer appears well satisfied, an extra 'invisible day' (or days) can be charged under such heads as 'consulting with colleagues', for 'explorations', for 'liaison', for 'research', or 'report-writing' – all of which are less visible than days spent on a site. In this kind of practice the consultant is then available to sell the same time to more than one client.

> The main point is always to make sure the client is satisfied. If he likes the job you've done – then you're away – then he'll pay you for it without haggles – irrespective – irrespective, that is, of the days you've put down. In fact, if you've done, say, a really first-class job, they often don't take it seriously *unless* you charge them a bomb! But it's always got to look reasonable, so I pad it out a bit, you

51

know – a day on here and a day on there – time that's not easily checked up on. Things like research and meetings with colleagues, travel – that kind of thing. But you can't just go into it like a bull at a gate. In the end the whole job, including the paying, has to satisfy the client who's going to settle the bill.

That's what makes consulting really exciting for me – you can make a bomb if you're good. Three months ago I had two jobs running together and I was able to squeeze ten days extra out of them – at two hundred pounds a day that's worth making. But it's not fiddling really – more a kind of payment by results. They thought the results were worth it – I've been called back on another job by one of those firms. (A self-employed management consultant)

Time, Time Investment and Personal Ratings

Another of the freedoms that autonomy and particularly professional autonomy confers is the freedom to choose collaborators. And this freedom gives the further freedom to choose terms by which work is done with these collaborators. Such terms are dictated by how time is allocated to them. In theory, in the fair-minded, free market milieu of hawk occupations everyone should have equal opportunities, which includes equal access to an individual's time. But since competition is crucial to hawks, ratings *vis-à-vis* one's colleagues and competitors continually need to be reassessed. Since time is the hawk's scarcest resource, time is therefore the principal measure used to determine how people are rated. As a result and in practice, access is easier for some than for others and in absolute terms more time is allotted to some than to others. The more 'useful' a collaboration, the more time a collaborator will get. This is how professional personal networks are built up and how followers are recruited. The same principle – time used as investment – also determines how freelancing professionals allocate their time to clients.

The UK hospital consultant has the choice to divide his time, in theory, between his National Health Service patients and his private patients – usually in the proportion of ten parts to one. In practice, he cannot divide his work into such watertight compartments. His difficulty comes because pressure over resources in the National Health Service often means long waiting lists for treatment: NHS patients may have to give months of their time for a few minutes of the consultant's time. But one way for a patient to gain immediate access to a consultant is for him to pay for private treatment, when there is no delay. This collaboration is profitable to the consultant, who is thus pressured by his own interests to make himself more accessible to a private patient. But what happens if a patient cannot afford the full cost of private treatment? In this case, the consultant may, for the price of a consultancy fee only, recommend immediate treatment on the NHS. The consultancy fee in effect buys up months of waiting and the generality of NHS patients bear the cost of preferential treatment that a patient would expect if he could afford to pay privately.

Upon payment of a consultancy fee, the patient enters a triadic relationship (see Chapter 6): he and the consultant are pitted against the hospital administration. It is an unequal contest: the administration is in no position to challenge the consultant's judgement about priorities or, more important, to check on his methods of working. Nor does it check, recognising that the consultant's private practice in effect subsidises the NHS by retaining him within the system. The fiddle is not seen as disruptive but as actually helping the system to function. In the Soviet bloc private fees for dentistry and medicine are expressly discouraged but they, too, are none the less built into the system (Kaiser, 1976, p. 129). 'Thank-you money' allows queue-jumping for those needing operations. It also gains access to the best doctors, an assurance of scarce anaesthetics in dentistry and places in holiday resorts through the issue of convalescent certificates. And it ensures personalised 'time-intensive' treatment rather than the rapid and formalised 'conveyor-belt' treatment available to the *hoi polloi*. As in the UK , the underlying cause is to be found in the low formal pay of highly skilled people where effective demand exists for a scarce resource. In the UK a 'consulting fee' is legal, whereas in the Soviet system 'thank-you money' is not. The effect, however, appears to be the same.

Status and Statelessness

Hawks are often protected from scrutiny, as I have suggested, by 'status' (the medical consultant's judgement) and by what I term 'statelessness'. It is in the nature of these occupations that they involve weak group affiliation. An individual may indeed belong to several groups – in fact, the bigger the hawk the greater the number of groups – but he will strenuously aim to remove any one group's exclusive control over him. And the more groups he is involved in, the easier this will be. It is in this situation and in this sense that hawks are 'stateless': they are *exclusively* bound only to themselves. In conveyancing work, for instance, which is the bread and butter of many solicitors, the solicitor deals with a number of different people and organisations: the vendor, the buyer's solicitor, the Land Registry, the local authority, the mortgagee's building society, and so on. Although superficially his exclusive loyalty belongs to his client, the structure of his occupation always puts *himself and his interests* rather than his client and his client's interests at the centre of things. Here a solicitor's position is structurally ambiguous, and he exploits this ambiguity principally in his use of time. If a client complains of delays in the conveyancing, which will cost him additional expense, the solicitor can always place the blame at someone else's door. In this way, delay as a fiddle is impossible, or at least difficult, to check out. No one other than the solicitor has the complete information which would be needed to do the checking.

The link between delay and incomplete information is implied in the UK Law Society's evidence to the Royal Commission on Legal Services (Law Society, 1977–9). The society reported that it receives about five thousand complaints a year, most of them dealing with 'delay in cases and the solicitor's failure to tell his clients what was happening'. Solicitors are the only professionals I know who never refuse extra work on the grounds that they are already at full capacity: they always take it and cope later. This is because, if pressed about delay, they find it easy to project the blame on other parties.

The canny use of delay can be compared to the prevarication of eighteenth-century European diplomats. Citing J. H. Plumb's account of the peculiar problems Robert Walpole faced in foreign relations, Mary Douglas (1978) saw in that diplomatic arena all the hallmarks of a weak-grid working environment that was also weak on group. Double-dealing (manipulated membership of several groups) and treachery (the unrealised promise of sole affiliation) were endemic, but were 'easily forgiven' (accepted as modes of operation which helped the system to function in its own way). Significantly, delay becomes a powerful device when linked with poor communications (incomplete information). In all these occupations, and in exactly the same way, the hawk offers partial information, while keeping the complete picture of what is happening to himself.

The environment that Adnam Khashoggi moved in and, in a sense, created (as all hawks do) strikingly resembles Plumb's picture of eighteenth-century European intrigue. Khashoggi was stated to have acted as a fixer for two rival American aircraft manufacturers, collecting around $100 million in commission from each. He early showed that he understood the importance of restricting information and registered his corporations away from scrutiny in Lichtenstein. Khashoggi himself actually became, in reality, stateless: he acted for the Belgians, the French and the British, as well as the Americans. His greatest achievement was to represent the interests of both Lockheed and Northrop, who were each pitching for a share of Saudi Arabia's defence budget. Again, he did this by keeping his collaborators in ignorance of each other's deals and of their dealings with him. In style, this is the treachery of the eighteenth-century diplomats. It is hawk fiddling on a global scale.

Public reaction to these disclosures illustrates again the ambiguous view people have of such occupations. Diplomats' treachery was easily forgiven because it was part of the way the diplomatic game was played. Even blatant treachery was no more than a rather too obvious piece of gamesmanship. Nowadays we are less tolerant of revealed 'backdoor' dealings. Allegations that British Leyland had paid slush money in its export markets to smooth through sales were hardly countered by 'If that's the way the game is played, that's how you have to play it'. Hawk occupations have everything to do with winning and with incentives to win, but public sensibilities have to be considered too.

Any Khashoggi needs to be stateless, in the sense of being free from group control, because the interests of one of the groups within his orbit are likely to clash with another. He needs, in these circumstances, to keep knowledge insulated. Where, however, the groups in his orbit do not compete, then the hawk has an easier task. An academic hawk I know frequently travels from the far north of England to London for what is to him a typical overnight stay. On these trips his aim is to 'bunch' appointments; to see people in at least three different organisations. He tries to arrange these appointments in close sequence, partly to save time – his most precious resource – but also to facilitate his extra earnings. By arranging his affairs in this way he can and does charge for three sets of travelling expenses, including first-class rail fare, and for three sets of overnight expenses. In fact he stays on these conglomerate trips with a colleague at no charge to himself and he usually travels in a friend's car for half the cost of the petrol.

The bigger the hawk's status, the bigger the scale of his fiddle. I know one senior medical consultant who has the buying rights to over a million dollars of specialised equipment. Three American companies are competing for his orders so he arranges to travel from London and visit all three of them:

> You can buy an 'all over' ticket that gives you unlimited travel in the States for two weeks – this costs three or four hundred dollars – but you've got to buy it in Europe. So one company pays for me to go and see them in New York. Then I go to another company in Los

Angeles and the third in Las Vegas – and I use my 'all over' ticket.
But I charge the regular charge from New York to Los Angeles
which is about nine hundred dollars – and from New York to Las
Vegas is not much different. They don't mind paying at all – it's
peanuts to them for a big order – but it means quite a bit to me. If
I was really unscrupulous, mind, I could charge all three from
London return!

The point here is not that this hawk carries out rather unremark-
able fiddles but that he is able to exploit several groups who neither
know nor care that he regularly claims similar expenses from the
others. They are prepared – are, in fact, keen – to pay for services
which include expenses, and each transaction is self-contained, a
separate contract to do work. So in real sense *no one* is fiddled,
everyone is happy and scarce resources are maximally used.

What further distinguishes hawk fiddles from other fiddles is
their open-endedness, their moral ambiguity and most important
their pragmatism. Whereas society or an organisation may overtly
resent fiddles, it covertly expects them of the hawk. If the language
can be read, the potential for fiddles is written into the hawk's job
specification. As one of Henry's (1978, p. 38) respondents said:
'There's a standard line that they try people out with . . . It's there
in every situation. You probe and if the bloke's with you you're
away.' The university or college lecturer, for example, has certain
prescribed duties which earn him his basic salary. But it is likely
that he will also develop other activities: write books, operate
consultancies, advise publishers, develop punditry, appear on
television. Indeed, he is encouraged to do these things; such
unofficial activities produce benefits, not just for the lecturer, but
for the institution that employs him. Original and publicised
research is fed back into duties (teaching), and punditry and
publishing reflect well on the institution. But all these links to
other groupings reduce the power of any single group over the
individual. Immediately he diversifies his activities, he fragments
the total information available about him and he insulates each
part from the other parts. Each group with which he transacts –
publishing firm, broadcasting company and college –

only knows what he is doing in terms of its own respective transactions. In his overall transactions and in the terms of these transactions he is bound to none of them exclusively. The ground is prepared for hawk fiddles.

Sometimes, however, an individual may be outmanoeuvred in political machinations. The hawk ideology emphasises that, in practice, because of the competitive tendency to control rather than be controlled, only a few can succeed. The rest, the relatively less successful, are pushed upgrid by the more successful, and it is because of this that organisations not infrequently have to allow a compensatory fiddle to keep these staff happy. An organisation, however, may not have such resources to allocate or would not so allocate them if it had. In these circumstances resentment over the advantages received by a few can cause discord among the many.

Where an overarching bureaucracy exists, envious, competitive and usually less successful colleagues can use it to bring in controls – practices which Harold Bridger (1971) calls 'institutionalised envy'. They attempt to create new rules or to activate old ones with which to limit the autonomy of their more successful colleagues. They will raise arguments concerned with bureaucratic precedent, the neglect of more formalised duties, or the fact that they have to do the work of these absent colleagues. Sometimes, of course, this last argument is well justified. Recent attempts in both US and British colleges to limit the consultancies of successful academics – or rules in the British National Health Service which similarly limit the private work of its clinical academic staffs – often, however, appear motivated by envy, if only because they usually originate from departments, subjects, or individuals whose skills are less marketable.

Hawk fiddles which involve the segmentation of control and the playing-off of different groups are, however, difficult to combat because they are difficult to identify. Only when someone is able to take a *complete* look at what is done, and can thereby gain full information about the whole range of a person's activities, do such fiddles appear disruptive. An investigation on behalf of the Inner London Education Authority took such an overview of its staff's activities. A confidential report concluded that private work by lecturers was 'full of potential conflicts of interest'. Lecturers had, in fact, set up private companies to deliver courses in their college rooms for commissions. In one case a commercial firm paid £95 a day to one 'college company', which then passed £80 to a second company, which in turn paid £60 a day to staff for giving lectures. Seen *together* different transactions did appear to impinge upon each other: 'The total time commitment of the individual may make it difficult for him to be effective in college work . . . time-tables of individual students may be subject to frequent changes to accommodate staff absences, resulting in a lack of continuity of teaching' (*Guardian*, 14 September 1978).

The report revealed all the features of the hawk fiddle: status, statelessness, the freedom to choose collaborators, to transact, to manipulate time. But the fact that timetables *could* be manipulated to make room for this private enterprise suggests that the college lecturer's job is actually structured to be potentially negotiable. It is designed so that it can be re-ordered to provide the kind of rewards the individual feels he is entitled to and which will benefit his status. Indeed, this is recognised by his employer. A Department of Education inspector disclosed that colleges regard private consultancies as useful incentives for senior staff. Indeed, it may be the only way they can secure and retain the most highly qualified, particularly when private industry is competing for the same class of labour. Fiddles, of course, need not involve the same sort of activities as the jobs which seem to encourage them. Because a reporter on a Fleet Street tabloid is able to fiddle time he is thereby able to run a sub-aqua sports shop from his newsroom desk.

It is possible now to look behind the often-made observation that the professional's drive to autonomy and the employing organisation's attempts at control lead to inherent and inevitable conflict between the two (Scott, 1966). It is the professional's involvement in groupings outside his employing organisation that necessarily reduces organisational control. It is his ability to exploit such groupings which gives him a degree of personal space not immediately apparent. And personal space in these occupations allows the opportunity for personal as against organisational advantage.

One further way of measuring success among hawks is gauged by the number and quality of an individual's followers, that is, of people who depend rather more on him than he depends on them. These can be junior professionals or clients. Khashoggi at one time, for instance, could number Richard Nixon and King Khaled among his followers. To succeed, to attract followers of this order, the individual has to corner a resource, to do something no one else is doing or at the very least to do it far better than most. But Khashoggi was expensive, not only because he could 'teach Lockheed the local customs' of Saudi Arabia but also because his followers complemented each other in ways that enormously increased his value.

Khashoggi, however, was a super hawk above the generality of most hawks. For more mundane professionals – the medical consultant, the journalist, the accountant or the academic – their control over others, that is, the number and significance of their followers, derives from their *status*: their 'magic' and specialised skills buttressed by professional monopoly power. If this attribute is high it enhances reputation, which increases the personal power of its possessor. As we saw, when a medical consultant enables a patient to jump the queue for NHS treatment his judgement will not – indeed, cannot – be questioned. The consultant is the equivalent of the competitive 'big man' in a New Guinea village (Forge, 1970); he is not unique like a Khashoggi, but it is only really possible for him to be challenged by another 'big man'. Armed with his reputation for special skills, the 'big man' achieves the power of a magician or *shaman* and his powers and scarcity have to be respected by smaller men. When it was suggested, for example, that UK Members of Parliament were making use of their secretarial allowance (about £3,000 a year) without making use of secretaries, the Fees Office which pays these allowances brushed aside any suggestion of any investigation. MPs, it pointed out, are 'honourable gentlemen' in title and, it followed, in practice. Either such 'big men' are impossible to cross-examine (like medical consultants) because of their real or imagined special skills; or (like MPs) their office puts them implicitly *above* investigation. 'Men like him', it was said of Benvenuto Cellini 'are not bound by the laws.'

Moonlighters and Breakaways

There are four main ways that an employed hawk is likely to find his position at risk. The first is when his immediate chief leaves his post and he has to renegotiate a new individual contract with a new contract-maker. A second is when he finds himself the political loser in bureaucratic action following a power shift. A third arises when flair-based organisations become rigidified by stultifying bureaucratic ritualism. Finally, there are external constraints that come from above the operating level or outside it – as, for instance in directives that come down from the board or from an imposed government incomes policy. All four reduce the hawk's ability to exploit his flair.

I have shown that hawks tend to circumvent such constraints: the individual can re-assert his individuality by moving into an area in which he is freer to negotiate. Yoric Wintergreen is a married accountant in his mid-twenties. In his job, the only full response to pay restraint is a change of job. The partial response, however, is moonlighting.

> They're very pleased if, when you move, you bring clients in with you, and they don't really care if they come from the firm you've been working for. But they hate the idea of you doing it yourself: they don't like moonlighting one bit – in fact it's against the contract of employment.
>
> What happens with moonlighting is that you get to know particular clients even though you don't sign the letters to them. Letters are always signed by the partners but clients soon get to know from the letter references who it is is actually working on their cases. Anyway, you build up a relationship. So when you

move you say, 'Well, I won't be dealing with your case after the end of the month'; and if he's built up a relationship with you he might say, 'Why not? I'd like you to keep on with it'; and then you'll say, 'No, I'm changing jobs, I'm moving to So-and-So'; and he'll say, 'Well, I've no reason to stay with Such-and-Such a firm, can I move with you too?'. And then you can say, 'Well, I'm starting a small private practice myself and I could fit you in on that. It'd be cheaper, of course, than Such-and-Such has been charging you, because there's less overheads.' And of course, he's absolutely delighted.

In the fullest possible way, the accountant here is re-establishing the essential freedoms of hawk dealing — the freedom to transact, to attract followers, to control rather than be controlled. The potential for this style of operation is always built into employed hawk occupations. Indeed, it *has* to be to retain enterprise, as we saw with lecturers, dental technicians, medical consultants and many others. So these fiddles produce a paradox. In return for a fiddle-prone environment, the organisation attracts a scarce resource — 'flair' — but it does so at a price. The accountant with flair applies it for the benefit of his firm but he is also likely to use it for his own benefit and the two are not necessarily compatible.

I took about twelve clients when I moved from the last company, and since then it's been growing because if you do a good service they recommend their friends. It's all much friendlier, too. Moonlighting is getting pretty well accepted — partly because of inflation. Inflation means that everyone has to do extra to survive. I'm not the only one in my firm who's moonlighting. Running your own practice in this kind of way has lots of advantages. You're not taking risks when you're moonlighting because you still have a steady job, and then there's the use of the firm's library. If I went independent, I know I could never afford to set up a library like the firm's got. There's not only the books, but there's also the subscriptions to all their intelligence reports. These contain details of things you can't do without, such as script issues for capital gains, movements in *The Financial Times* index, and so forth. In fact some of the cases and records go back to the eighteen-eighties.

You could never get that kind of back-up if you were independent. And then of course you can always get advice on your more difficult cases from more experienced members of staff and the partners. So you can see that it isn't so much the time that can be fiddled on your own cases that's so important. In fact, I often do my cases during the lunch hour (*laugh*). Then, of course, they think you're *really* keen!

As well as all the facilities such as the library and the records and the advice you can get by moonlighting in a company, you also get the benefit of their office equipment, particularly the 'phone and the photostatting machine which are big advantages – though they're really available to everyone who works in an office. But the really big advantage is that the clients you deal with in moonlighting are *your* clients. You're directly involved and you build up relationships with them. That's what I like.

Such moonlighting poses an increasing problem for professional firms in the private sector, such as associations of lawyers or accountants which, as they grow into ever larger units, come to possess an ever-diminishing proportion of profit-sharing partners. Because the firm, not the moonlighter, bears the cost of these overheads, the moonlighter can afford to undercut the firm. One result of the increasing bureaucratisation of professionals, therefore, is that we can expect to find an increasing move of such professional services into the hidden and black economies.

Organisations such as hospitals and college administrations which employ a high proportion of professionals, but which are firmly set in the public sector and therefore prone to the problems of private sector comparability, might well see this as a price worth paying to retain specialised individual initiative and scarce skills. If they object, they risk losing the hawk *and* the advantages he brings. As we have seen, there is constant pressure from organisations (which are by definition oriented around the idea of rules) to reduce this kind of freedom and to control their staffs' own methods of operating. But controls over hawks are almost always bound to fail. On the other hand, employing organisations still need to attract flair. This is why so many firms have a love/hate relationship with the professionals they employ. They both admire and need the individual who has room to manoeuvre and to transact freely with others (the accountant who brings his own clients with him; the cosmopolitan academic with prestige, extensive contacts and his own consultancies). At the same time they resent his liberties and their own lack of control. But if the firm is to survive, let alone prosper, there *must* be a possibility that the organisation can be 'abused'; there *must* in fact be a fiddle potential. The first clients of breakaway advertising agencies, recruitment agencies, market research firms, publishers and management consultancies are often acquired unofficially (sometimes illegally) in this way from 'parent' organisations which have lost their flexibility and therefore their fiddle potential. These are all firms where the amount of capital needed to set them up is relatively small but where their greatest, indeed their only *real*, capital is the often under-rated skill, flair and experience of their professional staffs. To a lesser extent the same is true of domestic tradesmen such as plumbers, carpenters, electricians and repairmen where personal relationships are important to the transaction and where the good can be very good and the bad disastrous. Other things being equal, the smaller these firms the better the level of personal service because they allow for individual negotiation and involvement in the job without bureaucratic intrusion, overheads and control. It is when they grow beyond a minimum optimum size that they become vulnerable to the more outrageous fiddles and tend to develop a high likelihood of fission. It has been rightly observed, for instance, that when a publisher acquires a smart new office block this is often the beginning of the end.

Breakaways, then, represent a constant effort within personal service and flair-based industries to overcome bureaucratic constraints and to re-establish flair: that is, a quick adaptability to the needs of the market and a responsiveness to change. The nearer they are to the action, the more direct their contact with the ultimate purchaser, then the more responsive they have to be. Enterprises like the fashion industry, the music supplies industry and firms within the youth market thrive best in *ad hoc* groupings which focus on creative people with flair and which permit a quick and easy turnover of their personnel. Such flair-based industries always have to allow individuals to negotiate their 'unofficial rewards' personally rather than collectively. It is the story in all occupations where flair is at a premium and where the most important input is human capital: the more competitive and turbulent the market, the more flair that is needed and the scarcer this resource, the more mobile its possessor and the more fluid his situation.

Hawk jobs are adaptable, constantly responding to pressures for change and innovation. They attract and reward people who successfully need to reconstruct their world a bit, who order it in a way that suits them. At the same time they penalise and reject those who cannot or will not adapt. And since innovation and inventiveness are vital aspects of entrepreneuriality and therefore of hawks' jobs, their bearers need a flexible work environment that is in their control. Being hawks, *if is is not flexible enough – they will bend it.*

Hawk fiddles are, therefore, part of the elasticity of these occupations. They are intrinsic rather than extrinsic: donkey fiddles stand outside the mode of work. Take them away and the mode of work remains unchanged; prevent a supermarket checkout girl from fiddling the till and you do not alter her job at all. But take away the fiddle in a hawk job, and you are likely to alter the mode of the task completely.

3

Donkey Jobs

The Supermarket Checkout Girl's Story

It's amazing, really. In six weeks, just by keeping my eyes open, I knew all that was going on. On a busy day you take in something like three and a half to four thousand pounds on your till. It averages, I suppose, something like one thousand, five hundred pounds a day, and when you remember there are six tills in the one shop, you can see how busy it is.

The fiddle is really straightforward — you don't fiddle the customer. You ring up on the till less than the proper charge and take the difference.

Very few customers bother about their ticket; it usually just falls amongst the pile of rubbish on the floor. If anyone does ask for their ticket, you just say: 'It's down there if you'd like to sort it out.' They never do. The other fiddle, of course, is when your mother or a friend comes in. Then they get away with a load of stuff and you put hardly anything through the till.

You've got to have a mind like a calculating machine: and at first it's quite a strain keeping check all day — specially if they check the tills several times a day. At first it was a fantastic strain, but after a few months it became easily managed routine.

After I'd been here a while I started to use a spare compartment in the till. There are three sections for notes and I use two and put my fiddle money in the third. There's not much risk, really, because you're supposed to find a place for foreign coins and the change that's sometimes left behind by customers. When you've made enough change to take out a note, then you swap over.

Position is very important. If your till is by a wall, there's a blind side, isn't there? There are always people watching what you're doing in a supermarket, but a blind side cuts down the chances of being seen. What you've got to do is to be brazen. Just look them in the eye – and look bored – which isn't difficult because it is boring, very boring.

When I got into the swing of it I used to fiddle twenty or twenty-five pounds a day, and then stop, but now it's tailed off and I mostly take out only eight to ten pounds. Whatever you take you've got to be clever, to know what you're up to. What's so surprising to me is that most managers don't know what's happening. They're very bothered by what they call 'petty pilferage' – taking stuff off the shelves. They've no idea of till fiddles.

The man who became my brother-in-law worked in this same store for eighteen months and he was astonished when, after he left, I told him what went on. Mind you, they have a very low level of management. He'd been a milk roundsman before taking on that job and he was pretty typical.

It's obvious they don't know what happens because when they close tills down during a slack time they often close the middle ones, leaving the side ones still working.

What they do is make an example out of petty things. They sacked one girl for petty pilferage because she was seen by someone to take two peaches on her way to her break. No one knew who'd told on her. She said she was going to pay for them and maybe she was, and maybe she wasn't, but they didn't give her a chance. And they told social security she'd been sacked for petty pilferage, so she couldn't get any dole. Another time they sacked a girl for stealing when she really hadn't stolen at all. It was all a stupid mistake. They sacked her on the spot, just the same, with no notice and all the time they're losing a fortune on the tills. While this was going on the under-manager's wife, who also worked there, was taking home her groceries without paying. I used to see her collecting the stuff in a bag and taking it through to her husband's office. I never said anything.

Of course, it's a lousy firm, a really lousy firm; girls are always leaving and so are managers. A friend of mine was once ten pounds down on her till. She never fiddled a penny but the manager said she must have taken it. She was so upset she said she couldn't work there if they thought she'd taken the ten pounds, so she left. Afterwards when they'd checked it all they discovered the error but they never wrote to her — just asked me if I saw her to tell her that it was OK. That's typical, they treat you like dirt, as if you have no intelligence at all. It's the little things like that, things you can't often remember, that makes them a horrible firm. It's horrible too because the pay is so low — even compared to similar jobs in other shops.

It's also a lousy firm in other ways. The girls are always backbiting and bitchy; there's a lot of gossip all the time. Nobody ever accuses anyone of fiddling the tills, though. That's never ever mentioned by anyone. Nothing is ever said — even by management — even when you first start. It's just not done to mention fiddling. New girls just have to find out for themselves. It's obvious to me, though, who fiddles and who doesn't. Some never will — the nervous ones and the stupid ones and those who can't cope with it. There are eight cashiers and three certainly do — probably four. You need a clear head and not everyone's got a clear head. I have one friend at the store who's been at school with me and she fiddles too, but we never even discuss it. If things are busy and packers are needed she'll always try to pack with me. There's never anything mentioned — no exchange of cash or anything — but if she hasn't been on a till much during the day and she's packed with me then I'll pay for drinks if we go out of an evening. Otherwise there aren't many friendships among the girls. Occasionally if you're checking a girl's own groceries you'll say something like 'Right, that's a pound for the lot'. But you have to be careful who you do it for — they can be very stupid and say something like 'But it should be a lot more than that'. No, there are absolutely no alliances or anything like that.

Another way in which it is a lousy firm is because they fiddle the customers. Every now and then one of the managers will come up to you, usually with a packet of tea, and put it close to the till, near the sweets and chocolates so that it can be taken as a purchase, and say 'put that through a couple of hundred times, will you'. There's never any explanation of *why* you're to do it, what it's for — but it's to sort out their stocks. It is usually done just before and just after stock-taking and it'll just be for a day. Not all the girls are asked to do it. Once a girl was daft, for instance, and she asked what it was for, and he said 'Oh, forget it'.

When you're there for a while you get to know who're the finicky ones. One man, for instance, comes through every Saturday and always checks every item. It's no good doing it to him. And it's no good doing it to anyone with only half-a-dozen items – it can show up too easily. You've got to be a good judge of character. But if someone does query it you've just got to say 'Oh, isn't it yours?'. Who isn't fiddled? Well, old people – you'd never do it to an old person – mind you, this is the girls' ruling, not the managers'. And you'd not do it to anyone with young children. You tend to take account of how well dressed people are. 'Oh', you think, 'they can afford an extra thirty pence,' or whatever it is. It isn't always tea, sometimes it's done with dented cans put close to the till, but the effect is always the same.

Another thing you may be interested in. They're always bothered about greengrocery. You see there is always a lot of wastage on greengrocery, it's a difficult class of goods to order properly. You have three buttons on the till, one for greengrocery, one for butchery and one for general groceries, and these mark the till rolls so that head office can know how much of each class of goods is sold. To stop head office knowing they've blundered in their ordering they'll come up to you and say 'Put the next half dozen through on greengrocery'. They never explain why, of course, and you're just expected to do it. I don't think management regard it as a fiddle, though, they think of it more as a way of stopping trouble. But when you get to fiddling things for them, you obviously get to fiddling things for yourself.

Donkey fiddles thrive in jobs where a person is both insulated from co-workers and constrained by rules. The extreme example, as we have seen, is probably provided by the nineteenth-century skivvy in a one-servant family who was tightly constrained by rules determining her position in time and place and who had her mode of work closely defined for her (Douglas, 1978). Such a worker could relate neither to other servants nor to the family who employed her and her life was minutely divided up and controlled. Insulation, however, may arise from a physical cause: the supermarket checkout girl is tied to her till; the lift operator to his lift; the bus conductor to his bus. Or the insulation may be more deeply etched into a job – the single storeman in charge of stock or the security guard guarding premises who must, by definition of their jobs, exclude outsiders and keep random intrusions to a minimum.

But these jobs have something else in common: they lack autonomy. Discretion over how they are carried out is minimal because they are all tightly controlled by rules that have an external source. The security guard must check in at his HQ at regular intervals; the supermarket girl cannot use her initiative but must follow laid-down procedures if anything out of the ordinary interrupts her routinised day. These jobs also share the fact that workers in them are likely to feel resentment at the constraints that bind them and where this is so it is reflected in their fiddles. Fiddles here aim to gain control – to overcome a job's constraints – and where jobs are so 'overcontrolled' that there is not even the opportunity to fiddle, then here we are likely to find, as a counter-response, the move into sabotage (Taylor and Walton, 1971, p. 38).

Donkey jobs differ from hawk jobs, then, essentially because in the latter a person can *choose* how he works and to whom he relates, while in the former he has very few areas of choice; the structured nature of the job removes such freedoms.

Jobs on long and noisy mass-production belts are good examples of donkey jobs. Not only are physical movements constrained from outside, by the pace of the belt and the 'rules' of the 'time and motion' men, but a man's freedom to relate to others is limited to his immediate neighbours – to those who precede and succeed him on the line. This is a severe constraint because his neighbours' usefulness and the benefits they can provide are in turn limited by *their* isolation. Though he works *with* people he does not *relate* to them and, in the terms used here, does not form part of a group:

> With the line you've got to adapt yourself to the speed. Some rush and get a break. I used to try and do that but the job used to get out

of hand. I just amble along now. Thirty seems a lot when you're working here. Some jobs you're on you can't talk or you'll lose concentration. When I came here first I couldn't talk at all. Now I can manage a few words with the man opposite me. (Beynon, 1975, p. 118)

The contrast in mass-production industries between men 'on the line' and managers and 'service' men is perhaps the most marked contrast in production today and one responsible for much resentment. Men who can physically move around a plant, applying their skills to different parts of the process, can temporarily attach themselves to groups or other individuals. Managers and specialist workers, like electricians and maintenance men, have this kind of freedom and the autonomy over how they do a job that goes with it.

The ability to move about through a production or retailing process is important because it lets the individual worker rather than his employer control his activities in both place and time. A favourite army dodge is to volunteer for part-time courses, not for the courses themselves, but for the increased control over time that they provide. A person cannot be in two places at one time, but he can be in *neither* place at one time. Because he is exclusively tied neither to his regular not to his part-time activity, his respective superiors in both cannot be sure whether the demands of one justify his being absent from the other.

Donkey workers lack this kind of mobility. A checkout girl's hours are not her hours, but the hours of a supermarket's trading; her time is not negotiable. Because she *is* a checkout girl, she has no business away from the till; her place is not negotiable. And since there is only one legitimate way of operating the till her *modus operandi* is also not negotiable.

The donkey type of fiddle is an appropriate response to this minimal autonomy. Since the job isolates the worker, the worker fiddles in isolation. Donkey fiddlers do not progress through a well-defined and socially set 'moral career' (that is, one which involves a moral transformation) such as is found in strong-group occupations where the group gradually introduces a new worker to the fiddles which it practises either *as* a group or individually with the group's approval and which Ditton (1977a) has carefully set out as occurring among the bread roundsmen he studied. Among donkeys the norm is that individuals both learn and fiddle in isolation. As our quoted supermarket cashier put it: 'It's just not done to mention fiddling. New girls just have to find out for themselves.'

This is not to say there is *no* induction among donkeys. The newcomer may quickly become aware of a climate of fiddling which affects all levels of an organisation's hierarchy. Manager's stratagems to set books right, particularly in sales and distribution, often supply the moral impetus to an employee's fiddling. This is because they periodically have to involve their staffs in the deception — as our supermarket cashier's management involved her. If this happens, as she observed: 'When you get to fiddling things for them, you obviously get to fiddling things for yourself.'

In extreme cases, then, and at crisis times such as before inventory-taking, there may be a quite conscious collusion between management and staff, by the placing of articles on checkout counters and getting the cashier to add them to customers' bills, as we have seen, or by 'marking up' items for sale without the clearance or knowledge of head office. This 'periodic collusion' sets the scene for a triadic shift in alliances (see Chapter 6); it might well explain why a US study found that although 90 per cent of supermarket staffs regularly created shortages of $1·5 million a year (quoted in Ditton, 1977a, p. 88), the figure for all retail outlets is less, and has been put at only 75 per cent (Zeitlin, 1971, p. 24).

For the most part, however, fiddles in these jobs are as insulated as are the job-holders themselves and they operate very much as the jobs themselves operate. For example, a salesgirl in a London store carried out a typical retailing fiddle. She made out imaginary refund dockets, sending them up to the accounts department and pocketing the money that came back down the Lamson tube. It can be seen immediately that the nature of her job suggested the form the fiddle would take. But her job also limited her to a narrow range of possible fiddles.

The salesgirl, like the mass-production-line worker, has a *repetitive* job. (Whether or not it is monotonous is beside the point.) She is pinned down at a single point within the retailing system. Unlike the production-line worker, she *does* see plenty of different faces; but always from the same standpoint. Transactions are always different, yet always the same. Contrast her with the manager or floor supervisor, who can move through the whole selling process of the store: supervising deliveries, checking stock, checking sales and dealing with staff problems and customer complaints. And he further has the autonomy to decide when he will do what. While the manager who has a hawk job within a strong-grid workplace sees the store's activities progressing cyclically like the hand movements of an analogue watch, the cashier sees merely a *repetition* of a single event, disconnected from whatever proceeds it, like the figure changes of a digital watch.

A hawk fiddler can take advantage of his overall view. A store manager can, for instance, recategorise goods as old, stale, or damaged, and then follow this through by altering stock records, accounts, or till rolls (Dalton, 1964, pp. 208–9). The cashier's fiddle, however, can take advantage only of the single-strand nature of a cashier's transactions; that is, taking money from, or refunding money to, customers. The more she wants to benefit from the fiddle, the more frequently she has to repeat it.

Thus the solitary donkey-type fiddler must make a virtue of the repetitive nature of her job. A bar steward who worked on the *Queen Mary* consistently short-measured drinkers on transatlantic crossings by sticking a dime to the bottom of a spirit measuring-cup. The amount fiddled in each measure was so small as to be barely detectable, but over tours of several weeks it provided the steward with an appreciable informal income.

A donkey fiddle therefore turns a job back on itself, and particularly in the way its occupants respond to rigid controls. In this type of job, the work situation controls the worker to a greater extent than the worker controls his situation. Controls may be explicit. Checkout girls, for example, are often forbidden to have money on their persons when working at a till, and are usually forbidden to serve friends or members of their own family. This last restriction recognises the system of personal morality which Henry (1978) sees as fundamental to hidden economy trading and which Stirling (1968) sees working against bureaucratic organisations in southern Italy. While the individual feels he has special obligations to friends and relatives, the organisation insists that its services must be dispensed equally and without favour.

Yet there are also implicit controls, which any fiddler has to recognise and counter. The till exercises the most obvious of these – the control of money. The cashier may simply over-ride this control by 'voiding' a transaction and pocketing the money. However, this is such a direct and unsubtle challenge to the control system that security-conscious managements have developed a rule of thumb about it: whenever 'no sale' is registered, someone is likely to have his hand in the till. The cashier may also try to keep pace with control by 'creaming'; that is, by removing small quantities of money consistently over a long period of time. Here the till may have a built-in advantage. Modern cash registers provide audit rolls which record all transactions throughout the day. This shifts the accounting control from the employee to management. The cashier has to have a quick mind to wrest back any of this control, as our cited supermarket cashier has explained.

A quick mind, however, is usually not enough. The cashier also needs an informal accounting system of her own to enable her to keep pace with the formal accounting system of the cash register. Cashiers have to be able to estimate accurately how many times they have rung short during the day to measure the extent of a repetitious fiddle, and to avoid detection. To do this, they may keep a small pile of pins or matches on their desks to keep tally. Each pin or match will represent, say, 10p which the cashier has fiddled. Or they may use sweets, either transferring them from one pocket to another or putting them in their mouths each time they ring a 'short' (Wright, 1971, p. 56).

74

This informal accounting breaches the principle that control of money belongs to the management, just as in earlier times the individual worker's possession of a watch was seen as breaching the principle that working time belongs to the management. As Ditton (1972) points out, it was not unusual once for factory-owners to forbid workers to bring their own watches to work. The present-day practice of presenting a retiring employee with a gold watch symbolises the emancipation of the worker from this kind of control: henceforth his time is, quite literally, his own.

Time-Cycles and Rule-Bending

We have seen that some people can increase their personal time at the expense of management time by 'destructuring' their activities (volunteering for a day-release course, for example) so that they are not pinned down to any one activity. Donkey jobs however, embed their workers in a set of highly structured controls — particularly over space. Though the cashier cannot leave her till, the security guard the premises he guards, or the bus conductor his bus, nevertheless some of these workers *can* fiddle time.

In these jobs the fiddling of time is common and it is focused *inwards* on the nature of the job itself, rather than *outwards* by playing one job off against another. To fiddle, the worker in a highly structured job has to make a virtue of its structure. For example, absence from work is, by implication, just as highly structured as attendance at work. It is, then, by recognising and working *within* structured absences, that the resentful worker fiddles time. In this way, absenteeism is a major fiddle.

In a shop the sales staff's time is rigidly structured: if they are not behind their counters, they are not doing their job. There is little ambiguity in their function, and therefore little room for manoeuvre. Absences from the counter are structured by management control of time: rest periods and tea-breaks are specifically limited to ten or fifteen minutes. The individual, however can manipulate this control to his or her own advantage. Because the

75

time allotted for breaks is unnegotiable, someone returning late from a break can argue 'I took my break five minutes late' (and therefore it had to over-run by five minutes). Unless the organisation keeps a constant check on the way its structured timetable is operating, individuals can turn it to their own advantage. If there is no give-and-take in a ten-minute break (no more than ten minutes and, obviously, no less), its very rigidity can be used to justify longer absences. On a larger scale, this can be seen operating in sickness absence. Because some systems of control allow two days of 'sickness' to elapse before an employee needs a medical certificate as proof of illness, fiddled sickness absence in these jobs invariably lasts for two days.

The fiddling of time is such an important donkey fiddle that it is worth looking at some of the assumptions behind the idea of 'management time' and 'personal time'. Anthropologists have long been aware that conceptions of time are culturally determined. The Calvinist work ethic adopted by 'advanced' industrial societies has produced the concept of 'linear time', where time is seen as a flow, where 'lost' time can never be regained – where time is, in fact, money. The seasonal nature of life in non-industrialised agricultural societies, however, operates on 'cyclical time' which is not conducive to ideas of urgency or punctuality. If a job is not done today, it can be put off until tomorrow. Cyclical time is repetitive time. Margaret Mead, comparing the Greek and American views of time, notes that 'Greeks pass the time, they do not save or accumulate or use it. And they are intent on passing time not on budgeting it' (1955, p. 70).

The different views of time held in different cultures have been used to explain the 'laziness' of certain ethnic groups in Western society. The West Indian, it is claimed, is unpunctual even in punctual societies because he has no concept of 'lateness'. The same applies to Greeks: 'the [Greek] attitude [to time] is still widely prevalent, even in the area of private life among the urban groups' (loc. cit.). But note the use of the qualification 'private'. There is no reason to suppose that a 'cyclical' view of time is not modified where a 'linear' view of time is the norm. Even though a Greek may 'pass' time in his home life, he will 'keep' time in his working life. The West Indian may be late for work, not because of his ethnocentric view of time, but for some less exotic reason. A study of urban American blacks found that of those who were consistently late for work, the majority had no alarm clocks. Other culturally insignificant factors may, of course, have contributed. The blacks had to travel in from the poorer areas of the city, where public transport was inadequate. It *could* be argued that both the lack of alarm clocks and the fact that the blacks lived in poorer areas of the city were culturally determined. Equally, though, the explanation for lateness may simply be that it is difficult for poor minorities to get to work on time each morning. This view of time as varying with perception is worth spelling out because it seems that the nature of production imposes a linear view of time upon individuals who naturally have a cyclical view of time; and that the mismatch results in fiddles of time.

But this is not what appears to happen. The division of labour among Adam Smith's pin-makers chopped up what had been a linear job – the manufacture of a pin by a single man through all its processes – into a series of cyclical jobs, in which different men performed different parts of the operation, *over and over again*. As with the digital watch, every operation is different in the sense of its being the second or third or fourth, but at the same time it is exactly the same. The checkout girl's job imposes not a linear but a similar cyclical view of time; her job-cycle is also repeated again and again. Only where control is relaxed and the individual is free to see the operation as a whole do the linear characteristics of the job appear. Management, as we have seen, can be – must be – aware of the whole retailing process from back door to front door.

Yet not every donkey job works in cycles. The bus crew's job is by its nature linear, a progression from the start of a journey to the finish in a set time. Their working day, however, is organised cyclically: the *same* journey is repeated in a shift. In turn, the shift is ordered in a linear fashion beginning at one point in the day and ending at another.

It seems, therefore, too simple to see the 'natural', pre-

industrial view of time breaking through the industrial organisation of time in the shape of time-fiddling. Instead it might be true
that in production work, indeed in all intrinsically repetitive
work, management time is 'analogue time' and the individual's
time is 'digital time'. In other kinds of work, where the nature of
the task is only extrinsically repetitive (like the repetition of a bus
crew's journey), the reverse may be true.

Speeding Up and Slowing Down

A theory of time-fiddling can now be developed which takes
account of the employer's and the employee's different perceptions
of the nature of employment.

Hypothesis 1   In occupations where the individual perceives his
task to be cyclical, he will fiddle time (and thereby
money) by slowing the rate of the task down.

Hypothesis 2   In occupations where the individual perceives his
task to be linear, he will fiddle time by speeding the
rate of the task up.

We can test the first hypothesis by looking at the way
production workers fiddle time. In her study of a manufacturing
firm, pseudonym 'Multiproducts Ltd', Lisl Klein (1964) shows
that machine-operators on piecework believed that the way in
which they worked while they were being timed by a time-study
engineer would affect the price they were paid for each operation.
They therefore slowed the job down and made it look more difficult
than it was. The fiddle was to create as large a gap as possible
between the time a job appeared to take and the time it actually
took. After the time-study engineer had set a price for the job, they
could then return to working their machines at an easy rate for the
same money. In this way operators could increase their earnings by
upping   the   work   rate   once   a   price   had   been   set,   or

alternatively they could enjoy a slower pace of work, or they could, as Roy (1952) shows, combine the two. They could work fast when they wanted to and 'bank' a surplus which could then 'fund' a more leisurely time later. They could thus beat the system and increase the choices open to them.

The fiddle here is double-pronged, and appears only partly to confirm Hypothesis 1. On the one hand, it consists of stratagems to make the job seem more arduous than it is. Klein noted that operators tensed muscles in a particular way, moved slowly and twisted tools more often than was necessary. On the other hand, it consists of stratagems for speeding the job up after a price had been set, such as putting up the rate of the machine, doing two operations simultaneously, or ignoring precautions.

In fact a rate was set according to the work a machine did rather than in response to the style of work of the operator. As Klein points out, the operators, and even some of the machine-setters, *believed* that how quickly or slowly they performed would affect the price that was set. From *their* point of view there was little point in slowing down if you did not then possess the choice to speed up. The one stratagem made the other possible; or so the operators believed. The hypothesis, therefore, seems to hold. Piecework is an intrinsically cyclical method of working, and the way to get control over it is to slow it down while it is being priced.

In this way the fiddling checkout girl also gains some control over her management's accounting procedures. The time-study engineer's function is roughly comparable to the cash register's. He too records the man—machine transactions and provides a 'total' (a price) of their value. Working slowly, therefore, can be compared with ringing short. In both cases the medium of control is given only as much information as the individual chooses to give it. The cash register may be programmed to try to regain lost control by having it carry out various additional checks; for instance, estimating and recording the change that should be given to a customer, thereby making short-ringing difficult for all but mathematical wizards. Likewise the time-study engineer may assume, as Klein says, that operators are going slow and allow for it in the price he sets.

Attempts by individuals to wrest control are normally countered by organisations imposing further, more stringent controls. The effect of these is to push the individual further upgrid. Often this will prompt fiddling through resentment where there was none before. At 'Multiproducts' the time-study engineers learned to watch out for fiddles.

> When I first started I had never met piecework before. I just had no idea that anyone might want to catch you; it never entered my vision. I assumed that everyone was honest, but I found that where wages are concerned that doesn't apply. As a time study engineer I find that though I try to be trusting, I don't really trust anyone. They're not always there, the fiddles, but I find that I'm always alert for them. (Klein, 1964, p. 20)

As a result, Klein says, the time-study engineer may overcompensate and assume that all workers are deliberately keeping the speed down. If he then sets a 'true' price for the job, adjusted to take account of this deliberate slowness, he may *compel* fiddling by the hitherto 'innocent' operator. Increased control thus builds increased resentment leading to increased fiddling.

Sometimes the introduction of new ways of working may inadvertently restrict freedom of movement and freedom to transact. The introduction of pocket 'bleepers', by which a management can summon its workers when it needs them, will suddenly restrict the freedom of a hotel porter, an electrician, or indeed anyone who, though not self-employed, is nevertheless self-*deployed*. The motorcycle dispatch rider may have chosen his job because, on the face of it, it allowed him a degree of personal freedom. But he soon finds that the radio link with head office cramps this freedom. More important, it limits his freedom to transact, to choose which jobs he will do and how much he will earn.

> You get paid according to how many trips you do and how long they are. So you try to do as much as you can. But sometimes when

you're out on one job, the office will come through on the radio and ask you to go to another job 'while you're out there'. This way they need only pay you for the one job. So sometimes you make excuses, you've had trouble with the bike or something.

From the office's point of view, putting a rider on to two or three jobs is more efficient than having him start out from the office three times. From the rider's point of view, the management is asking him to do three jobs for the price of one. In response, he can, like the checkout girl, simply 'void' the control system in his case by switching his radio off. But this is bound to be detected. More subtly, he can tie himself down to the one job until the office gives the other two to another rider and then return to base. This ensures that any *further* jobs he is asked to do will be paid for.

The dispatch rider provides a good example of a job where a simple piece of technology – in this case cheap radio receiver/transmitters – can transform the conditions of whole groups of workers. At one stroke it moves them upgrid: it can turn hawks and vultures into donkeys. In a similar way hotel security men and junior hospital doctors, large numbers of whom have been issued with 'bleeps', now find that their jobs have moved out of their control. As a hotel security man put it: 'It's like being on a bloody chain all the time now – you can't even slope off for a cup of bloody tea. The desk puts out the bleep for you and you've got to go and see what they want.'

In these jobs, then, an individual's time is not his own unless he can grab some of it back from the systems of control. Nothing more obviously controls a person's time than a timetable, and public transportation is therefore a battleground where the fight for control is based on fights over time. If we examine the experience of a Blackpool tram conductor we can test Hypothesis 2 – that if job structures are perceived as linear, fiddles will be concerned with speeding up time. A vehicle's timetable represents the transport management's notion of how long a journey is likely to take, given a certain number of mandatory stops and allowing for discretionary stops. How long the journey actually takes is up to the vehicle's crew. The advantage of speeding up a journey is nominal – a ten-minute break at the end of the run – but it represents an important switch in control.

> The main aim in being a tram conductor is to control the job and to stop it controlling you. This is why tram crews will go to all sorts of extremes to get a tram from A to B ten minutes earlier than it should get there so that they can get a ten-minute break the other end. The times are so worked out that if you follow the route properly you'll never get any tea-break at all and you'll be working your guts out for the whole shift. So the main aim of the job as I can see it is to fiddle time. (Blackpool tram conductor)

Since an important time-fiddling technique depends upon the conductor's quick ringing of the bell, it is important to have a driver who understands what is happening and who responds equally quickly. Although donkey fiddles are usually 'loner' fiddles, they do sometimes need an accomplice to make them work. The accomplice can often 'realise' a system of fiddling which has been devised individually but needs support to put it into action. The essential point is that with or without the use of accomplices, this kind of fiddle is an *isolated* action or mode of action within a heavily rulebound system of working:

> If your driver is slow on the getaway when you've given him the bell or you are slow on giving him the bells, you can lose all chance of any tea-breaks. The best driver I've ever worked with is Bill Walsh. I'd been casually put with him for one day at the start of the season and during the break he said 'By God, Gerry, I've never known anyone pick up so few passengers. Do you want a regular driver?'

This conductor had decided on his own that picking up as few passengers as possible was the quickest way to move the tram from A to B and the surest way to earn himself a tea-break at the journey's end. How he did this illustrates the way in which the donkey fiddler uses the rules of the job in such a way that the job's requirements are turned back on themselves to achieve the reverse of what is intended. Inspectors, as agents of management control, can only check that the rules are being applied; not that they are applied in the management's favour.

The conductor's stratagems can be broadly classed as (1) those directed at taking on board as few passengers as possible so that the vehicle can speed to its destination with few interruptions and (2) those directed at taking on an excess of passengers *at the start of the route* with the object of being able to legitimately speed past queues waiting along the route. Class (1) includes over-running the stops by thirty yards ('That way nobody can say we don't obey the rules') and providing passengers with purely negative information.

> I say, 'This tram goes to A, B and C (places at the end of the line that nobody's interested in) but it doesn't go to X, Y and Z', and I list a lot of other places they aren't interested in either. This way, instead of telling them the places we do go, which is where most of them want to go anyway, they're so baffled they don't know what the hell is going on. After this spiel, I look at them all – still with the door only open a bit – and say quickly 'OK?'. Then I ring the bell and we're off again.

Here, again, the rules are turned to the conductor's advantage. It is part of his job to tell passengers where the vehicle will stop, but he can be selective in providing this information. It is similarly part of his job to ensure that he only passes waiting passengers if his vehicle is full. Therefore Hypothesis 2 also appears to stand: that a worker who perceives this task as linear will fiddle time by speeding up the rate of the task.

False Collusion

Selective information need not always be negative in its effects. Instead of reducing the level of job efficiency it can sometimes increase it or at least appear to do so – which, where personal service is involved, amounts to the same thing. The waiter who is asked by a customer what he can recommend from the menu will be more than pleased to suggest the roast beef or saddle of lamb provided it stands on a trolley in the dining-room. This is because such dishes are not served from the kitchen. He thus avoids the security system of checkers who mark down every main course as it leaves the kitchen and thus keep a record of the number of meals served. The waiter, therefore, by avoiding this control, can pocket not only the price of the beef course but that of the whole meal (Mars, 1973).

The essence of this kind of fiddle is the 'false collusion' that is involved, the suggestion that a favour is being done for the customer, that the person working the fiddle is putting himself out in some way by giving an extra service, by making a special effort on the customer's behalf. I recall a waitress who, whenever she served a family with a small child, would slyly knock over the child's drink, spilling it all over the table. She would then rush to mop it up, exclaiming: 'Don't worry — he's only a baby, it doesn't matter — 'I'll soon get him another.' She was always rewarded with a hefty tip — because she was always so helpful!

The tram conductor's Class 2 fiddle has this flavour. By packing the tram with passengers, he is able to persuade those queueing farther down the line that there is no room for them, even when considerable numbers of passengers have got off.

> There's often a big queue at Cleveleys, all waiting to go to the Central Promenade. Now if you just fill the seats and have five standing passengers, which the rules say you should, you'll find two passengers getting off here and two passengers getting off there and really pissing you about . . . so what I do is to absolutely stack them in at Cleveleys. I play at being God's gift to passengers: 'Come on now, I'm sure we can get a few more in at the back. Can you squeeze up a bit, love?' That way I sometimes get forty standing passengers.

In this way, the waiter, the conductor and the waitress are able to gain far greater control of their situations than their normal work would allow. A conductor can run from one end of his route to the other with the minimum of stops. If only five are allowed to stand in the tram, potential passengers can easily see for themselves whether there is room for one more; but not if forty are standing. In this situation, people wanting to board the tram can only take the conductor's word for it that there is no room for them.

> The point about this technique is that every time you have to stop, you never have to pick anyone else up. You can say to the queues on the road if you let, say, eight people off, 'Now look, I'm absolutely crammed full, aren't I? I'm only allowed five standing passengers and I've already got twenty.' Nobody can argue about that.

The suggestion that the conductor is already doing the passengers on board his tram a favour will disarm anyone who is unconvinced by the loading mathematics. He cannot be doing it for himself, the queues will think, because he has already stuck his neck out for his passengers. Additionally, 'doing you a favour' sets the passengers already on board against those who want to board. The feeling on the trams is 'Keep off, you're rocking the boat; any more on board and an inspector might well turn the lot of us off'.

This kind of tactic gives the conductor opportunities to fiddle money as well as time. A sudden exodus of passengers at a central stop leaves him with money in his hand and no time to issue tickets for all of it. The ticket-issuing machine functions like the cash register and fiddlers of money have to get the better of it in the same way as the checkout girl paces her till. Simply omitting to issue a receipt carries the same dangers as ringing up 'no sale': it is easily detected by management checks. A more devious method involves issuing tickets which have been recovered from the floor and seats of the bus or tram. In the same way, checkout receipts in a supermarket are often picked up and used to cover shoplifting, and 'maxpax' coffee cups are re-used by British Rail restaurant car stewards.

Repetition and Excess

All donkey job money fiddles have a high risk of detection because, as we have seen, they are repetitive. If the conductor wants to make any sizeable profit from issuing used tickets, he must repeat the fiddle again and again. The more he repeats it, the more likely he is to be detected. Thus donkey fiddles have built into them the idea of *excess*. Hawks and vultures have flexibility to fiddle in different ways and in a variety of situations. They can accordingly lay off the odds of being detected. An expenses claim draws attention to itself, as does a tax return, if the expenditure in *one* category is disproportionately high or low in relation to other items or to other comparable people. But hawks are protected because they *disperse* their fiddles among different subjects and in different places, while vultures and wolves co-ordinate theirs — one to another — with group support. But the donkey is alone. Without group support and lacking the benefits of dispersion, he is the most vulnerable of all. The salesgirl who made out phoney refund dockets was discovered in the end because, since she fiddled excessively, she was almost *bound* to be discovered. Why, the counting house had only to ask, has *one* salesgirl handled a disproportionately large amount of refunds in a short time?

Donkey fiddles, as a bus driver put it, 'change a job designed by them for them, into a job designed by you for you'. But these variations do more than merely react against controls affecting time and space. When a supermarket girl goes into fiddling cash and goods, or a tram or bus conductor fiddles cash and time, they attach a whole new range of meanings to each repetitive act in their daily round. Every quick move to the bell, every passenger stop illicitly passed, each new matchstick added to the top of a till, gives meaning to an overall task that otherwise contains no inherent interest. And time now takes on a new dimension. Once he begins to fiddle, the fiddler gains new motives, new interests and new targets. Fiddling, for the donkey, converts repetitive meaningless acts into a wider personal mosaic. It means that now he is working for himself as well as for the company. And as well as challenge and a new approach to time, the activity also often gives fun.

Sabotage and Control

It is in donkey jobs then that the principal motive for fiddles is not just material gain but to obtain control – that is, to move oneself downgrid. But the very act of moving must in itself depend upon at least a minimal degree of control over a job. When even such minimal control is absent, however, then besides the various withdrawals from work such as absenteeism and sickness we are likely also to find sabotage – 'the conscious act of mutilation or destruction' that reduces tension and frustration. Taylor and Walton (1971, p. 219) quote a typical case.

> In the Christmas rush in a Knightsbridge store, the machine which shuttled change backwards and forwards suddenly ground to a halt. A frustrated salesman had demobilized it by ramming a cream bun down its gullet.

In some donkey jobs where a sufficient degree of autonomy does exist so that rules can be broken we find a paradox: that while acceptance of the rules implicitly makes for powerlessness, the breaking of rules brings considerable autonomy. England (1980) shows that shop assistants in clothing and shoe stores who move into fiddling sometimes do so to such an extent that we can regard them as operating 'a business within a business'. This involves the assistant buying his own goods at discount prices outside the shop and selling them on his own account in the shop. In moving downgrid, the donkey has turned into a hawk.

We can now understand why it is in these kinds of job that we find a mythology of scandals – of 'outrageous' cases that are part of the folklore of many establishments but which are often based upon fact. There is the tale of the shop assistant, for instance, who fiddled five times the amount of her wages every day for six months, or that of the short-order waiter who skimmed $150 a day for a year and of the sales girl who supplied a market stall with clothes from the firm's stock-room for over two years.

These workers were able to be excessive in their fiddling because of the absence of group controls in this type of job. As we shall see, where groups are involved, as in wolfpack and vulture jobs, excess is curbed by limits which are set and maintained by the group, while the acceptance of new entrants and their training is also a feature of the group. It is the absence of group and of group support in donkey jobs, coupled with their lack of legitimate flexibility, that are the principle causes of these workers' vulnerability.

4

Wolfpack Jobs

The Dustcart Crew

I went to the labour exchange and ended up at a crummy office in
the high street. They offered various jobs at different pay and the
pay of the dustmen seemed OK in comparison. I rather fancied the
idea, you know; at school they always said if you didn't do any
work, you'd 'end up a dustman'. It was nice in a way to prove them
right.

I'm lucky – it's a good gang. If you're unlucky, you can get one
of the big council estates; there are a lot in Extown. A good round is
one with hotels, shops and offices as well as where people live. One
where they want you to do things like take goods away you
shouldn't take, but which you will for money. Good really means
'good for extracting money'. It's a good round.

The job isn't especially difficult. There are things you have to
learn. You have to learn who to be careful about, who is likely to
report you, and so on; and you have to learn that there's always a lot
of fooling about among dustmen. For instance, dustmen always try
to hang things on each other's backs; if I go into a cafe I'd likely find
a line of condoms fixed to my back with pegs! There are also about
twenty council rules for dustmen that you've got to know about –
like not riding on the back of the cart and not leaving the cab
unattended. We break most of these rules every day.

In terms of making money, the first rule to break is the
non-gratuities rule. The second is that anything collected is the
property of the corporation. There are some old people who always
leave two pence on the top of the dustbin. You'll always be careful
emptying their bins, closing the gate, and so on. I suppose they

[i.e. the rest of the dustcart crew] tested me at first; if I'd kept the two pences I wouldn't have lasted long. One fiddle is that you can always sell dustbins. People approach us. That's why people sometimes lose dustbins. Any request like this that you get, you say: 'I don't know, I'll have to see the ganger.' Or if it's to take away stuff that we aren't allowed to take, we say: 'We aren't supposed to, I'll have to see the ganger.' Even if they ask the time, you practically have to say: 'I don't know, I'll have to ask the ganger!' Then Nick will go around and negotiate. This applies to all five of us on the cart – five plus Nick, plus a driver."

G.M.   Is the driver outside this system?

'Yes, he empties the cart and takes the wagons away. You have several drivers a day bringing back new wagons. But a driver never gets any benefits unless he gets out and humps bins. [Getting out breaks the rules.]

On the back of our cart, and it's the same for most of the others, you'll find a sack for each member of the gang. One collects brass, one collects gunmetal, one collects copper, down to the least important one which is me; I collect Babycham bottles. Even these mount up, you get about forty a week. Everyone collects for everyone else. While the wagon is away you have a 'good scratch', that's a poke around in the bin, and then you can always tip out a dustbin to see what's in it.

You occasionally find neat piles of clothing near a dustbin, cleaned and everything, that comes from someone who's died. You just say 'Who wants this?' You can easily equip yourself out, I get lots of gear. There's always co-operation in stealing. It is stealing, I suppose? First of all, it's council property. There's also a council arrangement with a scrap company who arrange to go through the litter; but they get very little after us. We also have our arrangements. For instance, if someone – a council workman – wants a bike, then one can be built up for him out of parts you collect.

Another way we make money is accepting tips or bribes. There's the Christmas box, of course, which is more or less accepted, but there's also money for taking away things you aren't supposed to, like mattresses covered in piss or blood. We aren't supposed to move these. If anyone asks me to, I say: 'We're not supposed to, I'll have to ask the ganger.' Then he comes out and negotiates, as I've said. What we get from these is always shared out at the end of the day, like everything else. There's a sweet factory on our round that has a load of waste sweets. It's a nasty job in summer because of the wasps. We do this in rotation – one of us each week. For that we get one pound plus a bag of sweets each. Bloody horrible they are, too. Some of the blokes give them out to the kids on the street.

When a three-piece suite or any furniture like that is thrown out, Nick fixes the tip for taking this stuff; fifty pence or a pound or whatever. This figure is based on what Nick thinks of the people. If someone says 'Dustman', with a hoity-toity voice, 'will you take this away?', Nick says: 'Oh, I'm sorry, we can't take that, it's against the rules.' If they're too objectionable, Nick would even stop them putting gold bars on the wagon!   As well as being paid for taking away furniture, we get money for the furniture itself. Nick gauges whether the suite, or settee, or whatever it is, is worth three pounds or not. If it's worth *more* than three pounds we sell it at a shop that buys these things. If Nick thinks it's worth *less* than three pounds we break it up and get the money that way. You nearly always get at least a couple of pounds, or two pounds fifty or so, out of furniture that's upholstered. If the shop offers too low a price, we break it up in front of them. That's a rule *we* have; *never* give stuff away. We also have arrangements with junk shops and antique shops.

G.M.   Are the people who work together very friendly with each other?

Yes they are. We always go for a drink after work on Fridays and because we work together and help each other, this makes us friendly. If you have a particularly heavy bin, you call out 'One up' and someone always comes and helps: either helps you hoist it on your shoulder or helps you carry it. You get the piss taken if you call out 'One up' and the weight doesn't justify it. One bloke has a double hernia so he always carries light bins and there was one old bloke on our wagon who was always helped. Dustmen aren't a lot of use after about fifty. Their guts get bad and they have bad backs. We always helped him out. But after about fifty they mostly move off the wagons and, providing they can read, they go to be parking attendants or something like that. There are really two extreme types of dustmen. There are the illiterate thugs – the stereotypes – but there's also quite a lot who are sharp, as clever as anyone you could meet. By no means are we all illiterate or thuggish – far from it.

G.M.   How much do people earn on the dust?

All these extra fiddles pull in about a third of your wages and this is tax free. Because I'm fairly junior, I earn less than the others; some earn more. Most of these extra earnings are pooled at the end of the day. 'The sparrow', it's called, is shared out on the bonnet of the wagon. Everyone gets the same in money. Nick the ganger gets his extra ganger's allowance from the council, plus his share-out from the collection in the sack, but everything else is very fair. Then again the big perk in this job is moonlighting. Most of the lads have other jobs they go off and do – that's why we rush around being dead efficient – to finish quick.

G.M.   Who do you dislike?

People who complain to you or about you. You particularly dislike them if they complain not to you, but to the Council. You also don't like people who fill the dustbins with glass so that you cut yourself, or half fill the dustbin with concrete so that it's too heavy to lift. You can always get your own back though, like not noticing a dustbin that's around a corner. Then you can leave jam-rags [sanitary towels] on the doorstep; that's common. Or not shutting gates which need to be shut, which lets the dog out. Or through bashing the bin and losing the lid, or by mashing it in the machine. There's lots of ways of getting your own back if people are nasty. That's perhaps why we're regarded as a bit wild by the other council workers.

In August 1974 baggage handlers at London's Heathrow Airport came out on strike when two of their number were arrested for pilfering (*Daily Telegraph*, 16 August 1974). In the same month warehousemen at Ipswich docks staged a twenty-four-hour strike to protest against police searches of some of their homes (ibid.). In December 1975 a team of London dustmen, the first of fourteen teams to be prosecuted, was fined £850 for demanding extra payments for emptying dustbins more than once a week (*The Times*, 10 December 1975).

A feature of all these cases is the strength of the team: these are the jobs that are worked by groups. Whether it is an individual who is threatened (the baggage handlers) or the group as a whole (dock warehousemen), the effect is the same: the group takes action. And when group members are prosecuted (the dustmen) they tend to be prosecuted as a group.

So far the fiddles we have considered have been freestanding fiddles: control of them belongs to an individual rather than a group. But in this type of job, where groups are strong, they are strong because the nature of the overall work task binds different individual jobs into an articulated and functional whole. When this happens control passes away from the individual and conditions are pre-set for such groups to become the true home, the only home, of the co-operative or wolfpack fiddle.

In wolfpacks the individual's subordinate interests are set by his first contacts with the group, since the group often has a decisive say in selecting its own members. It might arrange this by insisting on a long apprenticeship, as among printers, for instance, or by making it necessary for people to 'speak for' a new entrant, as among miners (Dennis *et al.*, 1956). It might insist on a rule that only the sons of existing job-holders be admitted, as occurs in some printing and dockland unions. When this kind of control is not possible it develops tactics to reject those who do not conform to its requirements. When a group needs to work together it is relatively easy to exclude someone who is not wanted.

Because of this control over its own constituency, a wolfpack expects and is able to demand that each of its members forfeits some of his personal autonomy in the interests of, and for the protection of, the group as a whole. The group also expects individuals to surrender their freedom to negotiate with whom they choose: that is, to attract followers or to become a follower of others. Instead, the group will rank them and through this means will decide their relationship one with another. It follows that the group, not the individual, will control resources. Among such resources will be the control of time: each individual's time, not only at work but also off duty, will — at least to some degree — be at the disposal of the group. So, too, will be his access to pilferage and fiddles.

This extensive and collective control is only possible in highly structured, that is, strong-grid occupations, where the group dimension is also strong and where the individual's place is clearly defined by and in relation to the people with whom he works. The ranking system of an army, for example, based as it is on a marked division of labour, provides an unambiguous definition of role: it is strong grid. This functional ranking system serves the operational needs of the army. But at the same time other, less tangible factors like morale and tradition, may well simultaneously demand other systems of ranking. Within them status is provided, not by formal means like the award of a commission, but by informal practice.

Newcomers may be given an unofficial status which may be lower or higher than their official one. Young subalterns in a guards regiment were, until recently, not allowed to speak to fellow officers in the mess until they were spoken to. Conversely, older members can have an unofficial standing that is often far higher than their official rank suggests. (A club's 'oldest member' is at the top of the club pecking order.)

Among occupational communities like fishermen (Tunstall, 1962), miners (Dennis *et al.*, 1956) and dockworkers (Mars, 1972), the intermesh of work and community permits the values of one sphere to be reinforced by controls available in the other. If the community ranks age higher than youth, for instance, the work-group will unofficially rank its younger members as lower in prestige than others. They will often then be considered fair game for practical jokes and elaborate rites of passage. Older members, on the other hand, will be rewarded for their continuity of service. They will be given lighter tasks, but the same or a higher share of the group's resources. In other words, these communities may put a value on youth and age which the job at a functional level does not and this community value will feed back into and affect how the group works.

The group's unofficial ranking always has implications for its unofficial allocation of resources. Where an individual stands with a group determines how much access he has to unofficial rewards and how much support he can expect in obtaining them. But even though older or perhaps more skilled people may be favoured, the group demands that *all* are rewarded to some extent. Though some group members will have more access to fiddles than others, *no* member has exclusive access. The structured nature of the group tasks in this type of job mean that individuals cannot work in isolation. They have to co-ordinate their activities with the activities of others.

Again, we need to make a distinction between the sequential collaboration of the production line and the co-ordination of tasks in a wolfpack. As Ditton (1972) has shown, it may be possible for an individual worker 'on the line' to achieve marginal fiddles of time, but only by collusion either with the supervisor or with other workers. We have already noted the difference between collusion and co-operation. In collusion, fiddling remains an arrangement between individuals, though they may have group support up to a point. In co-operation a fiddle just cannot exist outside the context of the group. Just as traditional dock loading and unloading needs to be performed by co-ordinated teamwork, so dock fiddles become feasible only within a team-based and co-ordinated fiddle system.

The wolfpack has the gene's determination to survive. It selects new members who it knows will co-operate with existing members to advance its interests. It protects itself externally by rejecting outsiders who threaten its interests. It protects itself internally by reducing the possibilities of disintegration by limiting competition. And it does all of this by controlling the access its members have to resources of time, information and rewards.

In these ways, the wolfpack as a group exercises the sort of control that the hawk fiddler exercises as an individual. Like the hawk, the wolfpack has an overall view of what is happening. Like the hawk, it will co-ordinate separate individual transactions to advance its own interests. But unlike the hawk, the wolfpack needs no motivation beyond the need to survive and it rates stability and continuity higher than advancement.

The fiddles of these groups operate and survive in the same way. Unless a wolfpack imposes control over access to fiddles and their distribution, the total amount available will be threatened. Outsiders will be brought in, as for example when the police were brought in to search the homes of warehousemen at Ipswich docks. Unless these fiddles are worked co-operatively, the resources will not be there to distribute. Because wolfpack fiddles are not accessible to individuals but need a group, the survival of the fiddle is linked to the survival of the group. The wolfpack fiddle does not need to promise extra benefits (such as 'if you fiddle as a *group* you can gain more'). It merely says that, for the fiddle to be possible at all, for it to survive – just as for the group itself to survive – individual group members *must* co-operate.

Wolfpacks therefore thrive on continuity and stability. They must seek to protect against internal schisms, rivalry and competition – those characteristics which so distinguish vultures. This is why wolfpacks universally take a hard line against change and why they seek to limit and control it, since change disturbs internal relationships. Vultures are much less able to control change; their internal competitiveness tends to preclude control over their environments and their lack of established rankings leads to ambiguities which preclude internal dispute settlement.

How do wolfpacks maintain this continuous management of events? Some clues are provided by a classic wolfpack – the family business. In the family business individual interests are subordinate to the welfare or survival of the group. Membership is tightly defined, because it can only, at least in positions of influence and trust, include members of the family. Or we might consider the example of the Japanese fishing boat, crewed exclusively by members of one family. Here the family unit is also the production unit. The rationale of the family – survival – is effortlessly transplanted to the family's business.

Cases where families form a complete economic unit are, of course, relatively rare in industrial society. But there are many occupations where kinship qualifications are applied to restrict entry to an economic system. Dockwork is a striking example. In 1951, 75 per cent of the labour force of the Manchester docks were the sons of dock workers (Liverpool University, 1954). Twenty years later the position had hardly changed. In the East London docks in the early 1970s that direct father–son inheritance accounted for 67 per cent of the men and 75 per cent of foremen. Only 10 per cent of the men and 8 per cent of foremen were unable to name one relative working in the docks (Hill, 1976).

Kinship provides dockworkers and many other wolfpacks with a system of positive vetting: it knows that it can trust newcomers because fathers will have implanted the values of the group in their sons well before they even start work. This 'quality control' of entrants also ensures that their moral careers develop in an acceptable way: that is, entrants will either have already accepted or will quickly come to accept the norms of gang working, and see fiddles and pilferage as a legitimate part of their total rewards.

Kinship ties are not a *sine qua non* of wolfpacks nor of their fiddles, but family obligations do provide a model of the mutual trust that must exist between members. Just as one member of a family is not normally expected to undermine another, so members of wolfpacks will not normally testify against one another when pilferage is being investigated. Instead, like a family, the group will close ranks, and is likely to take collective action to resist further investigation.

If a wolfpack member's trustworthiness *is* suspect, the group may hold him at arm's length for a while. It can do this through its unofficial system of ranking. A member without kinship ties (who is therefore, on the face of it, less trustworthy than those with) will be given a job in which access to fiddles is limited. In this way, the group can withhold its full acceptance from members whose moral careers appear retarded or not yet begun. Alternatively a new entrant may find himself 'tested' (Henry, 1978, p. 38), as our dustman showed that he was tested by his crewmates when he was first put with a gang: 'I suppose they tested me at first; if I'd kept the two pences I wouldn't have lasted long.'

Conversely, a member who refuses to fiddle, to take his share of the group's resources, is *ipso facto* considered untrustworthy.

When talking of the induction of new dock gang members one

informant recounted the case of a Salvationist who moved into his gang. Because he refused to take cargo, men were suspicious and reluctant to confirm him to membership. At this time police inquiries started into the theft of a valuable cargo of wrist-watches, and they 'grilled' the new member over a period of three months. 'All that time he didn't give anything away', said my informant. 'He was really firm in the gang after that.' (Mars, 1974)

In its determination to survive, therefore, the wolfpack resists external threats by controlling entry. But it must also resist internal threats. It must reduce the power of individuals to act individually (which includes fiddling independently). It does this by ranking its members according to scales which emphasise group continuity. To its employers, a dustcart gang will appear a group of equals, with the ganger merely *primus inter pares*. Payments to individuals will be made on this basis, and job descriptions might well suggest no gradation of responsibilities. But the gang will order itself rather differently. Older men, men who have got some service in, often attract greater respect than younger men, newly joined. The older will be placed higher up in any pecking order – including access to fiddles, as our dustmen showed in the allocation of salvageable items that were kept in different sacks.

Age and seniority are often the criteria chosen not only because they are unambiguous and therefore provide a good basis for settling disputes in such groups, but because the old also represent continuity and their extended experience is relevant to new problems. They are the storehouses of folk memories, providing younger members of the group with an awareness of group history and a sense of its own existence beyond the span of individual members. Even the role of newcomer is integrated with this larger whole. Not only does collecting Babycham bottles plug the new man into the fiddle system, but because 'everyone collects for everyone else' there is continuous reaffirmation of each man's status by everyone else. In this way the overall structure of the gang is maintained.

Such a system of ranking is functional to wolfpacks then, as it is to families, because it provides a ready means of controlling disputes that could otherwise prove divisive. Among vultures, competition brushes aside this reverence for experience, folk wisdom and established ranking. There is competition not just for a share but for the largest share of rewards, and not just for rewards but also for authority; the most successful salesman gains the largest commission and he also aims for promotion. Access to fiddles and access to promotion is gained as an individual's competence increases. The abler the salesman, the abler the fiddler. The field is wide open. Because turnover of labour is high among vultures, salesmen come and go. There is no continuity of status; in a new job the salesman has to start at the bottom and prove his competence all over again.

The dustcart gang, as is typical of wolfpacks, assures repeated recognition and affirmation of status. The senior men *always* get the best pickings. The newcomer *always* takes what is left; until he is no longer a newcomer, when another newcomer displaces him. The newcomer moves up, but the *role* of newcomer remains.

This ranking system stands *outside* the upward movement of group members over time. The upward movement of individuals does not change it, as it does in other quadrants (see Figure 1, p. 29). This ensures stability. And the *bases* of the ranking system, in this case age and seniority, also stand outside the ageing of individual members. This ensures continuity.

There is nothing personal in the relatively poor share of group pilferage that a wolfpack awards its junior members. It is not allocated according to the sort of people they are but according to their relative positions in the pack. The top man in a dustcart gang may be awarded all the valuable metal scrap, while the most junior man will have to be content with empty bottles. But he *is* content. He knows that his share is not a whimsical, arbitrary allocation, but that it proceeds from a structured view of his working career. And because it is based on this structured view, he knows he is bound to achieve a better share later. Growing older is, like death, a certainty.

Control of entry, control of ranking and control of resources: by these controls the wolfpack is able to maintain its own integrity. This integrity not only guarantees the wolfpack's survival; it also provides access to fiddles which are beyond the reach of individuals. At the production stage, goods are on the whole handled not by teams but sequentially by individuals. Since only individuals have access to them, fiddles tend to be 'one off' and isolated. At the retailing end of the process, only individuals have access to goods or money paid for goods. Again, fiddles are isolated. It is in the middle of the process, when goods are in transit in bulk, and where access is *denied* to individuals, that a wolfpack can come into its own.

Simply arranging for the 'accidental' breaking open and distributing of a crate of goods needs the co-operation of several individuals. This is why many wolfpack fiddles are a natural response to this middle stage in the production/distribution process. Here resources are in limbo, unaccountable yet unreachable without a group. Wolfpack fiddles therefore thrive in wholesale markets like London's Smithfield or Nine Elms. It was estimated that the recent move of the fruit market from Covent Garden to Nine Elms has saved £10 million in potential pilfered goods per annum. (Significantly, many old-established teams of porters were broken up by the move across the river.) And for the same reasons wolfpack fiddles thrive in cargo-handling areas at airports, distribution centres and, of course, docks.

We have seen that differential roles and strong kinship ties make dockers a model of what a wolfpack should be. Dockers' practices illustrate clearly the way in which the wolfpack fiddle springs naturally from an interdependent work-style. A good team, in effect, deserves good fiddles.

Dock Pilferage

The longshoremen of the Newfoundland port of St John's, which is predominantly an unloading port, form a close-knit occupational community of the sort that can be found in most dockland areas.

And though there is evidence that docking communities are now more dispersed geographically, social ties often remain strong, principally through kinship links. The traditional method of dockwork (rather than modern roll-on, roll-off techniques) is much the same wherever it is employed: cargo is shifted from the hold of the ship, winched on to the quayside, moved by fork-lift truck to the warehouse and there sorted, stacked and checked. If a cargo is being loaded the sequence is in reverse, but in either case the practices of St John's men are common to most of traditional dockwork.

The basic unit of traditional dockwork is the gang of, normally, between twelve and twenty men. Gangs are formed for specific jobs, for a particular boat. The system of hiring dock gangs in St John's is casual, and theoretically each new boat will produce a fresh coalescence of dockers into new gangs. In practice, this does not happen. Roughly the same gangs are selected for each new job but the members of each gang can be said to select themselves. This kind of self-selection is delegated to a group by their foreman. Since to function at all as a group wolfpack members must work together, men with experience of each other's working abilities provide a guarantee to the hiring foreman that they will perform well as a team and produce the output his superiors expect. In return for this guaranteed teamwork, the dock gang is given the security of the job itself – and access to pilferage.

Longshore gangs control entry by selecting themselves on the basis of mutual trust between foreman and gang and between individual members of the gang, and on the basis of skills developed as a result of this trust. And once the gang has been selected, it begins ranking itself. A ranking system of sorts already exists in the way the overall job is done; it is functionally divided into different stages with different responsibilities. The gang, however, decides who will get what responsibilities: it will itself allocate its members to the different jobs that are available.

How work tasks are rated and allocated depends upon a number of criteria. Is it hard work or easy? Does it give access to cargo or is it in full view of authority? Allocation depends on an individual's relative seniority in the gang, on strength, skills and sociability. The experienced/older man will be given lighter work than his colleagues. Stowing cargo in the sheds, for example, is not as physically demanding as are other stages in the unloading process, and stowing teams often contain older men. But this is a sociable task and a 'loner' would more likely be found working on the fork-lift. On the other hand the best place for pilferage is the hold but here work is hardest. Unpopular work is always allocated to outsiders, or people at the fringe of the group. Skidsmen, for example, who work on the quay at the side of a ship are physically and socially isolated from the rest of the gang and play no part in the pilferage of cargo. The job is also unskilled and for all these reasons is therefore rated low on prestige. It is a job often given to those who fill in for regular gang members.

The group's control of ranking and its allocation of people to jobs is crucial because it gives both overall control of resources, and specifically control of fiddles. From the foreman's viewpoint, a self-selected gang ensures that human resources will be used to produce maximum output of work. But from the gang's point of view, self-selection ensures that what the gang considers fair reward for the job is collected as efficiently as possible in the interests of the gang. In other words, the dock gang skills ensure skilful fiddling. To get the most out of a gang, employers must expect the gang to get the most out of them.

However, a skilful teamwork fiddle demands that an outsider or an incompetent is not trusted sufficiently to be given a key role in either normal working or pilferage. This is clearly understood by each member of the gang: each knows his place, and the place of his mates, in the gang's 'world-view'. But at the same time, boundary is also well defined; an outsider would not expect to take the job of an insider. When a St John's longshoreman was filling in for an absent member I asked him what would happen if he were put to work in the hold, the best place for pilferage. He denied it could happen. When pressed, he replied: 'They'd look at me as if I was a nigger.'

A sense of rank (a strong grid rating) is so powerful that it bears comparison with medieval concepts of 'degree' and 'harmony'. Medieval cosmology saw its universe in terms of nine spheres which enfolded the Earth like the skins of an onion, and the world-picture extended from the macrocosm of the universe to the microcosm of the individual's life. The human parallel to the harmony of the spheres was a society based on a respect for 'degree'. Once this respect was lost, discord followed: civil wars, squabbles, peasant revolts and family quarrels cracked the mould of harmonious human existence. In their own way, the longshoremen recognise this.

Access and Support

Why should degree, in terms of the job that each man is given, matter so much? Why should a job in the hold be more highly placed in the longshoreman's world-view than a job on the quayside?

The answer lies in the degree of access that jobs provide to the cargoes being unloaded. Only those with unhindered access to cargoes can actively pilfer them. These are therefore key jobs. The unloading is divided up in such a way that only some of the gang actually handle cargo. Broadly, these are the men at the beginning and end of the process: the eight holdsmen, working in pairs on the ship itself, and the eleven stowers, working in the warehouse. Theoretically, all these men can pilfer cargo. Yet supervision of unloading by the ship's officers at one end and the shed superintendent at the other greatly reduces *individual* opportunities. Those with *access* therefore need the *support* of those who do not have access, to distract the attention of the supervisors, to provide cover, to 'clear' documents and to enable the swift removal and distribution of goods once they have been pilfered.

This ranking system distributes both access and support as resources. The most powerful, the most prestigious, have the highest levels of both; the least powerful, the least prestigious, have the lowest levels of both. The hatch-checker represents an extreme of such power. He is the *only* member of the gang to enjoy both access *and* support. He is, moreover, the only gang member to have a complete view of the state of the cargo: by definition of his job, he knows what is being pilfered.

The skidsman, on the other hand, represents an extreme of powerlessness. Relatively isolated on the quayside, at the transit stage of cargo movement and always visible to those in authority, he has neither access *nor* support.

However, these are extreme positions. The majority of the gang enjoy some levels of access or support – but not of both. The division of labour means that one man's access will need another man's support. The holdsmen's and stowers' freedom to tamper with crates is severely constrained by the supervision of the ship's officers and the wharf superintendent. To pilfer cargo, holdsmen need the support of the winchman and signaller, while stowers need the support of the fork-lift truck drivers and the acquiescence of the hatch-checker. For fiddles to be possible at all, they must be worked as subgroup fiddles in the vessel and the shed.

If the vessel team can together load a crate safely, they can equally well load it unsafely. The signaller's hand signals, as incomprehensible to the outsider as a tick-tack man's telegraph, allow him to work as effectively at pilfering as at unloading. The skills of a team are put at the disposal of a teamwork fiddle.

Over at the shed, the same redirection of skills is necessary for a successful subgroup fiddle. Once a proportion of cargo has been 'legitimately' diverted by accidental breakage, it is up to the stowers to unload and distribute it. They can do this only if they are unobserved. Thus the skills of both fork-lift truck drivers and of stowers are employed in distributing crates in such a way that it shields pilfering activity from the view of supervisors. The effect of this interlocking of subgroup fiddles is a seemingly innocent sequence of events, which, to the uninitiated eye, appears part of the legitimate unloading of a ship.

The pilferage of thirteen of a consignment of a hundred men's suits provides a good example of this unofficial history of events. The hatch-checker knew from his bills of lading what sort of cargo was in transit. The vessel team then engineered an 'accidental' fall of two crates. The damaged crates were moved normally with the rest of the cargo to the shed. The shed team then engineered the undisturbed pilferage of the suits. To do this the fork-lift truck driver had to stack other cargo in such a way as to block off what was happening from the superintendent's line of vision. At the same time, he constructed, by skilful stacking, a changing-room where suits could be tried on by the men. The next day the hatch-checker reported that two crates were missing. By then the suits had disappeared – smuggled out of the dock under the men's clothes.

We have seen that goods are particularly vulnerable to group fiddling when in transit. This is because their handling is spread between so many different people. No one person is ever wholly responsible (as he is at the production or retailing ends of the process) for goods in transit. Neither, it follows is any one group. The clothing crates could have been opened at any stage between loading at Montreal, and unloading at St John's. In this way the group gains the protection of a larger group – comprising all those who handled the crates in transit. The reverse side of this coin, however is that the subgroup is often blamed for pilferage which occurs somewhere else and for which it was not actually responsible. Group protection is double-edged. Everyone and no one is suspected. Therefore when other individuals or individual groups are singled out by management for investigation or prosecution, the group tends to see such selection as random victimisation. Hence it takes retaliatory action as a group.

The system is worked so as not to draw attention to itself. It *appears* legitimate to the unskilled eye. It follows that the amount which is pilfered should also be kept manageable. The group gives and the group takes away. It can decide, for instance, how much of a man's time it needs and time usually extends beyond ordinary working hours. After work drinking is common among wolfpacks not only to dissipate earnings (see Chapter 7) but also because drinking sessions are a collective celebration of the group. Here, the old members strengthen continuity by reviving folk memories and the newcomer comes to recognise his place in group concerns as he moves through his moral career. He learns to accept the boundaries of the group's world-view, and the limits the group sets, including its limits on pilferage.

Group Controls on Limits

Limits on pilferage are *always* found and can apply to category of good and to category of victim as well as to amounts that are taken. But it is always the group that decides what is acceptable and unacceptable in pilferage, as Horning (1970) found in his study of pilferage in a factory — as it also decides what is permitted and what is forbidden in other areas it controls. Just as dustmen will always be careful of old people's bins and will see their gates are closed, so longshoremen will home in on 'rootless' cargoes, in transit between large, impersonal firms which are covered by insurance, and which are always fair game: 'It's all insured and nobody's heard of an insurance company going broke. In any case, they've made millions out of this port and it's us who do the work' (Mars, 1972). Individual cargoes, like personal baggage, are not fair game. The distinction emerges in the view dockers take of unacceptable pilferers. 'He'd take anything', said one of another, 'he's even taken baggage — he's nothing more than a thief' (Mars, 1974).

Terming a man 'thief' puts him beyond the pale of the group and its practices. A 'thief' not only pilfers unacceptable cargoes but unacceptably high quantities of any cargo. Such greediness casts him as an outsider just as fastidiousness cast the Salvationist as an outsider. A curriculum vitae *external* to group experience is suspect, just as the Salvationist's dogmatic principles are suspect because they are external to the developing moral career which the group demands. Unacceptable levels of pilferage, either too high or too low, will be expected from people who are themselves unacceptable to the group. Being unacceptable to a wolfpack means being ejected from it.

The 'right' people, conversely, will fiddle at the right level. The

St John's longshoremen had a formula they called 'working the value of the boat' to help them maintain this level. If the job of unloading the boat pays, say, 20 dollars, then cargo up to the same value is considered an acceptable reward. A group member is judged by how *consistently* and not to what *extent* he fiddles goods. 'He always works the value of the boat' is a compliment which recognises the particular nature of the wolfpack fiddle; just as, when the foreman consistently hires the same gang of men, he recognises the need for teamwork above any individual skills.

As we have seen, to accept consistency in legitimate teamwork, you accept consistency in illegitimate teamwork. Perhaps we need to modify the statement that if an employer wants to get the most out of his men, he must expect to hire men who will get the most out of him. The management of goods in transit requires *consistent* performance, and *continuous* movement, because it has to keep the supply of and demand for goods in constant harmony. The employer therefore wants men who will guarantee him a consistent rate of work. Men who can work consistently, on the other hand, will fiddle consistently – not excessively, but consistently.

We have looked in detail at fiddles among dockworkers because the formulaic quality of dock teamwork presents these fiddles in almost abstract terms. But the principles (of strong grid and strong group) that lie behind the organisation and practice of these fiddles operate in any occupation where ranked groups comprising a series of complementary tasks are the appropriate work unit.

Wolfpack fiddles are more than a 'fair' price to pay for group work. Paradoxically, they are evidence that management is getting it's money's worth. If a good story on a newspaper deserves 'good' expenses, then good teamwork deserves group fiddles. Police investigations of warehousemen and dockers usually occur when the group has lost control, and limits have been exceeded. But all things being equal (including the level of pilferage), employers would be wise to regard team fiddles as guarantees that in at least one respect they have hired the right teams.

5

Vulture Jobs

The Speciality Salesman of Photocopying Machines

They put us through a four-week training course. Two weeks on
the beat with an experienced seller and two weeks in the classroom.
Some of the fiddles you pick up on the training run [two weeks
accompanied]. You ask 'Couldn't I do it this way?' and the answer
is likely to be 'No, there's another way round that'. Mind you,
some of them will tell you fuck all. You have to pick it up yourself.
I had an instinct for it but I also had a good trainer – and you learn a
lot in the pub after work. Yes, it's very competitive. Salesmen tend
to be very highly strung, know what I mean? Everyone's watching
everyone else. If my best friend sold an Emperor (one of the large
machines), I'd say how pleased I was but I'd be jealous. Really I'd
wish it had been my Emperor that had been sold.

The course was very good. They told us about the different
types; the Blockers, the Nose-Pickers, the Wankers and Mr
Prospect. These are the people you meet as you go around trying to
sell. The Blockers are those who block access to a sale – people like
receptionists. Nose-Pickers are those who claim to have decision-
making power but really haven't. They just stand around wasting
your time – doing this (mimes nose-picking). Wankers are people
with executive authority but who just piss around wasting your
time. Mr Prospect is a man with executive authority who actually
might be prepared to buy. But he might turn into a Wanker, if a
Nose-Picker comes in while you're talking.

One way to sell is to use Nose-Pickers. They can be very useful in
situations where a sale is unlikely but possible. You chat them up
and offer them seventy to a hundred pounds if the firm buys an

Emperor. This comes out of your two hundred and seventy pounds [commission]. For this you explain what they have to do. During the next fortnight they have to jam the rival's machine just once or twice, and make a fuss about it. You have to be very careful how you go about this. If it goes wrong you can get a stinking letter to head office about it and the company gets a bad name.

You arrive in a fortnight's time and a Nose-Picker gets you to see Mr Prospect. He might say 'No, the machine we have is new', or 'It works well', or 'We are not interested'. You then ask if you can see it. You are new to the game. You are interested in all machines. May you have a copy from it? It's always best if you can get everyone around it – that way it's more embarrassing for them. The machine jams. The secretary has a rant about it and there you are – on the spot to sell.

A sale can be made by exploiting the discount, which always provides a fiddle. Sometimes the company might offer up to a fifty-five per cent discount. You explain that you can perhaps get it especially cheap – you show him the undiscounted price-list but you explain that for special sales you get no commission. So – if he can give you a cheque for such and such an amount – which you say is what you would lose in commission – you can swing a very cheap one for him. Actually you do get commission on discounts.

Another way to fiddle is to buy in at a good price an older machine for, say, fifty pounds when the company will offer, say, thirty pounds trade-in. The company doesn't really encourage trade-ins – it can't cope with the repairs, etc. – you then sell it at say a hundred and twenty pounds to one of the dealers – there are six in London. As well as this you sell a new machine and get your commission on that and you've got two benefits. This is all off the record – unofficial – nothing to do with the company. They would be angry about it if they found out.

A fiddle – which isn't a fiddle really – is to reduce the price of a machine in order to make the sale and lose the difference out of your commission.

To make a sale you might also give away paper: 'I can let you have twenty pounds-worth of free paper with this' – this sort of thing. You can get out of the office with all the free paper you need. You're not supposed to do this but the manager turns a blind eye. You can also have a fiddle on paper: some people sell it. Then there's fiddles on expenses, of course. Some of us have receipt books for petrol which we get from the garage. They give us the whole book and we fill in the details. You can get back a lot of VAT that way, of course.

A fiddle that I don't know much about at the moment is with the service blokes. Every day lorry-loads of machines go out – all for scrap. It's a terrible waste really – many of them are quite good. There's *bound* to be a fiddle there!

It's not a bad job, there's lots of rules but good selling allows the rules to be broken. As long as your sales are OK you can get away with fiddles or fiddled expenses or when you should be back in the office. For instance, you should be there at nine o'clock in the morning and be back there at five at night – but you can always get out of this providing you're a good salesman. The main thing – the only thing – is selling.

In vulture jobs, fiddles are not reactive (like donkey fiddles) or creative (like the individualist hawk fiddles) but responsive. They respond to the changing opportunities presented by management. An acceleration of pace, an increase in scale, alterations in price or incentives: it is changes like these that offer the individual employee the chance of fiddles. In this sense he can 'ride' the system, a system which is constantly bucking and threatening to throw him off.

In 1971 a group of workers at the Palatine Hotel in Blackpool was convicted of a conspiracy to steal £10,000 by overcharging for drinks sold in the hotel's six bars. At their trial, the hotel manager was cast as the group ringleader. In his defence, he said it was his job 'to make a profit for the company and to ensure that the stocks were right'. With these objectives in mind, he said that he was content to allow overcharging provided there were no complaints. He maintained:

> The directors' attitude was the same as mine, and on occasions directors have said, in a jocular manner, 'Are these visitors' prices or ours?' I told them they should be satisfied as we were getting our share – meaning that the company were benefiting – through good stocks. (*West Lancashire Evening Gazette*, 25 March 1971)

This manager was defending his part in the conspiracy, but he was also spelling out some of the characteristics of a vulture fiddle. Here employees fiddle individually but within a framework of action approved at a micro level by all the bar staff and at a macro level by the company. The fiddle was therefore institutionalised: it was built not only into the bureaucratic structure of the hotel's organisation but also into the objectives of the hotel management (to maintain profits and to keep stocks right).

Much of hotel work, like the work of many sales representatives, most truck drivers and the different sorts of roundsmen, fits snugly into the vulture quadrant. These are the occupations where workers do similar jobs but where competition hinges around good routes and bad routes; good territories and less good; preferred 'stations' of tables and those that waiters despise. But though competition is high in these occupations, their workers are thrown together by their sharing of a common employer, a common task and the need for at least a minimum level of mutual support in the everyday crises of their work.

In this kind of job, more than in any of the other three, there is always the possibility that individuals and occupations will shade off into other quadrants. The least successful are pushed diagonally upgrid and become more and more bound by the rules of their organisation. As our photocopying machine salesman explained: 'There's lots of rules but good selling allows the rules to be broken . . . The main thing – the only thing – is selling.'

If the unsuccessful are pushed upgrid and become more subject to control, the successful stay downgrid and escape it. Some of these occupations, in fact, allow the possibility of a greater range of individual dexterity than do others. This is so among travelling salesmen and fairground workers, for instance, where variations between individual achievements can be quite wide. It is less so among, say, truck drivers, where the range of possible variation is necessarily more limited. Even here the super successful can emerge – not only to bypass their organisation's control but even to transcend it altogether. Some truck drivers have been known to use their jobs as the basis of a one-man haulage company. One I knew acted as co-ordinator for a group of drivers and arranged private delivery terms on a regular 'business within a business' basis. Another regularly used his vehicle as a mobile shop to sell black economy clothing – 'cabbage production'. Both had in effect 'physically' moved out of their companies and into business for themselves. 'Star' salesmen can similarly transcend their companies, not by converting their jobs to their own account, but by being so successful that their reputations and contacts leave them never short of a job. These are the prima donnas; they move laterally and become hawks. But though the extremely successful and the least successful both readily merge into other quadrants, neither of these two extremes represents the position of the average vulture. His position is well illustrated by the two different types of cab driver.

The 'mush', or owner driver of a taxi, operates in quite a different way from the journeyman driver. The mush is his own man: his hours and his earnings are his own, and how he makes them is his own business. The journeyman drives for a garage, and (unless he works on a fixed rental) usually has to return a proportion of his takings to the garage. The mush *is* constrained, however, by strong grid controls (hackney carriage regulations). He operates somewhere between the hawk's quadrant and the donkey's quadrant. His fiddles reflect this. They show individual initiative but they also break extremely well-defined rules. The mush may 'stalk' for custom by leaving the meter set at 'hired' when he is unhired. This leaves him free to track worthwhile hirings – long trips to airports – or commission jobs 'steering' dupes to expensive nightclubs or young foreign girls to abortion touts (Powis, 1977).

The journeyman driver is in a different position: he is a vulture. Without capital he is personally vulnerable, being subject to the company that employs him. His firm may take on drivers according to demand, lay them off when hirings are slack, allocate them to non-preferred ranks, or change their hours. So insecurity is built into the job. To fiddle part of his earnings offers the journeyman further insecurity: he has to work in a way which is negatively acceptable to his garage; that is to say, his fiddles are tacitly allowed so long as he does not take too much for himself. But how is he to deduce what the limits are? The answer is that he must be taught.

Training for Vulture Fiddlers

Trainee fiddlers must pass through a process of education and transformation which will ensure that they do not threaten other workers already in post. This process of technical training and moral acclimatisation is sometimes called a 'moral career'. Like more usual careers, it involves stages and contingencies through each of which a trainee must pass before proceeding to the next stage. It is a 'moral' career because passage through it involves a moral transformation (see Goffman, 1961b; Becker, 1963; Ditton, 1977a). One of the key features of such a career as it applies to journeyman cab drivers is the teaching, acceptance and practice of a formula which governs how much of their takings is paid in. This is a method of computation that is devised, communicated and maintained by the drivers *as a group*, a group which draws its solidarity from mutual vulnerability and mutual self-interest. It is a group that is different in its essence from the relationships of mush cabbies.

A journeyman cab driver in a medium-sized northern town explains how these fiddles work and how he was taught about them. The firm he worked for was small, family-run, with a fleet of five cabs (though only three usually operated at one time). The drivers were paid as a wage half of their daily take.

What you are supposed to do, of course, is to hand in *all* your takings. What you really do is multiply the mileage you've driven by a multiple of six for a reasonable day and, say, five for a bad day like Sunday. Say, for instance, you've driven two hundred miles, which is about normal for most days, then you multiply two hundred by six and call it pence. That's twelve hundred pence, isn't it, which is twelve pounds. This twelve pounds now becomes your take, instead of, say, the twenty pounds it should be. From this twelve pounds you then deduct one and a half pence a mile for petrol which is three pounds. That leaves you nine pounds to be divided equally between the firm and you . . . if you don't fiddle anything out of a take of twenty pounds, you get only eight pounds, fifty pence. But with the formula, you get eight pounds [the difference between the real and alleged take] plus four pounds fifty wages [half the alleged take] which makes it up to twelve pounds fifty. On this fiddle you make an extra four pounds a day. (Journeyman cab driver)

New entrants to a job learn what to do from talking to people already in the job – often the contacts who enable them to get the job in the first place. And, though entry to most vulture jobs tends to be relatively unrestricted, the commonest method is to know someone who already works there. But since this kind of job comprises sets of people doing the same tasks under the control of a single overarching bureaucracy, we find a crucial role typically played by a single person whose real job it is to mediate between the two levels. He is usually that classic of marginal men, the foreman or overseer – the first-line supervisor whose role is to act as 'the man in the middle' – and it is on him that the operation of the fiddle system typically devolves.

Among the cab drivers already discussed the fiddle system was 'overseen' and moral career training was carried out by a senior driver whose position was totally ambiguous. This driver was identified with management to the extent that he had shares in the company. On the other hand, he virtually ran the fiddle system. He set limits on how much and how little could be fiddled. His bipartisan attitude allowed him actually to warn new drivers who, of the management personnel, to pay in to and who not.

'Just a tip. Don't pay in while Dollie's on.' There was no mention of why. 'Oh yes', I said, 'It's like that, is it?' 'Yes, she's the brains of the outfit. But pay in when John's on.'

The manager at the Palatine Hotel fitted this role exactly. He was also 'the man in the middle', the link man who reconciled the bureaucratic claims of the company and the individual needs of the men.

Such a link man *always* has an interest in teaching newly introduced colleagues. Since he is expected to teach a new entrant the formal requirements of a job it is most appropriate therefore that the same teacher should often be the one to link these to the teaching of a job's informal requirements. But more important, the new entrant *must* be made to walk in step with the rest of the group and here the group acts as a back-up resource to reinforce the training that is offered. He must be taught not to take too much – or, equally dangerous, to take too little – since either can have serious repercussions for the rest of the group. The acceptance and transmission of a formula as among taxi drivers – or as we saw in Chapter 4 among dockworkers – allows physically separated workers to fiddle in *alignment* and to account for changing conditions without the need to discuss each day's affairs and set common fiddle levels on every occasion they work.

Moral careers fall broadly into two stages: learning about the job (and more important, certain truths about the job); and learning to hold down and progress in the job (which invariably means fiddling). Where there is relatively little to learn then appropriately the teaching is simple and short as it is among cab drivers. Where there is more to learn, as when the market is extremely competitive or the range of goods complex, then a formal teaching programme for new entrants is required. But in all moral careers each stage must be 'passed' before an entrant is allowed to proceed to the next. And 'passing' means internalising a degree of moral transformation.

Among roundsmen on repetitive runs who deal in a wide range of commodities to a large number of regular customers, there is a lot to learn and a lot to teach. There is also, of necessity, a great degree of bureaucracy needed to support such a system, and the formal training of new staff also tends to be bureaucratised: there is usually a formal training period which emphasises formal procedures. But in all cases this formal training is linked to the learning of informal procedures.

Ditton (1977a) compared the induction of the bakery roundsmen he studied with someone learning to drive a car. The learner is
taught by the book at first until he can master procedures so
thoroughly that they become internalised: he stops thinking about
the use of the clutch and simply uses it. Only when the formal rules
have been internalised can he begin to cut corners – to drive in a
more informal way. The bakery roundsman learns about his job in
the course of three weeks' training during which he travels with an
experienced 'hand'. While he is being trained, he is impressed
with the importance of checking to avoid unnecessary mistakes
which have to be made good from his pay. But though in the early
stages this docking of pay is only a threat, the new roundsman is
allowed to make mistakes only for the first few months. This is a
'honeymoon' period; it is essentially temporary, with the implication that if losses continue he will either have to make them good
or be sacked.

At this stage, therefore, the idea of his subjection to the
company, of his vulnerability as an employee, is introduced. And
though the roundsman has considerable independence – his own
van, his own stock, his own round of customers – this vulnerability
distinguishes him from the genuinely free-floating entrepreneurial
hawks. For any sense of stability, he will have to look to a group
code of practice which provides him with an ethic and an objective
(you work for the company by working for yourself – but you still
work for the company). Very soon he realises that the official
objective of balancing his takings lith the stock he sells is unreal.
He may feel this is a discovery he makes for himself. But in fact the
truth is revealed to him bit by bit by his mentor or supervisor
during training:

> . . . well I never expect a round to work out dead right . . . and
> when I have a new chap, I always show him how to make a few
> coppers, and that helps cover that sort of thing . . . everybody
> makes mistakes . . . when you're adding up a load of figures,
> *everybody* makes mistakes, so you're going to lose a few coppers here
> and there . . . this is the best way to explain it to a chap. (Quoted in
> Ditton, 1977a, p. 33)

The introduction of a new entrant to fiddling usually begins when his 'instructor' is satisfied, by the way he tackles a job's formal requirements, that he has sufficient nous to grasp its informal requirements. He must therefore demonstrate his ability to cope with fiddles, not only to his mentor but also to others of his co-workers. Coping, however, involves far more than a mastery of the technical requirements of a vulture job and of its associated fiddles. The entrant must also cope with the psychological requirement of recognising that fiddles are acceptable to him personally. From outside the job, fiddles appear as excrescences, not integral to the job at all. Thus the entrant first sees them as something other people do, and something he might personally avoid. If he is not prepared to include himself in, however, he finds before too long that he has to throw in the job:

> I did six months at this job. I was amazed really. I suppose I was very naive but the extent of fiddling is fantastic . . . I eventually left because I didn't want to have to fiddle, and if you don't fiddle it isn't worth the effort for the money. (Processed food driver/salesman)

Six months or a little longer appears to be a common period within which many workers in vulture jobs decide that the job is not for them. I have noted that these jobs often have many entrants leave during this period, but that those that pass through it are likely to have very stable employment records: these are the ones who have internalised the demands of the job, have learned how to do it and have satisfactorily demonstrated their abilities to their workmates.

Moral acclimatisation has to take place gradually, and at first, to avoid shocking the trainee, a light tone is adopted. On regular rounds with myriad customers suggestions about adding a penny on here and there and advice on who to 'watch out for' (who not to fiddle) are made jokingly, as if only half-meant. At this stage they *are* only half-meant; if the trainee jibs at these suggestions, they can always be withdrawn and no harm is done. The joking tone, too, prevents suggestions being quoted against the trainer later on. In this way, the trainee recognises fiddles only when he himself is looking for them; that is, when his understanding of the impossibilities of reconciling the job's needs has grown to the point at which he realises he will have to fiddle or leave the job.

The deadline for this realisation is the end of the 'honeymoon' period, when shortages are no longer tolerated or when a low level of selling is no longer acceptable. Anticipating this stage of his career, the trainee's sense of vulnerability increases. Indiscriminate hiring and firing is threatened ('I could put my head out of this door, snap my fingers and fifteen men would be after your job!': Ditton, 1977a). The bureaucracy of the job becomes more oppressive, demanding impossible accuracy in book-keeping or a higher level of sales. The trainee by now looks for a way out, and the logical way out is through fiddles: one mistake can be cancelled only by another.

Since vultures work on the principle of mutual self-interest, an individual may be friendly with his colleagues but he never loses sight of the fact that they *are* competitors. Competition is most intense and the fiddles are more dramatic in selling jobs where the items sold are few or of high value, as in the arms trade – or, to a lesser and more mundane degree, among the less-established firms in high-value selling, as in the office equipment field. Here an individual's potential rewards are high but his sense of vulnerability is also high. Here, too, the bureaucracy is liable to be extensive because the sale of such items often needs a strong organisational back-up. Caught between the demands of such bureaucracy and the competition of his fellows, the individual is able to join the individualistic hawks only if he is outstandingly successful, but is most likely – with the majority – to remain in a tense and vulnerable limbo. As our salesman put it: 'It's very competitive. Salesmen tend to be very highly strung, know what I mean?'

These organisations tend to heat up competition with achievement league tables or by the monthly listing of salesmen's records, with large prizes for selling and upgridding for failure. There is therefore an incentive to reach the top, the move from the periphery to the core of the organisation which is linked to the award of a better round or a more lucrative territory. On the other side of the coin organisations play on salesmen's insecurity, making it clear, if they fail to achieve adequate sales or matching book-keeping after, say, a three-month training period, that they will be sacked.

The lesson is gradually pushed home that to survive, achieve and progress the salesman cannot allow his competitors an even break. There is limited space in the core and limitless space on the periphery. But his gradual introduction to a system of fiddles allows him to emerge from his training with a do-it-yourself survival kit. The trainee who accepts the go-it-alone philosophy that is appropriate to this quadrant easily takes to such a do-it-yourself fiddle system. It fits his world-view but it is a world-view that is different from the one he had before undergoing his training.

Most salesmen first learn a basic selling technique on a formal course, in the same way that a bakery roundsman or a pie salesman learns about his round. Our photocopying machine salesman was, for instance, taught about the different types – the Blockers, the Nose-Pickers, the Wankers and Mr Prospect – that he would meet, and the characteristics of each.

This training provides a guide to formal selling, to the 'cold canvas'. But it also provides a useful guide to who might and who might not collaborate in a fiddle. In other words, formal training (albeit in colourful language) provides the grounding for informal fiddling. In the photocopying machine case the fiddle amounted to straight bribery. Other inducements can be, and often are, less direct.

The bribe in this case persuades a quasi-decision-maker to act in the salesman's interest and his role thus becomes roughly comparable to that of the hotel manager who colludes in and oversees an overcharging fiddle, or the key taxi driver who limits how much other drivers hand in. The main difference is that though both collude with the fiddler, the last two teach the fiddler, while the first has to be taught to play his part *by* the fiddler. He has to explain 'what they have to do'; how to jam the rival's machine 'and make a fuss about it . . .' and how to set the scene to grant the salesman access to Mr Prospect and to cause him maximum embarrassment. Then with the machine jammed and the secretary having 'a rant about it . . . there you are – on the spot to sell'.

A proper reading of the target area for above-board selling is essential before a fiddle can ever be attempted and this must be understood implicitly or taught explicitly. To offer Mr Prospect a similar bribe could be disastrous. In the same way, to hint to the selling company's management that this is how sales are often made would be equally disastrous. The salesman must know from his previous experience, or he must be taught, how to talk to both in the language they understand. 'My machine must be an improvement on yours, because yours is demonstrably unreliable' in the first case, and 'my selling methods must be all right because I sell machines for you' in the second.

Formal training or induction not only shades into informal training for fiddling; it produces the conditions for fiddling. The trainee not only acclimatises himself to, but also familiarises himself with, a moral landscape. This driver/salesman working for a processed food distribution company, for example, has clear ideas picked up from a key senior salesman, of where fiddles are tolerated and where they are not:

> When it comes to fiddles – multiples are always the easiest – the staff often couldn't care less. It's not their money. I'm very friendly with two supermarket managers I have on my journey. One of them gives me a piece of wall space and says 'Fill it up'. So I fill it up with whatever I have spare and he'll always sign for anything – no problems . . . At the other extreme . . . are the one-man shops. They're likely to check everything. They say: 'What are you fiddling me today for, Joe?' I say: 'No – it's all there.' And it is.
> (Meat pie salesman)

Just as the idea of fiddling is passed on in a joking manner which 'defuses' it, so in the same way a constant harping on 'mistakes' and the likelihood of mistakes takes some of the moral weight out of the subject. And mistakes are a reality whenever stocks are exchanged for money. But the suggestion that 'anyone can make mistakes' implies that fiddles will be as inevitable as the liability to stock or money shortages of which a trainee is early made aware. The trainee is told that he is not going to be able to keep the books balanced in the normal way because everybody – even the most experienced – makes mistakes. And he is also warned, or soon finds out for himself, that when customers see a mistake to their advantage they rarely point out the mistake. And so he begins to take the 'anyone can make mistakes' line to mean 'anyone can make mistakes to put right other mistakes'.

This attitude to mistakes in mistake-prone occupations becomes internalised as the trainee's moral career develops. It is demonstrated to him that he is not exactly powerless and he now begins to view the landscape differently: it is one over which he, after all, possesses some control.

> Sometimes in some places they check – but often with one of the youngest girls. I say: 'I'll read out and you check.' I shout out, say, 'Two dozen Swiss rolls', where there should be three dozen. They'll say 'Yes' and then sign without checking the voucher. If anyone ever does query anything, you can always say: 'I made a mistake – sorry.' Anyone can make a mistake, can't they? (Driver/salesman of foods to the retail trade)

Over a long period of time 'mistakes' can actually be built into a round or sales area to become an unalterable feature of the landscape. The newcomer or trainee has a choice: he can accept the fiddle and by so doing implicitly recognise the whole landscape of fiddling; or he can reject it, and by so doing draw attention to an individual act of dishonesty.

> There's one woman . . . who runs the canteen at the tech. college. She orders trays of pies. Every day she orders three, every day she sells three, and for years she's always thought there were sixty pies to a tray when there should be seventy-two. This fiddle was passed on to me when I took the job on and the bloke who showed me had it passed on to him when he started. It must have been going on for years because that woman had been there thirteen years when I took

her on and that was two years ago. The fiddle is possible because she'll always sign for three trays with no mention on the voucher of the number of pies. (Meat pie salesman)

A salesman who could not accept this handed-down fiddle might well alert the customer to the fact that she had consistently been given thirty-six pies less than she should have been given every day for thirteen years. In doing so he might clear his own conscience though he would also, at the very least, lose his company a valuable customer. But it says much for the careful acclimatisation of newcomers, at least to this company, that the subterfuge should have lasted for so long without disruption.

It is in these ways that fiddlers adopt the important ethic of vulture jobs: that by helping the company you help yourself. The reverse also holds: by refusing to help the company you do a disservice to yourself. Ditton's (1977a) study of bakery roundsmen revealed a similar dilemma. The roundsman in a sense 'crossed the line' between the outsider's view of fiddling as a dishonest working method and the insider's view of it as just one of many 'adjustments' he needed to make to get on top of the job.

I've gone to the door, and the woman says 'Here's the money for the small loaf, baker', and she puts $7\frac{1}{2}$p in my hand, and I know that it's only 7p, but I've looked in the route book, and I've seen '$7\frac{1}{2}$'p marked right through it, so it's put me in a very embarrassing position, what do I do? If I tell the woman it's only 7p what happens? The new bloke has lost a customer . . . she's not going to think of the $\frac{1}{2}$p saved, but of all the other $\frac{1}{2}$p's she's lost in the past. (Quoted in Ditton, 1977a)

What is striking is not how the system isolates the roundsman but how it locks everyone – roundsman, co-workers, customer and company – together. Breaking out appears to do nobody any good.

The deviant worker among vultures, therefore, is not the worker who fiddles but the 'straight' worker who *refuses* to fiddle (or is unaware of fiddles). In other types of job the deviant straight can stand for principles of free enterprise in the face of collective attempts by his worker colleagues to restrict output. He refuses to conform with informal methods of production because he instinctively sympathises if not identifies with the aims of management (Snizek, 1974). But within vulture jobs, particularly where fiddles are a response to bureaucratic insistence on certain levels of sales each month, the straight worker dissociates himself from the sell-by-any-means ethic of his employer and takes the outsider's view – that fiddles are the dishonest excrescences of an honest job.

These 'straight' workers particularly threaten vulture fiddles, not simply because they throw them into relief by refusing to practise them, but because they increase rather than reduce other workers' suspicion of them and so further loosen the group. And they cannot readily be ejected as they can be from wolfpack groups.

A common hotel fiddle involves the ordering of coffee in coffee lounges. The waiter will take an order for four coffees but ask the kitchen for only two. He will then top up the coffee with hot water and add two cups, which he has hidden for the purpose, to his tray. He can then pocket the difference in price between two and four coffees, since only two will have to be docketed in the kitchen. An experienced waitress new to one hotel startled her colleagues by ordering six coffees. Six was an eminently fiddleable number, but an *order* for six was unheard of. Everyone assumed that she was either stupid or naive. In fact her reputation for deviant straightness allowed her thereafter to fiddle like the rest of them but with far less risk of detection.

Co-operation and Competition

The straight worker in this type of job does not threaten the fiddle system as severely as his counterpart in wolfpack jobs. There the division of labour means that fiddles have to be co-operative or they fail. Among vultures the 'straight' is less of a threat and more of a victim, refusing as he does to resist the upgrid tendency of bureaucracy which controls him and ignoring his opportunities to make the job more rewarding. It is as a victim that the newcomer is treated as a temporary deviant. He is given the least opportunity to fiddle. The new waiter is allocated the 'station' farthest from the bar and the kitchen and with the greatest number of eight- and ten-seater tables (where tips are proportionately less than for smaller tables). 'Chance' or casual custom, which is fiddleable because meals are not entered on hotel bills, is steered away from them and towards more experienced waiters who have negotiated arrangements with the head waiter. In exactly the same way the new roundsman gets the poorest round; the new driver the most demanding and least rewarding route; the new sales rep. the least lucrative territory. Vulture fiddles are competitive, not co-operative, because each man aims to maximise his returns but the overall supply of fiddles is limited. The individual has to earn his share of them and he often does so at another's expense.

On board passenger liners there is constant demand from couples for the essentially limited supply of 'deuce' tables (tables seating two) in the dining-room. Couples who gain these tables usually tip heavily to retain them. 'Deuce' tables, therefore, provide waiters with blue chip customers. Their supply is controlled – and it would appear limited – by the head waiter, and he allocates them to stewards who have shown an ability to cope and a willingness to tip him on each voyage. The system provides an unofficial redistribution of wealth: a system '*from* each according to his needs'. One steward, for example, tipped the head waiter his favourite brand of whisky for deuce tables, and also had to tip the chef (who in turn tipped his key men from the steward's payments).

> It's vital to tip these behind-the-scenes people because it's how fast they work that determines how quick you get your passengers fed and out of the restaurant. What happens is that all the money that flows around the ship comes from the passengers and all the staff are trying to get hold of it. So those that serve the passengers directly, like stewards, they get the passengers' money but have to make some of it available to galley chefs or bakers or other people who're in the background because you need their co-operation. It's a kind of teamwork.

This system is co-operative, but only to a point. The purpose of these transactions is to ensure that the steward gets as large a share of passengers' disposable expenditure as possible, and certainly a larger share than his colleagues are getting. The supply of expenditure is limited, and so vulture fiddling has a competitive edge ('I'd wish it had been *my* Emperor that had been sold'). The steward quoted above also commented:

> Stewards are really in business for themselves. Even though they recognise the need for co-operating with other stewards, they're still really running their own show for themselves. This is one reason why many stewards only stay in the Merchant Navy for three or four years, then with their earnings they buy a small business or home.

It is the competition in vulture jobs, and their competitive fiddles where these are linked to erratic product and labour markets, that add to the insecurity of these already insecure occupations. Particularly in the service industries it appears that managements find it difficult to forecast, and therefore to plan for, an inherently erratic demand. Management styles in this quadrant reflect this; they tend to a 'fire-fighting' response. Instead of responding with strategies for dealing with their erratic world most managements here adopt the short-term tactics of 'crisis management' – the constant matching of capacity to fluctuating demand which means that peripheral workers tend to be taken on quickly and indiscriminately and to be similarly fired. The individual who feels most at home here is the drifting peripheral, a person without much of a past and with no great hopes for the future. At the periphery's farthest edge we find the misfit, the hard to employ, the ethnic minorities, the socially stigmatised. Vulture jobs attract these people because their managements do not or cannot ask too many questions. Management here is likely to be imprecise about its needs, often calling for no more than an extra pair of hands. It may want to be more discriminating, but its immediate needs call for a less choosy policy of recruitment.

If workers are taken on indiscriminately they are also laid off indiscriminately; particularly the peripherals who do not have the time or the ability to establish any measure of their permanent usefulness to an organisation. In this environment fiddles — like employment itself — are also insecure. There is a constant risk that they will be uncovered, that management may tighten up, that key personnel be moved, or that deviant workers may give the game away — either through fiddling too much or through refusing to fiddle at all. As we have seen, the adoption of a fiddle formula can reduce some of this insecurity. The taxi driver's computation of mileage is finely calculated to be acceptable to management. But such a balance of interests may easily be upset. A deviant may emerge who may be dangerous not because he refuses to fiddle but because he refuses to recognise limits on his fiddling. Such a 'rogue deviant' takes only a part of the loose group ethic to heart — he becomes so engrossed in helping himself that he forgets the original reason for fiddling was to 'help the company'. In doing so, and by the likelihood of drawing management's attention to the fiddle, he presents it as destructive rather than supportive (the supportive fiddle is one where management may approve the result but cannot recognise the method).

The ship's steward on the passenger liner recalled a fiddle which went over the top in this way. On a cruise to Alaska the ship was entirely stocked with British provisions. Some of these, particularly the jams and marmalade, attracted the Americans on board as souvenirs.

> They literally knocked off the jams and marmalade right in front of our eyes. We had to take on more stores from sister ships at San Francisco . . . Then some of the stewards in the first-class restaurant started selling on their own. They sold jam and marmalade for about ten dollars a jar.

What might have remained concealed as a small-scale fiddle became dangerously obvious as a large-scale selling operation. 'Core' workers, those who had most to lose by having senior management's attention drawn to the whole system of vulture fiddling, began to get worried.

The chief steward and his assistant decided very quickly that this had to stop. It was far too risky; it went beyond the limits.

One member of the excessive fiddling group was identified as 'deviant', and labelled as the ringleader.

[He was] a right rogue, who had a reputation for petty crime . . . so nobody was really very sorry for him when he carried the can. Not only had he got the head waiter on his back, but the other stewards were already worried about working with him.

The rogue deviant always increases the instability of a naturally unstable occupation. In this case the group acted quickly, identified a 'ringleader' and got him 'to carry the can' — that is, it ejected him from the group. It was able to do this because, though a vulture group and therefore divided by individual competition, it was able to unify, assert its boundary and *act* as a group when its existence was threatened from a common source. In addition the common residence of its members in a 'total institution' (Goffman, 1961b), further helped this process. But in other cases destabilising a fiddle system is likely to lead to its complete break-up. The overcharging system in operation at the Blackpool hotel, for example, began to be threatened by the actions of one excessively deviant worker.

I was getting choked with her. Every week we were having stock deficiencies in her bar. She was letting the side down, and it was coming to bonus time. (Hotel manager, quoted in the *West Lancashire Evening Gazette* 25 March 1971).

Here 'letting the side down' meant that she was indulging her own interests to such a degree that her level of fiddling threatened the fiddles of the whole group. When the manager eventually removed her, as he had to, from the bar job, she then went to the directors, revealed all, and particularly expanded upon the manager's role as organiser and co-ordinator. The manager said that at first he was not unduly worried about being reported. To his mind, the fiddle and the overall objective of the hotel (to come out with a profit) had become so inextricably entwined that he believed the directors would accept the situation openly just as he knew they supported it covertly. He was, of course, wrong: what can be accepted – even colluded in when based on covert knowledge – cannot be tolerated when the pretence of ignorance is no longer sustainable: a point well explored by Henry (1978).

It is always difficult for link men to maintain an ambiguous position for long in an unstable environment without antagonising one or other of the parties. Since vultures are characterised by strong individual self-interest, someone is always going to accuse or at least suspect someone else of over-feathering his nest. And where authority is never fully legitimated the man in the middle becomes particularly vulnerable. But in one respect an 'outsider', someone who refused to or could not conform to the ethic behind the fiddle, brought this case upon the group. And in another respect, the group brought it upon itself – because it was unable to sustain adequate measures of control over individual aspirations.

This case reveals a constant danger for vultures: that ambiguity over who is an insider and who an outsider can destroy the whole system. Here the competitiveness and insecurity endemic to these kinds of job can put so much pressure on individuals that periodically the fiddle system, the unofficial redistribution of customer or managerial wealth, will be overthrown or at least deferred for a while. Indeed, a crisis of this sort may be necessary to resolve tension – to deflect heat from the generality of workers and re-establish equilibrium. Security is beyond the reach of these occupations as these are currently organised, but equilibrium is possible – though it *is* essentially an unstable equilibrium.

Scapegoats, Crackdowns and Cycles of Control

Equilibrium is not uncommonly achieved by a process which might be compared to the institution of witchcraft. Small-scale societies that encourage internal competition which is divisive, yet which need their members to collaborate in the essential tasks of living, have been observed as prone to periodic bouts of scapegoat selection. Vulture groups are in some respects structurally similar to such witchcraft-prone societies. The groups cohere under the pressure of threats from outside and individual action is always taken within the framework of this threat/protection regime. But individual interests are competitive and often run counter to group interests. Alliances are therefore rarely constant and individuals are thus kept in a state of secure insecurity – to such a degree that tension periodically rises and a scapegoat or victim has to be sought. The scapegoat is accused of disloyalty to the group and perhaps of alliances with outside forces; he is the threat made tangible ('a right rogue, who had a reputation for petty crime'). Once the scapegoat is punished, tension is resolved: new deals are struck and new standards are set. The process satisfies these workers since it reduces their tensions, overcomes their divisions and penalises only their marginal members. It also serves management needs since it permits them the comforting belief that they can solve a structurally determined situation by recourse to an *ad hoc* response. Their philosophic justification is likely to be some variant of the 'rotten apple' theory of deviance – that deviance is due to defective but essentially isolated individuals.

For these reasons we find that in some organisations crises occur with such regularity that they appear almost cyclical. This is especially true when the crises take the form of management purges (Ditton, 1979). It is particularly in vulture jobs that managements periodically attempt to restore control over their employees – to push them further upgrid – by bringing in new bureaucratic procedures, by tightening up on existing ones, or by bringing in 'new broom' managements. Firms employing sales representatives, for instance, periodically and typically clamp down on expenses and insist on the presentation of receipts – at least for a time. Hotel managements may for similar reasons attempt to bureaucratise the tipping system by including a service charge in customers' bills. They thus remove a profitable part of their staff's 'total reward system' and in doing so push them further upgrid. This is because the 'pool' of tips created by a service charge is then distributed on criteria deciddd by the management.

Managements sometimes crack down in other ways – by hiring a security firm, for instance (Henry, 1978) or by putting in 'straight' workers (Terkel, 1975). Such periodic purging is likely to run alongside efforts by the workforce to find scapegoats. In effect, workforce and management both become aware, often simultaneously, of a widening gap between an acceptable fiddle level and the unacceptable fiddles actually being practised.

The need to find scapegoats is important to the whole of such a workforce. When workers think a periodic purge is imminent, everyone feels equally threatened. No one knows where lightning may strike, the precise purpose of an investigation, or who specifically will be investigated. So everyone takes avoiding action. A waitress told me of such an incident when she heard a rumour that her hotel management had appointed private detectives with the power to search staff homes – a not uncommon fear among hotel workers and one paralleling similar periodic fears in other occupations of this type.

I was at the Embassy then, and it used to be very busy. Everyone was fiddling like mad when we got a leak through from the office that they were sending private detectives round the houses. Well a friend of mine, Molly, told me that this was going to happen. She didn't tell everyone – just me and two other girls. I was petrified because all my sheets and tablecloths and all my cutlery and silver were all stamped with the Embassy crest. Well, I didn't know what to do. As I say, I was petrified! So I made an excuse, I said I was ill, and rushed off home. I piled everything I could on to a sheet in the middle of the floor and tied up the corners. Laugh – the neighbours must have thought I was bloody crazy! I dashed into the garden – out there – and started digging a bloody great hole. I wasn't laughing at the time, though, I can tell you, because the more I dug down, the more I was digging up! There was a pile of coffee pots, cutlery and rotted linen already in the garden that had been buried there by the waiter who'd had the house before me! He must have done exactly the same thing as I did when the panic hit him. The only difference was that these all had the crest of the Splendide on them!

As in most such accounts, the rumour proved false. There were no actual searches and, as far as I could determine, there never had been. None the less, the crises revealed and created by these recurrent rumours indicate the degree of chronic insecurity that people have to learn to tolerate if they take employment in an insecure fiddle-prone occupation. Living with insecurity is one of the most important lessons to be absorbed during the learning phase. The cyclical pattern of fiddles and cover-ups, of equilibrium, instability and panics, follows from a management pattern of complaisance interrupted by bouts of tightening up. It is a pattern that reflects management attempts to counter group involvements on the one hand and a short-term crisis style of management on the other. Both together are implicit in many vulture jobs. But erratic demand can give workers an opportunity to assert their own controls and – through fiddles – to exploit the vulture characteristic of a group. Nowhere is this more strongly represented than in occupations where erraticism in employment follows from erraticism in the demand for its product. An extreme example is summer icecream-selling, where a workforce may be laid off in its entirety in the winter. With this high level of insecurity, the job does not encourage a sense of commitment.

> Turnover on this job is very high . . . most men had a high number
> of jobs beforehand. No references are ever asked for and most of us
> were sent from the employment exchange. (Icecream salesman)

The ultimate response to extreme fluctuations in these jobs is to change one job for another. But another response is for such seasonal workers to bind themselves tightly into vulture groups if conditions permit. 'We fiddled like hell all summer', said one icecream salesman. 'Everyone was in on it – there was a terrific spirit and everyone competed to do the most outrageous fiddles. It was making hay while the sun shone.' However, most job fluctuations are gentler – a hotel taking on additional peripheral staff for the summer season or a taxi firm taking on extra drivers at the weekend – and what is striking about the response to them, in terms of fiddles, is how precisely it mirrors these product market changes. The owner of the fleet of cabs, for example, could run five cabs but usually ran only three. On bad days, like Sundays, he would keep his fleet as slim as possible. The drivers as a group, however, made similar adjustments in their own way. On bad days they adjusted their 'take', that is, the amount they would pay in, by a sliding scale applied to their agreed formula: instead of multiplying mileage by six, as they normally did, they would multiply it by five. In this kind of way, both management and workforce can make adjustments that allow them to cope with changing situations and varied conditions.

Likewise, when a hotel has to take on large numbers of additional staff to cope with a banquet, the permanent staff can take advantage of the stretching, and usually overstretching of management control this involves. This is because the potential for fiddles increases with the scale of transaction. At a banquet for 200 people the prescribed number of bottles that is supplied will invariably be less than the amount paid for. This is because it is difficult to check quantities of anything that runs into the hundreds, let alone the thousands, and attempting to do so is no more than a futile gesture, as local authorities have found in the distribution of building materials to scattered sites. How *do* you check a stock of 100,000 bricks? No more easily than you can keep tally of 1,000 wine bottles or 3,000 pastries at a banquet. And especially so when the relationship is triadic (see Chapter 6) and the least experienced of the trio is the one who pays.

The Trained Vulture

The trained vulture has to recognise his opportunities. They arise not only from changes within his situation but from the changing opportunities presented by management who periodically alter pace, scale, prices and incentives. And we have seen how the vulture groups and collusive management will go halfway towards showing him how to recognise them. But only halfway. Once he has latched on to fiddles and the need for fiddles, his tutors withdraw and act thereafter as if only the job's formal technical requirements had been explained to him. He is deemed to have thought up any fiddle practices by himself and it is pure coincidence that his colleagues and competitors are practising the same fiddles.

Fully tutored, the vulture is on his own though he must work within group-set parameters. Yet he is not the same person as he was when he first took the job. What he has been taught is the preparatory grounding for certain rites of passage. Now he has crossed the line, and his initiation is complete. He is on his own again, but this time with the support that comes from sharing a group's knowledge and with the mental equipment to reinterpret his job in terms of a personal morality. And crucially, though this morality may be at odds with the demands of the bureaucracy which controls him, it will be in tune with the entrepreneurial ethic of his occupation – that if a man looks after the company's interests, he will look after his own interests.

The bureaucracy represented by more distant managerial control insists (because that is *how* it has to work) that services are provided justly and impartially. This, though, is *not* a moral insistence. Efficient accounting demands that people get what they pay for; that stock which is not bought is returned; that stock which is bought is accounted for. But as we have seen, the trainee is quickly told (and finds out for himself) that this is not how things actually happen. However 'just' he might be tempted to be, the nature of the goods-into-money process defeats him. His personal book-keeping is dogged by Sod's Law: his earnings are well below expected levels; his vulnerability to management control is too easily demonstrated. In desperation he looks not just for a way out but for an *explanation*. The fiddle provides it. It says that 'unless you substitute a system of justice for the bureaucratic system, its inbuilt unmanageability will defeat you'.

A personal system of justice (again without any moral overtones) lets the trainee vulture see the landscape anew. All shops need not get the same treatment from the salesman. Multiples (where 'they couldn't care less. It's not their money') are the greatest targets for fiddles. Small shops, where the owners *have* to care to maintain wafer-thin profits, are lesser targets. In hotels, if a customer is satisfied it is irrelevant whether or not he has been fiddled (again, this is not a moral but a purely practical point). The larger the round he buys, the more bottles a table consumes, the more likely fiddles are to succeed; no checks means no dissatisfaction. As we have seen, it may be better from everyone's point of view to continue a fiddle (as in the case of the canteen) than to stop it.

Vulture jobs provide the least stable working environment. This is not only because they shade readily into other quadrants but because individuals here lack the protective expertise of the hawk occupations and the tight support of the wolfpacks. They do not have the craft mastery and mystery of the watchmaker, the lawyer and the hospital consultant, which give unchallengeable status, and they lack the strong sense of group found in wolfpack occupations such as traditional dock gangs or mining teams. With none of the division of labour implicit in such groups, there are no established and stabilising hierarchies, no established and accepted means of settling disputes, and no organisational need for ongoing co-operation. Instead, the principal feature of vulture jobs, their instability, is compounded by and feeds upon the shifting competition that is the norm here. This is why companies can find it easy to dismiss emergent union activists by scapegoating them as thieves, which is often justifiable and difficult to refute. It is a policy that is endemic within one of Britain's largest anti-union catering chains, but it could never be applied in a wolfpack occupation without provoking collective action.

Throughout this range of jobs the unofficial management attitude to fiddling emerges as 'Do it, but don't tell me how' or 'Do it, but I don't want any complaints'. This contrasts with attitudes to deviance in donkey jobs where management collusion is entirely absent, and among hawk jobs where the distinction is blurred between what is fiddled income and what is legitimately earned. In wolfpack jobs we find a degree of collusion – managements are well aware of what goes on and are prepared to tolerate it within understood limits. Among vultures, however, managements positively encourage the fiddle practices of their workers, but at the same time aim to remain formally insulated from any overt knowledge. It is this which makes the position of their link men so vulnerable – in a crisis it is the link men who are both liable to be attacked from below and likely to be sacrificed by those above.

With competition on the one hand, and the lack of established hierarchies on the other, we find here a simultaneous source of conflict without the ready possibility of its resolution. As a result we tend to find undercurrents of envy and discontent, shifting alliances and frequent schisms and ruptures. This is why, when disputes do arise, they are likely to be focused upon scapegoats. And this, too, is why conflict can sometimes only be resolved by reference upwards and out of the groups to higher authority and to new sources of instability.

In no other type of job are fiddles so closely bound to these aspects of the nature of occupations. In no other type are fiddles so integral a part of the mechanics of coping. Fiddles by vultures are part of 'how things happen' rather than 'how things ought to happen'. Unless the very nature of selling, and of personal service, for example, is changed, the selling and service fiddles will persist. And perhaps ought to.

6

Fiddle Factors and Fiddle-Proneness

This chapter is concerned with where fiddles are to be found. I now attempt, therefore, to put fiddles into context — to identify the conditions that favour them and the places in which they are most likely to flourish.

In some occupations, particularly among wolves and vultures, positive pressures exist, as Ditton (1977a) has described in his study of bread salesmen, that not only encourage but which actually *coerce* workers to fiddle. They may have to deal with an accounting system too rigid to operate without the flexibility of built-in fiddles, or their membership in a work-group may be conditional on their participation. Sometimes a person may take on a job and find a fiddle so built into the way it is organised that many other relationships would be disrupted if he did not continue it.

Thus the opportunities and indeed the pressures for people to fiddle vary widely but they may equally well be entirely absent. A bank clerk, for example, has less chance regularly to skim the product he handles, that is, cash, than does, say, a shop assistant or a garage hand. This is not to assert that bank staffs do not fiddle, but to argue that if they fiddle less than shop assistants or garage hands it is because of structural factors: the units they work with are homogeneous, their systems of accountancy are more tightly controlled, and there is little ambiguity about what they deal in or the service they offer. None of these circumstances applies to the same degree in shops or garages. It is important, therefore, to identify the factors which promote fiddling in some contexts and which limit it in others, and to note that they apply or not

136

regardless of the personalities, characters and attitudes of the bank clerks, the shop assistants and the garage hands concerned.

When we try to unravel the conditions influencing a person's behaviour in a particular place and time, it is therefore useful to separate factors stemming from the way a job is designed and structured from those inherent in the personality of the job-holder. It is clearly not enough to explain actions solely in terms of a person's mental state, whether we are studying pilferage or anything else. This is not to suggest that personality does not affect behaviour, but to focus attention more persistently and insistently on the *situations* in which people find themselves. Of course, personality factors cannot be ignored. Some fiddle-prone jobs pre-select certain kinds of people and during their training and socialisation the 'straight' ones tend to be rejected or decide to move. This therefore leaves a residual category of 'non-straights'. But it must be emphasised that it is their *situation* that is fiddle-prone and that this is a prerequisite for them to fiddle. I do not argue that all people who work in a 'fiddle-prone' context necessarily become fiddlers. Rather I argue that socialisation into such a context is likely to exert a definite bias toward maintaining the existing practices of that situation. We can work on the assumption, therefore, that it is *situations* which fix the broad limits of behaviour and which indeed define what is considered permissible and appropriate. Variants in personality can then be seen to operate within limits set by the situation.

It should be noted that for any particular fiddle a number of factors occur repeatedly and it is when several occur together that we find 'fiddle-proneness' (Mars, 1977). This I define as 'any work context where a propensity exists for a job to offer regular material rewards that are excluded from formal accounts or which are included under ambiguous or deceptive headings'. It is a definition wide enough to cover the arms dealer with his doubtful commissions and payments for consultancies on the one hand, and the employed icecream salesman who provides his own biscuit cornets on the other. But it also covers jobs where there is a built-in propensity to avoid or evade taxes – especially where these activities are colluded in by the management. It is important, too, to note that fiddle-proneness is involved in the fiddling of time – and this includes the opportunity to engage in colluded moonlighting.

In this chapter I suggest a number of 'fiddle-prone' factors which so structure economic activity as to facilitate the regular payment of a significant part of people's total reward in the form of fiddles. If fiddles are found in a context that reveals them as significant and regular, then there we are likely to find not one dominant factor but a range of factors. I have identified five of these which I consider of major importance. These are 'passing trade', 'exploiting expertise', 'gatekeepers', 'triadic occupations' and 'special skills/effort'. All these factors depend on the underlying structural differences of knowledge, control, power and ability held by some groups over others. Fiddles arise because workers creatively exploit these differences for their own economic benefit.

Passing Trade

Passing trade exists where two sides to a transaction typically meet only once. Because a high degree of transience precludes the possibility of a build-up of goodwill, we find that this increases the likelihood of fiddles. This can be illustrated by the relationship between an established village resident and the village shopkeeper where transience is low and the possibility of goodwill high. Here there is least likelihood of this kind of fiddle, since any one transaction is part of a longer-term flow, and damage to the relationship at any single point can destroy the flow. The chances of being fiddled, however, increase if there are many weekenders who use the village shop only occasionally, while the high points of this kind of fiddle-proneness are reached in the 'one-off' transient transactions which are so much a part of life in urban centres. Indeed, the larger the urban centre the greater the likelihood of employee–customer fiddling, since a high proportion of its total transactions are transitory. It is the transience in passing trade that helps to explain the near-universal vulnerability of travellers and tourists to being fiddled. Since tourists are travellers with the added problem of being cultural strangers, their vulnerability is doubly increased.

At one restaurant in the centre of London passing trade provides the basis on which its staff are paid and maintains the differentials between their different levels. Its two most senior staff reserve to themselves the right to serve Japanese customers. This is because they hold a stereotype of the Japanese, who are thought not to understand English money since they typically do not count their change. Japanese customers are, therefore, particularly vulnerable to being short-changed. Since this restaurant is in the centre of the city's entertainment area it is frequented by drunks, especially at weekends. They are allocated to all waiters on a strict rota – but with the greater number going to those with the greatest seniority.

In this restaurant it is the situation in which waiters find themselves, not their personalities, that is the primary cause of their fiddling. And though passing trade is a necessary condition, the presence of conditions affecting pay and bargaining power also contribute to its high fiddle-proneness: its waiters' wages are low – below the legal minimum; most are foreigners working illegally without work permits; and this restaurant is one of a chain whose management is resolutely anti-union (see Mars and Mitchell, 1977). At the same time it helps our understanding not at all to see the drunks or the Japanese, the waiters or their supervisors, as individuals; they are the climate – the wallpaper of the situation.

A way to further understand the implications raised by passing trade is to look at relationships as ranging from 'single-stranded' to 'multi-stranded' (Gluckman, 1955, pp. 18, 19, 20). Passing trade involves not only transient relationships – the purely one-off, contractual encounters typical of the city – but they also involve people who have no other basis for contact. In a village, however (or in any fairly close-knit social field), we find people not only relating to each other in an ongoing and continuous way but simultaneously relating to each other in a *variety* of ways. The man keeping the village shop is not only a shopkeeper but also a neighbour and perhaps he also sits on the rural council. He is likely to have kinship links with at least some of his customers. He may support the local football team and join in other communal activities. His customers similarly relate to him in ways other than as a shopkeeper and he relates to them in his other social roles as well. Not only do these relationships span time, they also span depth. Goodwill is thus able to be built up not only over time by repeated contact but also in depth on a variety of different dimensions. Goodwill generated through repetition is buttressed and supported by multi-strandedness.

In multi-stranded relationships it is potentially expensive in social terms to risk damage to even one strand. This is because in any transaction there are always other strands involved, which is why reputation is more highly prized in a village than in a large city. This also incidentally explains why disputes, when they do occur in a village (or in any 'close-knit' field), are likely to be particularly disruptive, bitter and divisive.

It is not only customers in passing trade who are mobile relative to the trader. The mechanics operate equally well when the trader is mobile relative to his customers. The 'relief hand', the 'filler-in', the 'temporary replacement' is thus more likely to cheat his customers than the regular man he replaces. A milkman I knew was adamant that I should never pay my bill to the temporary relief workers who took his place on holidays. Relief workers have only transitory relationships with both workmates *and* customers and they have less to lose if they disturb either set of relationships.

A further aspect of passing trade has to do with social distance between parties to a transaction. The more we consider others as different from ourselves, and the less contact we have with such people, the more likely is 'normal' morality to be suspended or modified. This was the case with the Japanese visitors to the London restaurant. It is when the relationship of trader and customer is not only transient and single-stranded but is also between those who are socially distant in this sense that the chance of fiddles rise steeply. The victim is then outside the rules governing morality that normally govern our excesses (Leach, 1977).

I demonstrated this in a highly unsystematic way in a number of food shops. In working-class districts it is not common for food shopping to be done by men. A middle-class male in a working-class grocer's is therefore doubly out of place, and the social distance between him and a female shopkeeper is greater than normal. I therefore went shopping in ten working-class food shops in different areas where I was not known. In each shop I emphasised my social distance from the assistant. I wore smart 'middle-class clothes' and I raised the social level of my accent. Unlike most regular customers, I was vague about my purchases, showed an ignorance of prices and paid more attention to what was going on outside the shop than to transactions within it. Finally I produced a five-pound note without apparently noticing its value. In three of the ten shops I was offered change for only a pound.

Some selling techniques, although not strictly fiddles, also exploit both transitory relationships and social distance. Certain classes of door-to-door selling have faced such adverse criticism that they are now legally restrained in most Western countries. Extreme examples are found among some sellers of encyclopaedias to aspirant immigrant families where social distance is particularly wide. A variation in similarly exploiting social class as a form of social distance is also found among insurance salesmen. In the north of England most working-class insurance policies are serviced by weekly payments to 'the insurance man' and salesmen are trained to find ways of becoming friends of the family — to build up a relationship so as always to be available to sell new insurance. When this established contact fails, recourse is made to a transitory, socially distant salesman: the 'friendly' salesman is advised to introduce his area superintendent into the home 'to explain things a bit more'. A highly successful salesman described what happens next.

> These are very simple people, you understand, and the poor buggers are absolutely dominated by this pompous middle-class bloke who comes in and uses all sorts of high-powered language. It's amazing how often it works, though — bringing in the 'super' often clinches it.

141

Passing trade has many faces and its associated fiddles are widespread. Its central feature – the transitory nature of many relationships – is increasing as people become more mobile and as urban society increases, though of course urban society cannot be considered monolithic. I have only sketched in broad outline the principles involved. The reader is invited to extend these to enterprises such as main road and motorway petrol stations; to cafes that cater principally for tourists; to motorway breakdown services and indeed to other 'twenty-four-hour emergency services' such as locksmiths or plumbers; and particularly to the various 'once only' offers that might well be 'in your neighbourhood now'.

Exploiting Expertise

A widespread fiddle factor is found where real or suggested expertise is involved in a transaction and where at the same time it may be assumed that the customer is ignorant about what it is he is paying for. This factor therefore depends upon an imbalance in power which is based on an imbalance in knowledge.

These conditions *typically* exist in garage servicing, though they are by no means confined to it. They are indeed well represented among repairmen of all kinds and are also found, to a degree, among the professions. It will be useful, however, if we begin this discussion with garage servicing – treating it as a perfect type for this class of hawkish fiddle. This is not only because experience of it is so common, but also because there have been series of impartial and sophisticatedly planned tests both in the USA and in the UK (Riis and Patric, 1942; *Motoring Which?* 1970–81) which show that this is indeed an industry with a structure that makes it peculiarly fiddle-prone.

The economic base to garage servicing (following O'Brien, 1977) lacks two conditions that normally operate in pricing: the first is that consumers should have speedy knowledge of defects in what they buy; the second that they are free to move from an unsatisfactory supplier to a more satisfactory one. In competitive trading these conditions exist and the price system benefits the consumer. Thus, says O'Brien, in normal trading a firm offering defective goods or service is less competitive than one giving its customers what they want at a price that compares well with what other firms offer. If a customer is unsatisfied he moves. Other things being equal, then, the competitive price system allows at least some degree of consumer choice and, benefiting the consumer, benefits the producer who best caters for him — and penalises those who do not.

Those two conditions are absent from garage servicing. O'Brien uses the phase 'perverse incentives' to explain how a garage that performs poorly is likely to do better than one that performs well. He argues that bad garages drive out good ones because the typical customer cannot judge whether a service has been done properly, and it is difficult for him to check. Thus a garage can, with impunity, charge for a full service which has been only half-done. O'Brien's evidence is clear and, as he says, the economist's profit-maximising 'model' of the firm predicts that this not only occurs but *is the norm*:

> For if a garage habitually does half the service its costs are very much lower than if it has done the full service; and since it can charge the full price, because of the ignorance of the consumer, its profits are maximised when it does as little of the service as it can get away with.
>
> There is probably some lower limit below which the garage will not go in skimping the service, because the risk of detection then becomes too high. Casual observation would suggest that, for most garages, this minimum involves an oil change, together with two other operations which are themselves the result of perverse incentives — the unnecessary replacement of plugs and points. It now seems to be normal to replace both of these items when they are only half worn out.
>
> The consumer of garage services generally does not know enough about the manufacturer's recommendations to argue about this; he lacks knowledge and he has no alternative as he is presented with a *fait accompli* when he goes to collect his car and he either pays

143

the bill or does not get his car back. The garage makes a profit on the supply of unnecessary items; while their inclusion in the minimal service performance makes the customer think that the rest of the job has been done. (O'Brien, 1977)

The garage benefits even further since faults from defective service are unlikely to occur immediately after collection of a vehicle. An ignorant motorist is likely, therefore, to absolve the garage from responsibility and pay it further to rectify these new faults. Nor, as O'Brien points out, can he easily change his garage. The franchising system ties him for the first year of a car's life to its supplier and

> If the car is at all unusual he is limited to the manufacturer's agent thereafter. This can be an acute problem in the case of some imported cars which are handled through agents and where spares are very specialised. (ibid.)

Finally, with cars becoming more complex, owners are less able to do their own maintenance which further increases the power of their servants. Garages, then, are notorious for bad and dishonest service — not only because of the operation of perverse incentives and the garage's control of expertise, but because this is so often linked to passing trade — and also because the inconvenience from a defective vehicle involves a lack of negotiating muscle.

In 1941, in a five-month survey that covered 19,900 miles, two researchers travelled 'up and down and back and forth across the United States from New England to Florida, from coast to coast'.

> [They] stopped at every kind of garage and service station — . . . the results of . . . sampling allow but one conclusion: *that the automobile servicing and repair business of the United States does not give its customers a square deal.* (Italics in original.)

More specifically, they found that

> Three out of five times our investigating motorists stopping for repair at a strange garage were gypped. Three out of five garage-

men (218 out of 347) overcharged, lied, invented unnecessary work or charged for work not done, for parts not needed, for parts not installed. (Riis and Patric, 1942)

The position in the UK forty years later is little different. In January 1977 *Motoring Which?*, the UK Consumers' Association magazine, disclosed that it had investigated garage servicing three times since 1970 and that its latest probe revealed 'results as appalling as in the past'. It concluded that many garages were 'incompetent, untrustworthy or both'. This should hardly surprise us since the *structures* that facilitate such fiddles are the same as existed forty years ago in the USA.

There is little that the ignorant motorist can do. One strength he does possess, however, is to insist on the receipt of all worn-out and replaced parts. Indeed, garages should be expected to return these as part of normal practice. The real answer, however, lies in the motor companies themselves who, one would have imagined, might have a vested interest in seeing their products properly and fairly maintained.

What applies in its purest form to garage servicing applies in different degrees elsewhere. The same conditions are likely to be found wherever the customer is essentially one down through ignorance of what he is paying for. Where technical or professional complexity exists, so too does ignorance.

Another example, also from the USA, subjected watch repairers to a similar inquiry. Four hundred and sixty-two watch repairers across the country were presented with an identical problem: a standard watch in perfect condition but with one simple fault – when opened it revealed a single loose screw (the crown gear screw) which could be instantly tightened and was obvious to even a scarcely trained watch repairer. Of those approached, 226 – 49 per cent of the sample – offered diagnoses that 'lied, overcharged, gave phoney diagnoses, or suggested extensive and unnecessary repairs' (Strodtbeck and Sussman, 1955–6, p. 605).

This fiddle depends upon the customer's ignorance of technical changes in watch manufacture and repair during the past fifty years. Few people realise, as the authors point out, that parts for watches are now mass-produced, standardised and mostly available in gross lots extremely cheaply. And the skill needed to replace one part by another is almost negligible: 'interchangeable parts have so reduced the value of metal working skills that it is fair to say that the bench lathe is more frequently used as a show piece than as a tool' (ibid., p. 607). Despite these technical changes, the watch repairer still trades on his role as an independent craftsman deserving of high prestige and high reward. How does he manage this?

He typically does three things. He will argue that in addition to its special fault a watch needs cleaning and a complete overhaul. He will offer a service guarantee – usually of a year in the event of further trouble. And he never offers to repair a watch while the customer waits; there is always a wait of at least a week and often a fortnight.

The time taken to repair a watch is always vastly longer than it need be in order to obscure the essentially simple nature of most watch repairs. In offering the unwanted service of 'a complete overhaul', a watch repairer meets his customer's need for reliability at a known price, while the guarantee confirms this and can be offered at negligible cost.

One further point deserves emphasis. Since repairmen of all kinds typically trade in the products they repair, there is frequently a blurring between these two aspects of activity. This means that if the quoted price for a repair is more than the customer appears willing to pay, then it can be pointed out how the repair price rates relative to the cost of replacement. This information can then be used as extra persuasion to have the repair done or as part of a sales pitch aiming to have the customer scrap or trade in his old model and buy a new or reconditioned one. In both transactions it is the customer's relative ignorance that makes him (but more often her) particularly vulnerable to being ripped off.

Where a dealer deals in both new and reconditioned products as well as offering a repair service, there are likely to be fiddles to do with spare parts. There are three fiddles here: second-hand parts can be supplied and charges made for new parts; relatively new parts can be extracted from a customer's model and older parts substituted; and finally, little credit need be given on a trade-in model which may even be disposed of 'as a favour' but which may well contain salvageable parts.

An ignorance of exactly what is involved in a job can, then, form the basis of fiddle-proneness and it is here that professionals come into their own. And this kind of ignorance, as we saw in Chapter 2, is also likely to be associated with an ignorance about the amount of *time* a job is expected to take and the particular vulnerability of those to whom the time taken to repair an appliance or do a service is crucially important – as it often is with domestic appliances. Riis and Patric discovered the higher vulnerability of women to the depredations of repairmen – partly because of their presumed technical ignorance, and partly because of their heavy dependence on domestic appliances: 'throughout this survey the man encounters crookedness in 46 per cent of his cases, and woman in 56 per cent' (ibid., p. 178).

Gatekeepers

A third fiddle factor is found where there exists an imbalance between supply and demand. This can apply to information or to goods. Whatever the resource, however, this lack of balance will be most evident at the boundary between supply and demand and it is at this point in production or distribution that benefit will accrue to gatekeepers who control what is required.

In a command economy it is the supply side of the demand/ supply equation that is dominant at the expense of demanders. As Nove points out for the Soviet Union, in a land of chronic shortage it is the supplier who is king.

> a key factor ... is the seller's market plus monopoly. In an economy of shortage, the supplier is powerful. He can insist on his own terms, knowing that he can cause great inconvenience. This attitude is frankly analysed by one Soviet critic, who roundly says 'the producer, the supplier, dictates'. (Nove, 1977, p. 110)

In Chapter 2 I discussed the role of a UK hawk, Sydney Stanley, who operated in the UK command conditions of shortage that followed the Second World War. As an illicit broker he balanced strong demand against a fixed supply of scarce materials and centrally controlled building licences; he really dealt in information.

The 'opposite' of a command economy is a competitive one, where the consumer is sovereign. Here there is a surplus of supply relative to the demand and it is therefore the suppliers of goods and services who have to make the running. The Poulson scandal in the UK which broke in the 1970s revealed an almost standardised bribery system by which John Poulson, who headed a large firm of construction architects, was able to bribe a variety of local authority officials and elected councillors to give advantage to his firm. The Poulson affair had its structural base in the excessive number of competitors such a firm faces – all supplying a service relative to a limited demand, in this case the demand for the construction of large-scale building projects. Corruption was further encouraged by the individual companies' need to maintain steady production when, as in this industry, demand is necessarily erratic. Where processing officials are, on the whole, both low in the hierarchy and lowly paid, as they are in the public sector, then their liability to corruption increases (Montias and Rose-Ackerman, 1980).

Often the metaphor of 'gatekeeper' applies to an actual physical role. A leaked management report indicated that in London's underground transit system the physical gatekeepers who control exit from the system were estimated to be fiddling an alleged £2 million annually in surplus fares, collected but not remitted to the authority (*The Evening News*, 2 April 1979). What is surprising here, however, is that London Transport have never fitted locked glass boxes at all exits, as is common in the USA, nor made any systematic attempt to stop their losses in the three years since their estimates were made public.

Triadic Occupations

When we think of employment we typically think of a two-way relationship – that between employer and employee. We need, however, to look also at those occupations which are involved with customers or clients. These *triadic* occupations deserve special attention because they enable alliances to be made by any two parties against a third. Such occupations are a feature of the personal service industries and it is here that the regular presence of triads increases fiddling because they offer the constant chance of making alliances. The most common fiddling alliances occur among vultures through collusion between employers and workers who are able to fiddle customers by short-changing them and by making reduced deliveries. Various kinds of driver salesmen – such as roundsmen and milkmen – provide good examples.

In these occupations, managements gain through the effective subsidisation of their wage bill while the worker gains in independence and income; it is the customer who usually loses. Sometimes, however, collusion between the employee and the customer enable them both to cheat the employer. Sales clerks and cashiers in retail distribution, or warehousemen who overload and undercharge their friends and relatives, provide good examples. I have noticed, too, that as catering becomes more bureaucratised there is an increasing tendency for waiters ostentatiously to charge less than the full price on a bill. By listing, say, three meals for a party of four, the waiter can hope for a larger tip – in effect obtaining a share of the diners' benefit from his 'error'.

The most thoroughly recorded example of triadic fiddling is described in Ditton's *Part-Time Crime* (1977a). He points out that a baker's roundsman on regular deliveries (particularly where he sells to retailers) is, in effect, forced into fiddling because he is made accountable for shortages on his round. There are always shortages because the system of accounting is inevitably geared against him. In addition there is the likelihood that he can be short after being fiddled by the loaders of his vehicle or by his customers. Ditton carefully describes the collusive training whereby man-

149

agements teach their staffs how to overcome these liabilities by learning to fiddle customers. Their training encourages them to protect themselves by 'adding a bit on' or 'leaving a bit less'. One of my own roundsmen informants explained:

> We talk about 'turning the customer over', meaning to fiddle him – and, of course, don't forget there are always customers ready to turn you over if they can get away with it. That's why you have to fiddle to an extent – to cover any losses you make . . . all the fiddles are against customers: none are against the company . . . so there's no bother. No one has ever been prosecuted.

The question of 'who pays' is crucial in triadic fiddles. It is crucial, as in the case just quoted, not only in determining management's attitudes to fiddling but also in setting the whole tone and climate in which these fiddles are set. In retail shops, for example, the cost of most fiddles falls upon the employer. Jobs are therefore likely to be tightly controlled and attempts are made to prevent close alliances between staff. These become donkey jobs. The position is therefore very different from that found among driver salesmen who are permitted to project most of their fiddles on to their customers. These jobs are less controlled and insulation is less enforced. Such workers are likely to be hawks or vultures. When a retail sales clerk is found fiddling he or she is usually instantly sacked and occasionally also prosecuted. A supermarket manager in the retail arm of a national company supplying its retailers from its own wholesale depots said:

> If I catch any of my girls fiddling then they're sacked straight away without notice, they get nothing. I cannot abide fiddlers and I've had a few . . . it's always the same – out they go.

He then discussed the firm's policy as this applied to its depot drivers:

> What gets me, though, is the depots. I've actually caught their drivers fiddling us by dropping shorts – I caught one red-handed

only a month ago. Of course I reported him. Do you know, he was back here the next week, back in my shop, and all he got was a ticking off? Well, what good is that? I told him straight, I'm not having you delivering stuff to me again. So what do they do? They just move him off on to a different round. Now he's fiddling someone else I suppose.

Here we have examples of two different policies from the same firm – but it is a firm where two accounting units are involved: moral censure can be seen to flourish in the one that pays.

Triadic fiddling in retail outlets (customer and employee allianced against the employer) has always been an accepted liability of companies which have expanded their concerns from a single unit. These are able to be run effectively by a single person or by a family, but have typically developed into organisations of linked units requiring the employment of outsiders and a growth in bureaucratic controls involving numerous levels. For this reason retail distribution has had to build into its accounting systems a loss item called 'inventory or stock shrinkage' which varies usually from 2 to 5 per cent of turnover and sometimes more. Shrinkage is meant to cover loss from damage in storage or transit and irreducible hazards such as soiling, as well as pilferage and shoplifting. It is, however, an amorphous, ambiguous entity. Most managements project the largest share of it outside the company to shoplifters British government inquiry, however, estimated that at least a third of stock shrinkage is attributable to staff, though my own discussions with store detectives and commercial security firms suggest this figure to be closer to two-thirds (Home Office, 1973).

There is a clear connection between these estimates and the low pay in retail distribution. When British government wage inspectors check whether minimum wages are maintained they *always* find the two industries most at fault to be catering and retail distribution. Here they regularly find that about two-thirds of employees tend to be underpaid. A spokesman for USDAW, the union covering retail selling, argued from the 1980 figures that shopworkers therefore need stronger union representation. But an alternative deduction could be that in many cases shopworkers refuse to join the union *because their official wages are less than their total rewards*. And it also seems likely that employers keep official wages down either because they are aware there is a 'fiddle entitlement' or because their workers' wages plus their fiddles equal the labour market's 'valuation' for that class of work.

The triadic fiddle frequently makes a victim of the state. It is common in the catering industry (Mars and Mitchell, 1976; Mars *et al.*, 1979), and in building construction (see the trials of J. Murphy & Sons Ltd, *The Times*, 19 November 1974 *et seq.*), for both management and employees to collude in order to cheat the Inland Revenue of income tax. One fiddle is to re-employ workers for special overtime tasks and allow them to be hired using false names and addresses. In catering it is common to keep two sets of books for the 'tronc'. One set of books forms the basis of the division and another, showing lower figures, goes to the Inland Revenue. Where deception such as this is endemic, waiters often accuse or at least suspect the head waiter of keeping yet a third set of books and of thereby milking the 'tronc' for his own benefit.

Since triadic occupations are predominantly found in the personal service sector of the economy and since this sector is growing, we can expect a growth in triadic fiddles.

Special Efforts/Skills

A fourth fiddle factor exists where levels of effort and skill in an occupation vary widely — where economic return is directly relatable to individual effort or skill and where, therefore, there exists economic pressure for rewards to be brought into line with the market for them.

This position exists among employed professionals and tradesmen where formal rewards are bureaucratically, often collectively, fixed, but where the *real* market price of labour is adjusted not through collective means but by individual arrangements. These, then, are essentially the fiddles of employed hawks. They flourish where some impediment exists to limit differential payments through more formal and orthodox means and they need the collusion of management. This is often arranged through facilitated moonlighting or collusion about expenses.

Journalism, as we saw in Chapter 2, is an occupation where rates of pay are relatively compressed as a result of tight union organisation, but where special efforts or special skills can make for vastly disparate results. In these circumstances extra differentials *have* to be fed into the reward system, not only to reward past efforts but as an incentive for future ones and as a way of retaining staff against competition in a similar line of business.

One sector of the economy is particularly vulnerable to crises in day-to-day affairs. This is the personal service sector and especially the hotel and catering industry which, as I have shown, is already fiddle-prone because of the presence of passing trade and of triadic relationships. Here demand tends to be erratic and intrusion from the environment unpredictable and often severe. Management's problem, therefore, is to match supply to this fluctuating base (Mars *et al.*, 1979, p. 3). In addition these are industries where there is often an immediate feedback of satisfaction or dissatisfaction and an important and valued skill, therefore, is to be able to avoid customer complaints or, if this fails, to diffuse them.

In these circumstances management must be quickly adaptable to crises and is heavily dependent on workers who can cope with the varying and unpredictable demands upon them. The problem for employers is that they tend to depend on an erratic supply of low-quality labour who, through government or union rulings, have to be paid a standard rate. They often solve this problem by offering differential but covert rewards above basic pay to essential, knowledgeable and experienced workers who are able to keep the organisation going and cope with its repetitive crises. These workers' real earnings are based on their access to fiddles, many of which are at the expense of customers (Mars, 1973). It is useful to describe such essential staff as 'core' workers, and their less-favoured workmates as 'peripherals'. Despite the law, there is a tendency to pay peripherals less than the prevailing market rate and even below the legal minimum while core workers are allowed, through collusion, to boost their earnings to a level closer to their market value. Their total rewards are never collectively set but are achieved by a process of individual negotiation that fixes the level of their 'individual contracts' (Mars and Mitchell, 1976, 1977).

This duality, of course, effectively negates the spirit of equal pay and equal opportunity laws, since it allows discrimination that can hardly be formally challenged. This is because a worker's normal career progression is from the periphery through to the core, but it is one that not everyone has an equal opportunity of making. People who are socially stigmatised are over-represented among such peripheral workers because they are never given a 'fair' chance to get to the core.

These five main fiddle factors have in common that they all involve the creative exploitation of a structured imbalance in power between the fiddler and his victim. In addition, however, there are a number of supplementary functions. I have identified four of these. They have to do with control systems, the ambiguities surrounding certain classes of good, the ease of their conversion to private use and the anonymity arising from large-scale organisation. None of these is decisive in determining whether a specific context is fiddle-prone or not, but they all act in common with one or more main factors to facilitate fiddle-proneness. Whereas the main fiddle factors are concerned with power, these facilitators derive from the nature of goods and the structures which mediate between them and the people who handle them.

Control Systems

Sometimes control systems are too expensive or complicated to install or to operate. Garage forecourt owners and shopkeepers argue that it would be too involved and too expensive for them to check on their staff's issuing of trading stamps. This in part explains why, in the days when I collected stamps, I always seemed to find myself queueing in the stamp company's discount store behind two or three petrol station staff! The expense of control is also an explanation offered by bar managements when challenged about the depredations of their staffs. 'How can we control them', they ask, 'without setting up impossibly complicated control systems?' In many bars and garages the distance of employers from the scene of action and the 'passing trade' factor of one-off custom combine with this difficulty of control to make fiddling a near-certainty. But the other part of the explanation is that while the cost of control systems would be borne entirely by management, the incentive to install and operate them is often minimal – since the cost of many fiddles, especially those in triadic occupations, is, as I have shown, often not borne by the company but borne instead by its customers. Cheaper electronic controls, however, are beginning to facilitate their wider introduction.

Ambiguity

Where ambiguity over the quantity of a good, its quality, or its exact category is inherent in its nature, this may not only cloak fiddling but be specially developed to do so. It is not easy, for example, to compute the quantity of drink consumed at a wedding; or, in the building trade, the number of bricks delivered to a site, the thickness of concrete on a path, the exact amount of copper used in a building, or the gauge of zinc on a roof. At busy times (and especially in a seller's market) ambiguity is likely to be deliberately increased. Price lists go missing and cash register windows tend to become covered over or otherwise obscured when icecream is sold on hot days, when customers are surging about at a New Year sale, when drinks are ordered at theatre bars during crowded intervals, or whenever market conditions move against buyers. I once demonstrated this last example in an extremely unsystematic way. Faced with a crush of bodies and dodging outstretched arms in a London West End theatre bar, I shouted:

155

'Here! – haven't I been short-changed?' There was no argument, but with alacrity my hand was filled with silver!

Ambiguity over quality and category is, then, particularly exploited where the customer cannot physically check the quantity of a good he pays for, and where he lacks expertise and comprises one of a triad. In bars after a few drinks customers are usually unable to distinguish dear drinks from similar but cheaper ones, which encourages a plethora of bar fiddles, short-changing and overcharging. Bar staff, for instance, smear gin around the inside rim of a young girl's glass, fill it with tonic and pass it off as gin and tonic. Taverns sell tarragona as port wine – especially at Christmas – while some wine waiters in even the best restaurants, after careful assessments of their customers, sometimes sell them cheap wine as château-bottled. It is also not uncommon for them to collect the ends of other customers' bottles and to sell them in carafes as 'house wine'. Organisations supplying food and drink combine a concentration of fiddle factors.

The Conversion and Smuggling of Goods

When working in the RAF stores I found watches and micrometers were categorised 'V & A' – that is, as 'valuable and attractive items', which were well known as more prone to 'consumer conversion' than, say, the side of a fuselage. Storemen who guard these convertible items often operate 'away from the light'* – that is, with little supervision. They can therefore juggle records over time to match them to physical stocks during checks (but in my experience these rarely match *between* checks). Such goods, if stored in warehouses and store-rooms, need to be smuggled out of their lawful situations. Thus valuable and attractive items which are small or can easily pass as the property of the pilferer, and items in or awaiting transit, are particularly at risk. Shops, warehouses and stores, as well as vehicles moving goods to or from these places, are all prone to pilferage which is often linked to 'core' and 'peripheral'

---

* A neat point suggested by Nigel South.

staff categories and to the triadic linkages between workers, customers and deliverers. Probably the main source of warehouse loss arises from collusive arrangements between warehousemen and drivers.

Anonymity and Scale

The most common facilitator is the question of scale, of the impersonality of large organisations. This point has been noted elsewhere. Cahn (1955), for instance, comments: 'As soon as the owner becomes too large or too impersonal to permit an imaginative interchange with him then his property rights are likely to be negated' (p. 199). Smigel and Ross (1970) go further in suggesting that since our ethics are developed from small-scale communities, we lack appropriate rules to govern the moral relationships of the individual to the corporation. Whatever the reason, many people appear to regard theft from a corporation as qualitatively different from theft from an individual (Henry, 1978).

The five main factors that structurally predispose situations and the people in them to what I call 'fiddle-proneness' and the 'facilitators' that apply across the board have been looked at as if the economy were static. But changes constantly occur which affect the way rewards are distributed. These can arise through the policy of governments or business or through changes in market or technical conditions beyond the control of anyone directly involved. From whichever source it comes, change means disturbance and where this affects reward it is also likely to affect differentials. This is particularly so where one wage level has traditionally been linked to another, but where the market for one type of labour has changed while the other has remained the same. In these circumstances managements are under pressure to collude in measures which increase fiddle-proneness. Though they may well prefer to respond to market forces, the cost in terms of disturbed relativities of workers' ratings may be too great, or the 'political' implications too extreme. One easy way of responding to changes in the market is to acknowledge them by permitting fiddles. Zeitlin makes the point that 'By permitting a controlled amount of theft, management can avoid reorganising jobs and raising wages' (1971, p. 24).

Changes in technology and in the nature of marketing, changes in the move of populations to towns, as well as changes in company and industrial organisation, have all contributed to increased fiddle-proneness. The growing complexity of the motor car, as was shown, provides only one example of technical change that increases the vulnerability of laymen to the depredations of specialists. But the motor car itself, by encouraging travel and changes in residence, has also created a whole new area of passing trade, of transient transactions ranging from those concerned with tourism to those affecting the housewife. This growth in movement has, in its turn, brought about and responded to changes in marketing that have further revolutionised most day-to-day transactions. To offer only one example, most food shopping has now moved from the small-scale neighbourhood shop to the larger, more impersonal supermarket. It is now one unit only in a chain of units organised and managed from afar; a place from where people buy spasmodically in bulk rather than repetitively in detail, and one, therefore, where the moderating and repetitive links of local involvement between the parties are likely to be absent.

But there are also countervailing trends that limit fiddles – particularly those arising from cheap and efficient control systems based on electronics and micro-computers. In attempting to identify and locate fiddle-proneness, therefore, we must not be deluded by ideas of its continuity in any particular location. Some developments, like the growth of supermarkets, certainly encourage it; others, like the increasing trend to electronically controlled hypermarkets – and indeed to electronic control of all stocks – certainly limit it. But none of these changes acts in perpetuity: Though the five main factors are a constant, their *incidence* in any specific location can be altered by the kind of changes I have discussed. There is nothing sacrosanct about the underlying structural differences of knowledge, power and ability that some groups hold over others. While changes affecting facilitations occur all the time, change is a constant and its pace is accelerating. This is one reason why fiddles are not, and never can be, readily controlled: control itself, once applied, becomes in its turn subject to change. And subject, too, to more refined ingenuity.

Part Two

The Wider Implications

7

Fiddling as Crime

For de little stealin' dey gits you in jail soon or late. For de big stealin' dey makes you emperor and puts you in de Hall o' Fame when you croaks.

(Eugene O'Neill, *The Emperor Jones*)

Big Stealing and Little Stealing

The naive might expect society to take a view of crime which increased in severity with the degree of offence. It might be thought that society would rank the big stealing above the little stealing. In practice it does not. As we have seen in earlier chapters, society has an ambiguous attitude towards the actions of its 'big men'. In a perverse way, the corrupt means such men employ to achieve success and power is seen as part of their achieving-style: to have succeeded, the individual must have 'fixed' things for himself. On the other hand, society's view of the actions of 'little men' is unambiguous. The supermarket cashier who rings short is seen as nothing more or less than dishonest.

It is tempting to explain this distinction purely in terms of class: to suggest that working-class crime, however small in scale, is treated as if it is more reprehensible than middle- or upper-class crime, however large in scale. The class argument is based upon the view that opinions are moulded and social agencies activated by the most powerful elements in society in their own interests. There is a lot in this argument and yet, as the preceding chapters have shown, individuals, as far as their fiddling goes, are not so much simply the victims of a class system as the victims of its mediation through occupational structures which determine the nature, type and scale of fiddles that are practised.

How people behave is a product of where they stand within the social, class and occupational structures. Where they stand, however, comprises not only an objective class position but also a relationship to a specific occupational setting. The Poulsons and the T. Dan Smiths are able to fiddle on a grand scale because their whole style of operating belongs with the individualistic hawks. The supermarket cashier has to confine her fiddles to ringing short on the till because her physically and socially restricted style of work belongs with the insulated and subordinate donkeys. The alternatives offered by the nature of her work are as limited as the nature and variety of her possible fiddles. Here constraints flow from features of her technical work setting, not from the direct unmediated pressure that comes from occupying a low class position (see Marx, 1972, pp. 369–80, where he discusses the distinction between the division of labour in society and that in manufacture). The cashier's situation qualitatively resembles that of a member of a royal family, who is equally restricted by the strong grid of protocol. Prince Bernhard's involvement in the Lockheed affair caused a scandal not solely because of the scale of his actions but because of where he was placed. Although he himself belonged in a strong-grid occupation, he appeared to have become involved in a weak-grid hawk fiddle.

The basis of the different views society takes of different offences can be seen in the different words it uses to describe them. Throughout this book I have tended to use the word 'fiddle' rather than pilferage or theft. The word is not used lightly, but it is a 'light' word; morally it is relatively neutral. It is what Ditton (1977b) calls a 'weasel word'. It allows us to look at part-time crime not so much with complaisance as with empathy. Using the word 'fiddle', we can more readily appreciate the world-view or cosmology of the fiddler. And through its use we can then, in effect, move into the fiddler's quadrant, and ignore, for the moment, the view of what goes on in it from the standpoint of *other* types of job. If, on the other hand, we use the word 'theft' we stand *outside* the fiddler's view of his own actions. Theft is a 'heavy' word which belongs to a strong-grid world-view. In strong-grid environments ambiguity is kept to a minimum, and definitions of action are made as precise as possible. Strong-grid agencies need a less ambiguous word than 'fiddling' to describe illicit transactions. Theft is 'heavy' because it is precise.

To enforce the law, the police need the precise definitions produced by the law. They are reluctant to use 'lighter' words like 'fixing' and 'dealing' to describe what they see as corruption and fraud. If they were to do so, they would move out of the certainties of strong grid into the ambiguities of weak grid. Individual policemen may indeed have to do this, in the short term, to get information. The plain-clothes detective who pays informers moves down-quadrant. But he is allowed to do so only in the interests of long-term strong-grid enforcement. And he then finds himself placed in the same kind of anomalous position that faced Prince Bernhard. This is the basis of the structural dilemma that confronts detectives and, to a lesser extent, policemen everywhere; that they are governed by the constraints of strong grid but in fact must operate in a weak-grid environment.

We must be careful, then, not to adopt a holistic approach to the idea of different world-views. Though our society is *on the whole* a weak-grid society – since the growth of technology and of knowledge goes hand-in-hand with competition and social mobility – it none the less needs precise definitions to operate some aspects of its economy and to enforce its laws. Society therefore employs strong-grid agencies when it finds them necessary (for example, to enforce the more precise rules of market exchange). However, we *can* say that the view society takes of financial transactions belongs essentially in the realm of strong grid. It is a single-strand view of how business is done. In this view, money is crucial, because it is a medium that allows precise dealing. In the money transactions that govern market exchanges, people get what they pay for. Transactions are fully documented, with invoices, receipts, bills of lading, all of which are designed to reduce ambiguity.

Yet if we look at what goes on *before* transactions are finalised we can see that there are other systems of dealing. For a sale to be made, a product may have to be sold by a salesman. The salesman, operating in an occupational structure where grid is weak, transacts in quite a different way from his firm's accounts department which operates within a strong-grid structure. Whereas the accounts department will tend to keep transactions as impersonal as possible, the salesman will attempt to make them as personal as he can. He might, for instance, modify the strict system of distributive justice implicit in the pricing of goods. He will do potential customers 'a favour', offer discounts and suggest overall that the customer can get *more* than he is paying for because of his personal relationship (Henry and Mars, 1978).

Now if we accept that there *are* different methods of transaction, even within the relatively 'straight' operation of market exchange, we can see that fiddling is not necessarily the 'wrong' way of doing something but rather that it is *another* way of doing something. And we can now appreciate that the use of 'heavy' words like 'theft' and 'crime' by people who are outside the operating quadrant excludes (because it has to if these terms are to have meaning) the possibility of there being such alternative methods of transaction. If effectively prejudges because it recategorises the acts that are being discussed. Therefore when I use the word 'fiddle' I do so not to condone theft, but to allow for the possibility of other systems of dealing which 'theft' does not adequately describe.

It is because people are in a sense 'trapped' in their own cosmologies that they do not have the ability to split up the image of what they see. Their view of fiddles is determined by where they stand, since a specific cosmology not only orders the world, it also precludes alternative orderings. The use of words to describe what is seen suggests that different viewpoints need different words to describe the same view. A businessman, as a hawk, might describe his expense allowance as a 'perk'. Viewed from outside, it will, however, look like a 'fiddle'. And viewed from a strong-grid position – by, for example, the Inland Revenue – it will look more like 'fraud'.

When a 'perk' is classed as fraud, perhaps because it oversteps acceptable limits and becomes the subject of prosecution, it is prosecuted *as* a fraud and the charge has to be answered in these terms. Generally there is no answer. The 'facts' are indisputable, as Henry (1978) has clearly shown, because they are interpreted within the unambiguous terminology of market exchange. Taxable income is undeclared, liable tax is unpaid, and a precise monetary value is placed on the 'fiddle'. The transaction has broken the rules of 'normal' dealing and it is for this that punishment is appropriate and recategorisation becomes a necessity.

Now and then a defendant refuses to answer the charge in these terms. In Chapter 5 I considered the case of overcharging at Blackpool's Palatine Hotel. In his evidence to the court the manager told of an 'understanding' between the directors, the manager and the staff that overcharging in the bars was acceptable in the interests of the hotel's profits. Here, we glimpsed *another* form of 'management', besides the more rigid bureaucratic management which market exchange transactions demand. Here we found a system which relied on personal obligation rather than impersonal dealing; where the directors could say, by implication, to the manager and his staff: 'You look after us and we'll let you look after yourselves.'

These glimpses are rare. The market exchange system, the normal and (to auditors, police and magistrates) the *only* recognised method of dealing, predominates to such an extent that the individual is compelled, consciously or unconsciously, to explain his motives and actions in terms of it. Fiddled goods are *cheaper*; fiddles allow people to 'make an extra bob or two'. As Henry (1978) has argued, the explanatory emphasis is always on money and it is expressed in monetary terms, since money is the common medium of 'legitimate' transactions. The offence is set out in terms that the agents of control will understand. And the motive that is assumed and often admitted also has to be offered in the same vocabulary that these agents can recognise – that is, in terms of economic gain.

An obvious analogy is with the inquisitional examination of witches in seventeenth-century England or the famous witchcraft trials at Salem in the USA. If the 'witch' attempted to defend herself in the terms of her *real* actions and *real* motives as she perceived them, the administration of justice was hampered and there was no possibility of a transaction between the accusers and the accused. But once a witch accepted the court's interpretations of her actions she became 'manageable' in a judicial/administrative sense. This is why it was so important to get witches to confess. Similarly, a heretic who admits his heresy (the court's term, not his) is forgivable, while one who does not just cannot be accommodated within the prevailing system of thought.

Witchcraft provides, perhaps, a better analogy than heresy. Heresy implies an alternative world-view which precludes the alternatives forgone. Witchcraft, however, belongs to a *diffuse* multi-stranded world-view: a linkage of the internal and the external rather than a replacement of one by the other. It could and it did coexist with prevailing views of causality. It was, in fact, just *one* way in which people accepted that things happen, and it supported the prevailing world-view. Fiddling, too, can be understood within a multi-stranded view of transaction. It is just *one* of several ways in which people deal with each other. It is heretical in the sense that it lies outside the orthodoxy of market exchange and distributive justice. But it does not *challenge* that orthodoxy and nor indeed need it do so. Ditton has suggested in his book *Part-Time Crime* that fiddling, far from comprising a counter-economy, is a bastard of the capitalist economy. At its own level, says Ditton, it reinterprets or misinterprets the rules of the orthodox system of market exchange. Like the Black Mass, it apes the forms of 'white' religion.

Yet because an alternative system of transaction does not counter orthodox systems, it need not follow that it mirrors them. When we look at fiddling we are looking at something that coexists (as long as it is unchallenged) with other transactional systems in the same way that pagan custom can coexist with Christianity: neither challenging nor supportive, but complementary. And yet the complementary nature of fiddling is not generally accepted. As we saw, outside the quadrant of its origin it is regarded as theft. A problem arises, therefore, in interpreting the rationale of fiddling at the level of the fiddler. In short, how does he cope with this definition of fiddling as theft and of himself as a thief?

Coping with Fiddling: the Split Self

In most societies ritual plays a much greater role in everyday affairs than it does in our own society, and transgressions against the prevailing norms are normally 'corrected' by rituals of purification (Rock, 1973). Such rituals acknowledge that a man plays many parts – that he simultaneously occupies a variety of roles – and that it is normal human experience for people occasionally to fail in one or other of their roles. What a ritual of purification does is split off the role-related offence from the total persona of the offender, thus providing a basis of expiation for the offence by allowing the individual to segment his personality. He can have another self, a 'sinful self', which is *bound* to offend and bound to be punished. And this leaves his coexistent everyday self free of guilt.

A secular and scientific base to morality such as we possess, however, and an emphasis on single-stranded relationships leads to what Douglas (1970) has described as 'ritual poverty'. We have a shortage of rituals from which to select one means of splitting one role off from another. As a result, in modern secular society the individual cannot segment his personality in this way. (In this sense Protestants are 'poorer' than Catholics.) The whole self offends: the whole self is contaminated.

The implications of this for the fiddler, the 'part-time' criminal, are clear. When he fiddles he divides his life, as Ditton (1977a) skilfully shows, into a working life, public and impersonal, and a fiddling life, private and personal. However, he lacks both the psychic equipment and the split-level moral framework needed to cope with this division. Strong-grid agencies of control like the law will take only *one* view of fiddling. The individual has to square his fiddling self with his working self.

This squaring of the working self with the fiddling self is often achieved, as we have seen, with group support. When Ditton's bread salesman was shown the ropes by an experienced salesman or supervisor, he was also shown certain truths about the job. He was shown how to balance his books and then shown, in the course of learning, that the books would never balance; that he would always be down at the end of the day. He was gradually led to realise that only through fiddling could he stay on top of the job. He then adopted the cosmology of the group of bread salesmen, in which fiddling is intrinsic not extrinsic to the job. In the same way the docker's world-view is also pressed home by the group — that because managements are perceived as inherently untrustworthy, the group itself is the only secure defender of members' interests. It is the group worker's acceptance and absorption of group assumptions that allows him to square his straight self with his sinful self. The two are insulated at one level but coalesce at another and thus ambiguity is resolved. Without group support, however, ambiguity remains unresolved. In jobs where the worker is isolated, there is an individual but not a group view. Hence the personal, 'sinning' self threatens to overwhelm the working self.

This has implications for the morality of fiddling. Where the group provides an interpretation of the job, it also imposes a morality in the form of both qualitative and quantitative limits. Dockers will decide and enforce what sorts and amounts of cargoes are out of bounds; cab drivers will relate amounts taken to common levels; fairground barkers work to a common 'weed'. Operating on his own, however, the individual has himself to impose limits on the scale and nature of his fiddling. The temptation *not* to do so is strong, particularly when the insulated nature of a job encourages repetitive fiddling. The sales assistant who fiddled enough through issuing false refund dockets to pay for an abortion was betrayed by the *quantity* of dockets she issued. The sinning self overwhelmed the working self because there was no group restraint and therefore no culture that could develop, be added to and be passed down. The hawk fiddler is vulnerable in the same way, but for a different reason. He too lacks a supportive culture, but it is because he operates freely and on his own initiative that there are no limits on his legitimate dealings. Why, therefore, should there be limits to his illicit dealings? And because he operates on the borders of change there are no precedents that exactly fit each new situation in which he may find himself.

Most fiddles, however, remain undetected because they are self-controlled – that is, they are kept within limits – or they are colluded in by managements. It could be argued, and policemen in particular periodically do argue, that 'little stealings' lead to 'big stealings', and that society is right to regard fiddling as no different from other criminal acts. Yet this argument assumes that part-time crime, like full-time crime, always threatens to disrupt or short-circuit the operation of 'straight' dealing – the money-based system of market exchange. Because it has the same ultimate aim as legitimate transactions – economic gain – full-time crime clearly does short-circuit the market exchange system. Fiddles, however, *need not* have the same aim as normal transactional systems. Obviously *some* gain is necessary, but money is only part, and rarely the most important part, of this gain.

Trust Relations in Obtaining and Distributing Groups

However anarchic the suggestion may seem, *controlled* fiddling, far from being anarchic, is one of the factors that contribute to equilibrium in normal economic activity. The single dimension of market exchange does not recognise the multi-dimensional nature of human dealings. Much of what has been discussed as fiddling does. Indeed, the characteristics of the fiddle strongly suggest that it has more in common with quite legal 'sub-transactions' than with criminal activity. Crime acknowledges the importance of a single, dominant market exchange system, and sets out to short-circuit it. Fiddling acknowledges no such dominance. It is itself proof that *other* exchange systems exist, systems which complement rather than challenge the dominant system.

In everday life we can see these alternative transactions smoothing out the sharp edges of normal market exchange. Cash with orders, cash on delivery, cash only – or hire purchase where the terms of payment are closely defined – these are the unequivocal demands of a sphere of material exchange where money and goods change hands at the same time and 'one-off' transactions are completed. Something on account, on the slate, tick, is the language of another sphere of exchange, one where a sense of personal obligation is created by the provision of credit, and where transactions are never completed because they become part of a flow of transactions.

The local pub, the neighbourhood bar, normally deals with its customers in both ways depending upon whether they are new customers or regulars. Dealings with new customers are a sequence of separate transactions which are completed when goods and money change hands. But when trust develops the publican may agree to put something on the slate or to cash a cheque.

Two things happen then. The time a transaction takes to be completed is lengthened and the balance of the transaction tips to emphasise the social rather than the economic. If a cheque is accepted, this can mean credit from two days to a week. If straight credit is given, the time needed for completion is as long as the publican wishes. The transaction may *never* be completed, since settling up one account provides fresh credit for another; the deal has changed from a sequence of separate transactions to a single open-ended transaction. In this case the publican is doing the customer a favour which he can repay only by providing more of his custom. But the same kind of dealing occurs when payment for goods is made in kind, as has always happened, for instance, in farming communities; and this is a practice which is growing elsewhere in the economy. The point here is that payments in kind rarely match exactly the value of the goods provided. The mismatch puts one of the transactors in the other's debt. No debt is ever *precisely* paid off, and a sense of obligation is sustained.

However, when a trust relationship does break up the debt *has* to be paid off — precisely and immediately. The open-ended transaction is closed, and the method of final settlement reverts to normal market exchange. The transaction is, in effect, depersonalised and rematerialised as it was among working-class families in the north of England where I grew up. The credit account at the local store would be broken through a dispute. Then the bill was paid and the family's custom removed to another shop. A similar situation is recorded in Ireland marking the traditional relationship between farmers and their suppliers in the town (Arensberg and Kimball, 1940).

The social relationships that derive from dealings in fiddled goods, what Henry (1978) calls 'the amateur trade' of fiddling, work, as he has shown, in a very similar way. In a hotel a head waiter may give a new waiter 'something to take home'. The favour has to be repaid, but only when the opportunity arises and only with whatever comes to hand. And 'whatever is to hand' may not be material at all. It is as likely, for instance, to be the offer of extra hours without pay in a crisis or dependency in a political power shift. There is no time-limit on repayment, and because no value is put on the 'knocked-off' goods there is no actual amount that has to be paid. The goods that were given have been dematerialised and the transaction has been personalised.

We have seen that goods in transit, as in docking, warehousing and airport cargo-handling, are fiddle-prone. One of the problems (and part of the excitement) of fiddling in these situations is that workers do not know precisely what is going to be available and when. Situations where there are large *quantities* of 'unmeasurable material' like bricks and coal are equally fiddle-prone, because the agents of control do not know precisely how much is there at any one time. Therefore amateur trading lacks the certainty of normal trading. One of Henry's informants nicely reveals this uncertainty (1978, p. 83):

'I'll have some bricks.' So he says 'How many do you want and what colour?' So I looked at a few, and I met him in the pub and said 'I think I need about 150 of such and such', and he said 'I can't promise anything, but I'll keep my eyes open'.

The opportunity to get hold of the bricks may never occur. Such uncertainty would be intolerable in normal dealing. Legitimate car sales, for example, depend on the meeting of delivery dates at every stage from production line to the point of sale. Yet, in spite of this uncertainty, the amateur dealer will take *precise* note of his customer's needs. By putting himself out in this way, he unbalances the normal dealer-customer relationship, he offers more than the normal dealer. By doing the customer a favour, he assures *himself* of a future supply of reciprocal favours. In other words, he opens up an 'account' with the customer, providing himself with social credit that is infinitely extendable.

It is infinitely extendable because the system of payment ensures that the account, in normal terms, will never be paid off. To quote another of Henry's informants (ibid., p. 85):

> I was in the pub and saying 'So many coal mines round here, where can I buy coal?', and someone says 'Oh, we'll send George round'. So George appeared with two or three hundredweight of coal, and there was I, money in hand, about to pay him, and he says 'Oh, you owe me a pint', something like this.

Drinking and its Role in Distribution

It is not accidental that pubs have long been traditional places in which to do amateur business. Custom is predominantly local and customers can therefore be positively vetted. Relationships are informal; no one pulls rank (hence the deep suspicion of policemen and vicars who tend, even off duty, to be bound by the strong grid of others' expectations). Therefore it is natural that drink should be used as a method of payment. If money is the medium of exchange in material dealings, drink is often the medium of exchange in personal dealings.

Drink is a medium ideally suited to encourage the growth of personal relationships. Dissipating capital in shared drinking enhances individual and group relationships – not only through the encouragement of a communal activity but also because it precludes the development of insidious and divisive differences that come from differences in capital accumulated (Douglas and Isherwood, 1978). Thus, by dematerialising money into the social and personal currency of expended drink, the system ensures that value is set not on goods but on relationships. Even the insulated and isolated donkey job need not preclude its holder from entering an integrated social life. His work can provide him too with the means to prestige and a valued place. The dealer does not think of himself as a thief trying to fence goods but as a benevolent provider trying to do the best for his friends. The reinterpretation of role is reinforced within a pub-based trading group: 'Oh, we'll send George round', they say, casting him, in this instance, as the problem-solver, the provider.

The trading group does this 'casting' by drawing on common assumptions about amateur trading which assert its boundary – which define those who are trusted insiders as against the threatening outside. As yet another of Henry's eloquent informants puts it (1978, p. 39):

> There's an unspoken understanding that everyone is willing to buy stuff cheap, and the bloke who won't buy it cheap becomes an outsider and dodgy for a start.

The importance of a defined boundary to a group is valid whether the group is an amateur trading group concerned to *distribute* goods obtained by its members from their work, or a wolfpack or vulture group, concerned to *obtain* material. Both depend equally on unspoken understandings. The longshoremen discussed in Chapter 4 had precisely this kind of boundary and they asserted it when they cast the Salvationist who refused to pilfer as an outsider. (Only when he withstood weeks of grilling by security men about the group's activities was he 'cleared' and admitted to the group.) The

bakery roundsman and the pie salesman similarly had group
support for 'unspoken understandings' – that the job they had to
do was impossible *without* fiddling, that since you were bound to
lose money on normal dealing you had to make up the loss
whenever you could. Here the understanding is in the form of a
rationalisation of what would otherwise look like criminal acts.
Rationalisation *backed by group assumptions and group support* allows
people to cast themselves in roles that make sense to them.

When the pie salesman understocks a supermarket, he is not, in
his eyes, performing a criminal act; rather, he is demonstrating
that he is on top of the job and that the job is not on top of him. The
same functions are served in distribution within amateur trading
groups. Roles like the 'provider', the 'problem-solver', the 'super
salesman', allow people to play a part that *they* rather than *outsiders*
cast them in. But it also allows them to reconcile the part they play
in two different spheres of trading: to square their 'sinning' self
with their working self. Cressey (1953) suggests that this is how
the 'trust violator' comes to terms with what he is doing. He
internalises group assumptions about the nature of the job ('In the
real estate business there is nothing wrong about using deposits
before the deal is closed') so that he can rationalise his own
behaviour. He does this by casting himself, not as a trust violator,
but as a 'borrower' or a 'businessman'. Group assumptions tell him
which actions and which sorts of people are acceptable. Borrowing
money is acceptable, so the 'borrower' becomes an acceptable role.
What is particularly significant is that he can sustain this role only
as long as his 'trust violation' stays within bounds. Once it
over-reaches itself, and becomes obvious and detectable, the role of
'borrower' can no longer be sustained.

The Vocabulary of Fiddle Groups and the Vocabulary of the Law

It is because individuals cannot easily sustain an identity that is not
backed by a group that group controls of fiddling are so important,

whether these are in obtaining groups or in distribution groups. Initially, like the controls in any other group, they protect it from outsiders and prevent disintegration. But more fundamentally they sustain the group's own idea of itself as beneficient and achieving. Such groups can be compared with masonic lodges. The careful screening of entrants, the induction of those who satisfy certain tests, the use of recognition signals – these control devices create the right conditions for an alternative but not disruptive way of doing things. In distribution groups members are helped without the expectations of any reward, save that they may repay the favour *in kind* at a later, unspecified date. No one questions too closely *how* things are done. Personal relationships are crucial, and this is *why* things are done. To sustain this 'otherness' needs a special language: a vocabulary which reflects the nature of the group's relationships with its own members *and* with outsiders. Words which seem overtly innocent to outsiders must covertly alert insiders, and raise their awareness of their obligations to each other.

As we have seen, market exchange and the agents who control it use unambiguous words to describe precise activities. Goods are 'stolen' or 'pilfered' or 'thieved' only in the terminology of official or external social control. But this vocabulary is not appropriate or acceptable to those engaged in fiddling. It is not appropriate because it is too heavy and it is not acceptable because it does not tell the truth as the actors see it about the exchange relationships on which fiddling is based. As Henry has argued (1978, Ch. 6), when fiddlers are prosecuted, fiddles appear as 'theft' on the court charge sheet. The charge sheet is, as he shows, in effect a misinterpretation of actions, because it assumes the sphere of exchange in which they occurred is the normal sphere of exchange. It uses the *only* vocabulary available to describe aberrations of the *only* system of exchange that society officially recognises. A general language has to be used to describe misappropriations of a general-purpose currency – money.

The vocabulary is not acceptable to individuals for the same reason. It does not tell the truth about the role an individual adopts

177

when he fiddles. 'I only borrowed the money – I was going to put it back' is often a quite *genuine* response of the accused. The provision of goods on an open-ended basis – with an obligation to pay it back at *some* time but by no pre-arranged time – lies at the core of amateur trading. Yet, except in the case of 'taking away' (rather than stealing) cars, the legal code does not recognise this.

Amateur traders, therefore, have to use a 'desensitised' vocabulary, which is morally neutral yet ambiguous enough to act as a masonic code. The non-mason will not recognise a masonic handshake because it does not obtrude. In the same way what Ditton calls 'alerting phrases' alert the fiddler but not the non-fiddler. The bread roundsman will ask for or offer 'extra bread'. The lorry driver, part to a petrol pump fiddle, will ask if there is 'any over the top'. The fairground worker looking for a job will ask 'Is the weed decent?' These innocent-sounding questions plug the fiddler straight into a fiddling circuit, but because they *are* innocent-sounding they cannot be used against him by non-fiddlers. They are all the call signs of amateur trading, yet are unexceptional to people engaged in normal trading.

Alerting phrases are useful at the induction stage of a newcomer's entry to a fiddling group. They test, first, the acuteness of the newcomer (stupid people, people bad at their legitimate jobs, are unlikely to be any better at coping with fiddling) and, secondly, his potential dishonesty, that is, his willingness to adopt the norms of amateur trading. As another of Henry's informants says (1978, p. 38):

> In our works there's a standard line that they try people out with. They say 'Would *you* like to sell me this? Not the firm, but *you*?' If the bloke doesn't twig, he's a berk. If he doesn't see it, it's forgotten and they don't push it any further. It's there in every situation. You can probe and if the bloke's with you you're away.

Henry shows that the tone of altering phrases is always determinedly light. As we saw, the language of fiddling avoids words and meanings which are 'heavy', which define actions too precisely. The fiddler must put some distance between what a magistrates' court might decide has happened and what he himself believes has happened. If goods are offered with the information that they are stolen, people tend to shrink from the *implicit* value-judgement of the word 'stolen'. It interferes with a personal interpretation of transactions. If, however, people are told that goods 'fell off the back of a lorry', they are free to extend the morally neutral explanation of their own actions: 'I'd be a fool not to take my share of what's going.'

This is similar to the distancing that occurs in 'management by exception'. A manager will expect to have to take action or make decisions when things go wrong. Otherwise he does not expect his staff to bother him. In a hotel the manager may wink at overcharging by his staff, but in the interests of good stock control and high profits; he accepts the *end* of the fiddle without wanting to know about the *means*. Only when a customer complains or a co-worker 'splits' does the system 'arc'. The manager can no longer refuse to interpret his staff's action in the way the outside world does. A fiddle then has to be recognised as a fraud.

We have already seen what happens next. The system of fiddling which investigation reveals is 'depersonalised' by a precise but in fact untruthful description of it. 'Handling stolen goods' says nothing about the doing of favours. 'Receiving stolen goods' does not hint at the relationships this receiving establishes. We would not expect the legal machine to be able to explain what was actually happening, since the language of market exchange is the only one it has. The language of amateur trading is a non-language, it is a *refusal* to define or describe what is happening. As Henry argues, to compound the lack of comprehension, fiddlers *themselves* will explain their actions in terms or motives which can be understood by outsiders. This happens because the normal transactional mode of market exchange predominates to such an extent that the fiddler recognises that any explanation in other than the terms (profit/bargain) of this mode will not make sense to others *or* to himself.

Control

It is no wonder that managements act clumsily in their handling of employee theft. The normal workings of market exchange cannot explain the relationships of alternative exchange systems. *Crime* is seen as individual, just as normal transactions are individual. Fiddling can thus be blamed on *individuals* rather than on groups, so supporting a 'rotten apple' theory of management. Managements therefore introduce outsiders to investigate employee theft and dig out the rotten apples.

Sometimes they recruit 'undercover' workers employed by security firms whose job is to infiltrate workforces. But because group relationships within fiddle systems are not recognised, or their extent is unappreciated, these planted workers are usually quickly recognised. The results, however, can be catastrophic for managements. Workers will leave, possibly in groups, or they may strike in groups. Either way they offer a clear warning that if the individual fiddler is threatened, the group as a whole reacts.

Social control of fiddling is obviously necessary. The question is, what sort of control should this be? Control exercised by outside agencies, as we have seen, cannot be expected to recognise either the sound structure or the transactional style of fiddle groups. This again is a point already well argued by Henry (1978, ch. 8), who further and rightly argues that this is a management rather than a policing problem. He suggests that in the allocation of power and authority at work managements might devolve some degree of control to workers *themselves* in the form of community-work-based 'courts'. Such a suggestion would build upon controls that already exist. The use of a mileage 'formula' by taxi drivers, as we saw in Chapter 5, is such a system of control exercised from *below* rather than above. And it works. Fiddling levels are kept up, in the interests of other taxi drivers, but they are also kept down to an acceptable level which is presumably in the interests of management. The same kinds of control have been found in the docks, where longshore wolfpacks 'work the value of the boat' but no more than this. Their fiddle is worked in percentage terms; it is limited to a certain quantity of each cargo.

Henry argues that community courts not only work well as a source of control in Soviet societies but are also well established (though not widely known) in the UK. He shows that firms such as Cadbury-Schweppes have operated these 'tribunals' for many years and that both management and staff appear well satisfied with them. It may be, however, that these courts are well suited only to certain industries – probably those which contain a high number of donkey jobs, since people in such jobs have little countervailing power and are the most vulnerable to managerial discipline. At the same time managements are still concerned to control pilferage and courts do this for them better and more cheaply than any alternative method.

It is less than likely, however, that courts would operate well among hawks, vultures, or wolfpacks. Hawks, as was shown in Chapter 2, would be likely to move to less constraining environments, while vultures and wolfpacks would resent what they would certainly see as formalised and externally based limitations on their group autonomy. This reaction would be strongest among wolfpacks which, as we saw in Chapter 4, operate behind well-defined boundaries and use fiddle allocations as a buttress to their internal authority and structures.

There are, however, options which can build upon Henry's ideas of 'self-controls' but which do not extend to the degree of formalisation envisaged by work-based courts or tribunals. These involve the participative restructuring and redesign of donkey jobs, the institutionalising of entrepreneuriality among hawks and the radical alteration of workers' relationships to their employing organisations that would come from franchising and subcontracting and which would affect vultures and wolfpacks. These alternatives are discussed in the next chapter.

8

Some Implications for Industrial Relations

Resistance to Change: Attempts at Staying Loose in a Tightening World

If students of industrial relations, let alone managers, want to find out what people are capable of rather than what they are actually required to do in their jobs, they must learn to listen to 'the music behind the words' (Bridger and Wilson, 1947). This is equally true in interpreting action, only here the music is louder.

If we exclude sabotage by workers (Taylor and Walton, 1971; Dubois, 1979) and various forms of 'withdrawal from work' (Hill and Trist, 1962) that are open to discontented workers, we are left with two basic actions that workers can take when management's plans for them are unacceptable. They can collectively and temporarily withdraw their labour, or they can individually and sometimes permanently take their labour elsewhere. Strikes provide the most dramatic index of industrial discontent. Yet most strikes occur in the diminishing industrial sector which in the UK employs just over a half of all workers and in the USA fewer than this. Even in this sector strikes occur infrequently: only one UK factory in fifty suffered a strike in 1977. A much more common response is for individuals to change their jobs. And this occurs chiefly in the service sector. The typical gesture of dissatisfaction here is a turnover of labour.

What do these gestures actually tell us about satisfaction and dissatisfaction in the workplace? If we listen to 'the music behind the words' it tells us that individuals need to stay loose in their working lives. When outside pressures threaten to tighten up working conditions generally by weakening covert institutions and specifically by limiting people's ability to fiddle, then people invariably take action. But such action cannot be openly explained by those involved, in the real terms of their complaint. As we have seen in Chapter 7, people relate their motives to market exchange and they use the dominant language of market exchange to explain their behaviour in industrial affairs. People therefore say they strike for more pay, or for parity with other groups, or for any one of a number of other declared interests – a point also noted by Gouldner in his classic study of a strike at a gypsum plant (1954). This too was apparently a strike for more pay, but was in reality a response to the disturbance of what he called an 'indulgency pattern' – a series of unofficial arrangements by which men were allowed all sorts of resources and indulgencies, all of which were removed by a new efficiency-conscious manager.

Changes in the Docks
We can distinguish two broad changes which intentionally or unintentionally tighten the working environment: technological change (which brings organisational change) and organisational change alone. Technological change is always, of itself, likely to provoke conflict, because it involves a trade-off between manpower and efficiency. The worldwide move to containerisation of cargoes throughout the 1960s and 1970s meant faster handling by fewer dockworkers. Faster handling was not their union's main concern, but manpower was and dock unions throughout the world were therefore set to negotiate about this threat to the size of their memberships. Their workforces, however, had their own worries to do with containerisation and these were concerned not only with redundancies but with reductions in permitted pilferage that containerisation was in part concerned to prevent. There is, however, no overt way of expressing a concern over the loss of pilferage rights. Instead the unions' legitimate worry about

reduced manpower was invariably used to channel their members' less legitimate concerns. No one could object to dockworkers' proper concern with saving their jobs. Equally no one could pretend that such concern did not cloak an improper fear that containerisation would greatly reduce the opportunities for 'working the value of boats': that is, pilfering a proportion of their cargo.

Yet dockers, whether their concern was improper or not, were right to be worried. The covert institutions governing all their conditions of work, including tolerated rights to pilferage, enabled them also to hold their employers at arm's length; to retain control over their work conditions within the basic unit of dockwork – the gang; and to resist the constant pressure to tidy their jobs. They used their system of informal organisation which had evolved over many years to balance what they saw as an exploitative contract, and in doing so they reduced the likelihood of more open industrial action (Mars, 1972). But if employers tighten up the job and reduce the opportunities for pilferage then, other things remaining equal, they increase the incidence of withdrawals from work. In occupations where a consciousness of group is as strong as in dockwork this is likely to be manifest in strikes.

In this case the overt grievance was visible to everyone as a concern over loss of jobs, so that opposition to containerisation seemed understandable if not justified. No matter that the introduction of containerisation threatened covert institutions: it threatened *overt* institutions as well. But what happens when change is introduced which, appears on the surface to *benefit* the workers involved? The answer is something like the UK dustmen's strikes of 1973.

The Dustmen's Strikes

The dustmen had no previous record of industrial militancy, yet suddenly and, to most observers, inexplicably, they lodged a pay claim which was so unreasonably large that it stood no chance of success. Since the size of the claim infringed the government's current pay policy, it was rejected. Consequently, the dustmen went on strike.

Just as a doctor would ask a patient who comes to him with a complaint of illness which is difficult to diagnose, 'Is anything *else* worrying you?' so it would have been useful to have put the question to the dustmen. For something else *was* worrying them. Around the same time that the dustmen put in their claim, local municipalities were introducing a 'maceration' system of refuse collection and disposal. In this system householders put their refuse into plastic bags, seal them and put them in the bin. The sealed bags of refuse are then ground down by 'chomping trucks'.

The system was environmentally an improvement on the usual method of collecting and dumping untreated garbage on landfill sites, because the pulverised refuse takes up less space. But it was considerably more expensive than the usual method and provided little overall financial saving to the municipalities. The dustmen, on the other hand, *did* benefit. It was argued that they would no longer have to deal directly with dirt, since it would now be sealed away, and there was much talk in the press about the new dignity of the white-coated dustmen that the system would bring. It also brought a small increase in pay, negotiated to ease the introduction of the new technology.

The new system had been negotiated by local government officials and officials of the General and Municipal Workers' Union. Perhaps none of them had worked on a dustcart or they may have forgotten what the dustmen's job was like. Most likely, however, the problem that arose was due to an inability to communicate.

Because the parameters of discussion were locked into the narrow mould of market exchange, neither the union nor the management appeared to realise, or if they did they ignored the fact, that the clean-handling maceration system would also effectively macerate the unofficial system of 'totting'; a dustmen's fiddle which, as was shown in Chaper 4, involves the raking and sorting-through of refuse and the taking-out and selling of anything salvageable. Since at no point in the new system did the dustmen's hands come in contact with refuse, the opportunities for totting in effect disappeared.

The dustmen took strike action because they were being squeezed on two sides. There was, first, pressure from the government. An interventionist policy of arbitrary pay restraint had allowed the government, with the unions, to 'rationalise' a substantial part of the wage bargaining process. As a result many groups of workers found they had surrendered their right to take part in free collective bargaining. When one avenue is closed, however, people look for another: when formal pay is limited, informal pay assumes a greater importance. However, the dustmen found that *this* avenue, too, was closed to them. By accident, a technology which had been introduced primarily on their behalf trampled over an informal system which could increase their wages by a non-taxable third.

In losing the totting system dustmen, like the dockworkers, stood to lose something other than money: they were to lose substantial social benefits as well. The new technology of the chomping trucks threatened not just unofficial rewards but the system of ranking through which they were allocated. Dustmen, as we saw, distributed totting proceeds among themselves on the basis of a pecking order, a hierarchy of desert: first come, in terms of seniority, is first served.

This system of hierarchical reward gives the man at the top, the 'ganger', an autonomy and a freedom to transact that do not appear in any formal description of his job. But not only does he get prime pickings from totting, he alone negotiates, on behalf of his gang, a second set of benefits: informal deals with 'clients' to take away, for a price, items which dustmen are not formally allowed to collect. He then, as we saw, shares out these takings (sometimes called 'sparrows') among his gang, sometimes equally, sometimes on the basis of their ranking, and in doing so he reaffirms his authority and the system of ranking that totting represents and buttresses. This system of self-selected and self-maintaining ranking appears to be a valued feature of stigmatised groups, minute divisions of prestige within their groupings compensating for the undifferenti-ated view of them by members of the wider society.

Under the old system the dustmen, and specifically the ganger, were thus at the centre of a *radial* pattern of relationships. They were free through the ganger to transact with householders and shopkeepers, jockeying for business and obtaining a share of the proceeds. But a new technology that reduced the opportunities for totting also dissolved the established ranking pattern on which this second system of radial relationships was based — thus further reducing the dustmen's control of their environment.

The ganger and his gang, through the totting system, achieved a more independent status than the job was designed to give them, and they obtained a system of internal ranking which allowed them to negate the overall assessment of them by the wider society. The clean-handling system offered in exchange status of a different and, to them, an inferior kind. Since they no longer had to handle other people's refuse directly, it was argued by outsiders that dustmen would no longer be inferior to other people. The job would move from blue collar towards white collar. Yet the shift, in exchanging the status conferred by independence of action and transaction for the status of 'clean' work without independence, appeared a bad deal: in their own eyes they stood to lose more than they gained.

New Technology in Hotels

Because 'well-meant' change may inadvertently disturb relation-ships it can bring unforeseen effects that managements would often prefer to avoid. A good example here is provided by recent changes in technology that have affected food preparation in hotels, and which have led to an increase in the unionisation of chefs. The chef's skills and responsibilities have traditionally given him autonomy and the freedom to transact. In buying food for the hotel he deals with individual suppliers. Since much of what he buys is 'loose' (fresh meat and vegetables) and therefore its quantity is ambiguous he has opportunities for keeping a proportion for his own use and of making deals with suppliers which ensure him a kickback in return for placing orders. Only the fiddler himself knows how much the suppliers have supplied him with, which may not be the amount stated on receipts. Only he knows, because of his skills and his judgement, how much food actually needs to be used in meal preparation.

A technological shift has dramatically reduced his freedom to 'monarchise'. The introduction of frozen foods implicitly acts as a stock control device and thus limits food-buying fiddles. In addition microwave ovens, pre-packaged foods, and catering systems all reduce the need for a chef's skills, and therefore challenge his judgement. He is effectively 'de-skilled', and moved upgrid. But at the same time he shares this fate with others and he therefore becomes more susceptible to group. Progressively stripped of his independence, he now looks increasingly to unions to negotiate his rewards (Chivers, 1973).

The Spy in the Cab: the Tachograph
Conspiracy theorists might see *all* technological innovation as an oblique but intended challenge to the individual's freedom. Certainly the EEC's requirements for tachographs, the 'spy in the cab', to be fitted to lorries weighing over $3\frac{1}{2}$ tons, or carrying dangerous loads, is *intended* to limit the lorry driver's freedom. The tachograph is a combined speedometer and mileage counter which records for each day the distance a lorry travels, its time on the road and the speeds it reaches throughout its journey. It directly challenges the individual driver's control over his time and freedom. Drivers' 'total rewards' include income gained through travelling at faster than lorry speed-limits, for longer than permitted periods, travelling through the night and claiming subsistence and lodging allowances, and doing other work or extra driving in the time saved. In this case, the drivers' union, the Transport and General Workers' Union, saw the threat as clearly as did its membership; and its strong opposition and political muscle for several years delayed the introduction of the tachograph to Britain, despite EEC regulations, European Court decisions and the pleas of road safety bodies.

This case is exceptional. The use of a tachograph *recognises* that drivers work beyond the formal requirements of the job. The covert institution has evolved to become overt and visible: it now belongs with 'custom and practice' procedures rather than with institutionalised fiddles. The lesson of the dustmen's strike, however, is that it is not technological change *per se* which is resisted but the disturbance of *unrecognised* patterns of working relationships. Being unrecognised, they cannot be negotiated about – or even discussed. It follows that *any* change which disturbs these informal relationships will encourage reaction, but that this will be directed somewhere other than at the source of the disturbance.

The Firemen's Strike
The UK firemen's strike in 1977 puzzled most observers. First, the firemen were behaving out of character; they had no record of militancy, and had never before held a national strike. Secondly, their action appeared to have a suicidal quality. There was no strike fund and apparently, therefore, nothing to sustain the firemen during their strike. And finally, since the strike was the first important confrontation with the government's new pay policy round, it was certain to be resisted. The truth was that though the strike was aimed at the government's pay policy, it was not *about* that policy; though about more pay it was not, paradoxically, about the pay of firemen at all. In effect, strike action in support of this *formal* pay claim was again an indication that an *informal* pattern of work had been disturbed. It was a sign, to anyone who could understand it, that the firemen's real earnings, their *total* rewards, were being squeezed.

How, in organisational terms, could this have been so? Firemen work in a strong-grid occupation, ranks and uniforms are the norm, discipline is almost military, and the brigades have traditionally recruited solidly from ex-servicemen. Hours, duties and earnings are all tightly prescribed and there appears to be little elbow-room. In fact, there is considerable room for manoeuvre. Most firemen work a weekly shift system of forty-eight hours spread over six days. They are usually divided into seven groups, two groups being on duty at any one time. The two groups will not necessarily be on duty together all the time. The day shift typically runs from 9 a.m. to 6 p.m. and the night shift from 6 p.m. to 9 a.m. It can be seen that this results in fairly lengthy 'rota leave periods'.

The trump card in the fireman's hand, however, is the night shift. In a city like Manchester, for instance, only 8 per cent of a shift's fire calls are made between midnight and 7 a.m. Firemen are allowed to sleep unless they are called. So that after an *average* shift, not an abnormally quiet one, they are physically able to take on more work. And they do take on more work, not only work that exploits their skills like window-cleaning and driving but work within the 'moonlighting' trades such as building and decorating. A government social survey in 1969 (Thomas, 1969) found that 'moonlighting' in the fire brigades was well above the national average (and this was probably an underestimate). Official attitudes to 'moonlighting' by firemen were, and still are, ambivalent. Regulations forbid it, yet it is useful to employers since it provides a fire service on the cheap: moonlighting, in fact, helps hold wages down (Quinn, 1977); it has become a perk so much recognised that potential recruits were and are often told about it to encourage them to join. Unofficial rewards, which were largely untaxed, had become part of the total package of a fireman's working life.

By the late 1970s, however, the *whole* package began to look, to the firemen, much less enticing. The government's pay policy imposed a 10 per cent ceiling on formal pay increases, and the economic recession began to cut back opportunities for earning informal pay: people were cleaning their windows themselves, leaving decorating, and generally cutting out the services of the sparetime driver and the entrepreneurial handyman. And this was happening at a time of unprecedentedly high domestic inflation. The government's policy, although on the surface more provocative, hurt less than this 'making do' by the firemen's unofficial customers. Wages had always been low – and the pay ceiling was not in itself going to change anything very much. But an overall downturn in the economy at large does not have an equal effect in all sectors and some employers of moonlight labour are liable to cut back disproportionately.

Now that moonlighting was threatened, firemen began to look hard in the direction of their formal pay. And it was at this moment that the government decided to limit formal pay negotiations. The conditions were ripe for a strike which was as uncharacteristic as it was understandable. Though segmented by the variety of their informal moonlighting, the firemen were united by their formal jobs and their sense of common grievance. Indeed, this was the *only* aspect of their total rewards over which they could exert any control.

Their tendency for collective action had always existed even though it had lain latent for many years. The firemen's shift system, besides providing elbow-room to moonlight, contributed to the strength of group; it created some elements of an 'occupational community', that is, a community which spills over into off-duty life. In an occupational community workers socialise more with their co-workers than with other workers. They talk shop off-duty. Their *world* is their job and their grievances are not dissipated at the end of the shift as they are, for instance, with office workers or sales clerks who disperse after work (Kerr and Siegel, 1954). Firemen whose moonlighting normally separates them physically and socially from their fellows were thrown together when these opportunities were reduced. When such workers are firmly moved into the wolfpack quadrant and take action they tend, therefore, to take it collectively and with strong resolution.

Individual Contracts, Total Rewards and Core and Peripheral Workers

Collective action is taken chiefly in the industrial sector, and then for less often than is popularly imagined (in terms of days lost,

Western industrial countries suffer far more from industrial injuries than from strikes). Far more common, indeed typical, is the action an individual can take by walking out of his job, which is more usual in the service sector. If many individuals 'walk out' in this way we talk of a high rate of labour turnover. But to say that a high rate of labour turnover is endemic to certain jobs is to grasp only a part of what is happening.

The 'right job' for a person implies more than just the individual's possession of straightforward characteristics. In fiddle-prone occupations it implies a meshing of fiddle-prone occupation and fiddle-prone worker: someone who is able to take advantage of the opportunities given to him. An expenses system, as we have seen, provides a litmus paper test of this. It *can* be used quite straightforwardly. An employee may indeed charge no more than the expenses he has actually incurred. Yet the built-in fiddle potential (uncheckable entertainment expenses, travelling second class and claiming for first class, private car mileage charged as business mileage) invites exploitation: the journalist's rule-of-thumb that 'a good story deserves good expenses' spells this out.

The right person for the job, in turn, implies an acceptance of rules — or, in some cases, no rules. Some occupations, as we saw, will in a sense force fiddling on to workers. Fiddling may be the only way an employee can make his books balance. But if, as happens all the time, the person stays the same but the job changes in some way — if, for instance, expenses claims begin to be questioned or rejected — then the 'right man' will move on to where rules are still low, where the potential for fiddling is still real. Conversely if a new entrant to an occupation cannot accept its total rewards system, he may soon move on to where rules are stronger and rewards fully provided by a basic wage. The constant factor behind both kinds of rejection is the total rewards system. The individual either accepts it — and always looks for it in any job within the occupation — or he rejects it.

Some occupations are marked by a particularly *consistent pattern* of rejection. Milk roundsmen, bakers' roundsmen and delivery drivers, as we have seen, are expected to make up shortfalls by fiddling. And it is among these occupations that there is a particularly high labour turnover during the first six months. After six months the situation stabilises and workers tend to stay on, often for several years. This suggests that the first six months is a necessary period for adjustment to the mechanics of fiddling in these occupations and, more important, of the *need* to fiddle and of the self-acceptance of the role of fiddler. Those workers who cannot adjust, leave; those who can adjust find that the working environment satisfies them and they stay on. To a degree, this process of moral adaptations through a moral career works in all occupations, but it is more noticeable in fiddle-prone occupations because here the range of adaptations is greatest. This is why experienced store detectives insist that the stereotype of the deviant sales clerk as 'the new girl who is improperly socialised' just does not square with the facts as presented by store managers. They find instead that their most typical deviants are in fact trusted and experienced middle-aged women employees. But they are also difficult to catch!

On the other hand, an individual's acceptance of a total rewards system means that he takes it with him when he goes. The situation changes, but he does not. If an individual contract is broken, a total reward system fails, and the worker feels free to move on to where a new relationship can be established in terms of his understanding of the old.

This is why, in order to break the expectations of a total rewards system, one needs a radical solution. Such a solution was achieved by one enterprising restaurant owner who, through careful planning, bypassed the expectations of a total rewards system. He realised that fiddling was part of the catering industry's culture: it was passed on through 'generations' of catering workers and travelled with them as they moved from job to job. He broke with fiddling in his establishment by developing a range of strategies one of which was to recruit only from people *without* experience in the industry. And he made up his staff levels of reward by increasing formal pay and through linking this to turnover: it proved highly profitable (Mars *et al.*, 1979, case 4). An alternative and increasingly common response – one favoured by many hotel chains – is to bureaucratise their staffs' conditions of service and to stamp out informal contracts. It appears to produce many unanticipated effects (see Mars and Nicod, 1981).

The hotel and catering industry in all Western countries has high labour turnover. The accepted explanation is that since the industry has an erratic demand for its product, its workforce will be temporarily expanded – as for the summer holiday period and for one-off occasions like banquets. It therefore, so the argument goes, attracts itinerant, rootless workers. Yet, as we have seen, hotel workers tend either to stay on the periphery of a hotel's organisation or to gravitate to the centre. 'Core' workers are both self-selected and management-selected. Beyond their basic wages they have to exploit the total rewards system. The enterprising worker, then, will build up his total rewards by tips, perks and fiddles. In turn, his initiative will be recognised, and management will put the pickings his way.

Head waiters, head porters and chefs are typical 'core' workers, each of them negotiating his own individual contract and making himself less and less dispensable as he colludes more and more thoroughly with management. The management thus knows it has a cadre which in pursuit of its own interests can be relied on to serve the hotel's interests and cope with its recurrent crises.

This kind of organisation, however, is not static, but is in constant flux. Peripheral workers will continually be edging their way towards the centre. They do this by transacting with 'core' workers. They become followers, growing in their leader's trust and gaining an increasingly large share of the resources at the leader's disposal. A head waiter, for example, has the unstated but crucial job of deciding what each of his waiters is worth and negotiating their individual contracts accordingly. How much he gives them from the 'pool' of tips, which 'stations' he gives them (and therefore which guests), will depend upon this assessment. As he moves his waiters into 'core' jobs, so their potential for fiddles increases. A waiter given responsibility for the dispense bar is given access to the whole range of bar fiddles – for which, of course, his contractor will require some payment in kind.

The 'covert institution' here is a network of social and working relationships which operates in the interests of the organisation because, paradoxically, it operates independently of it. Detailed control by management stops at the level of the head waiter, the head porter and the chef. At this point power is delegated and its exercise is a matter of negotiation with other workers, core or peripheral.

When this network is disturbed there is a domino effect, as when a head waiter leaves. The waiters who have stood to gain most from him, who have moved into the core and negotiated good individual contracts, find themselves back where they started, at the periphery. All their individual contracts with the head waiter and their relative standing with other waiters fall to nought. For a period they have no pedigree, no record of worth, and it is in that period that they are liable to leave. Waiters may leave in groups soon after a head waiter has left, possibly to follow him to his new job where they can pick up their individual contracts with him where they left off. This is, of course, a phenomenon not restricted to the catering industry. It is particularly a feature of personal service occupations where there is an erratic demand and it is therefore found, with variations, in other luxury occupations such as hairdressing or interior decorating – but by no means exclusively so. It is also found in the building trade, where erratic demand is a constant and where informal earnings form a high proportion of total rewards.

The vacuum left by the departure of a 'core' worker is never easy to fill. A new head waiter, a senior hair-stylist or a building foreman who has a clean slate in terms of contracts with his assistants may find his *own* position suffers. He does not get all that is due to him, in status, or power, or pickings. *He*, too, may leave. Labour turnover in these occupations can therefore quickly snowball; not because formal working conditions have deteriorated, or because the people employed are somehow inherently shiftless, or for *any* perceptible reason, but because here 'covert institutions' are easily disturbed and these institutions involve a network of relationships so sensitive that one falling can knock off ten others. To be sure the loss of resources is important and cannot be discounted. But these people are reacting individually for the same reasons that the firemen, dockworkers, dustmen and truck drivers acted collectively: much of their resistance comes about because they want to stay loose in a tightening world.

Uncovering Covert Institutions: the Outsider's Dilemma

To an outsider, no occupation is quite what it seems. Nor do employees, when they talk to outsiders, always say what they mean, let alone behave as they are expected to. These differences have implications for the conduct of industrial relations; people expect rational responses to what seem to them to be rational measures. Yet often the response to change, even well-meant change, appears from the outside to be 'irrational'. And it is change in particular that seems to be resisted, sometimes to the point of collective strikes or individual walk-outs, and often when what appear to be generous compensation terms have been built into an agreement.

Whenever covert institutions are threatened by change, the individual is vulnerable, first in the way his job is organised, and secondly to changes in the way he negotiates for and obtains the reward he believes is due to him. But he cannot actually say as much; there is no official language in which to protest about such threats. The most common language he can employ is the language of action: he can withdraw his labour. Such withdrawals can be total or partial and they may be organised and collective or spasmodic and individualistic. They can range from the individual act of sabotage, through absences due to sickness or breakdown, to changes of job, go-slows, working to rule, or out-and-out strikes.

Commentators on industrial relations who fail to recognise

the significance of covert institutions find themselves in the position of the press, which signals its bewilderment by its use of language: unofficial strikes are invariably labelled 'lightning' or 'wildcat', heightening the sense of mindless, unconsidered opposition to sensible proposals. And even the established body of industrial relations study – what in the UK is still sometimes called the 'Oxford school' – has all but ignored covert institutions, concentrating most of its attention instead on what is visible: on the formal workings of unions, management associations, wages councils and arbitration schemes.

Clegg, perhaps the school's most eloquent voice, rightly suggests that the academic approach to industrial relations must be through a study of job regulations, through the study of 'procedural' and 'substantive' rules by which conditions of work are settled (1972). But with a few exceptions (e.g. Batstone *et al.*, 1977), apart from noting rules of 'custom and practice' this school has barely considered the informal rules, practices and particularly fiddles which affect the real conditions of work in a more basic way. Phelps-Brown, in a recent and influential work, tackles payment systems without any mention of their informal aspects (1977).

These limitations are serious enough, but most industrial relations study has also focused on *manufacturing* industry at the expense of other sectors of the economy. Nearly every paperback in this field published in the last twenty years has, for instance, featured a cover design suggestive of manufacturing – either men in overalls, or abstract designs involving machinery and gears. Yet manufacturing is declining in importance.

The real way many rewards are allocated in much of the economy – particularly in the service sector and especially in personal service occupations – is *not* through the formalised collective institutions typical of manufacturing. It is largely done, as we saw among the vultures in Chapter 5, through covert institutions. The chief of these is the total rewards system (which I define on p. 8) and which works alongside an arrangement of deals with specific supervisors: what can be called *individual* contracts. These depend on the competitive bargaining power of individual workers. They are essentially covert and are the means by which first-level supervisors illicitly distribute aspects of total rewards between competing subordinates.

To put it bluntly, the ruling analysts of industrial affairs may well be looking at the wrong areas of the wrong sectors of industry, and missing or dismissing hidden practices which directly and increasingly bear on major incidents of industrial strife. Fiddling, of course, is not the only covert activity which affects overt industrial practice. Much of it is part of a spectrum of counter-productivity (that is, counter-productive in terms of a firm's balance sheet: it is often extremely productive to the individual), and which takes in industrial sabotage at one end and absenteeism at the other. This counter-productivity is informed by a lack of involvement which is the equivalent in employment terms of a lack of involvement in political affairs (which is considered in the next chapter). It is the individual's or group's indifference to work and what it stands for to management that is such a feature of strong-grid jobs. And this lack of involvement has grown as many jobs have come to be strongly constrained by the design of management on the one hand and as the overt institutions of industrial bargaining have grown in size and influence on the other.

Unions have certainly grown – mainly through amalgamation. Contrary to conventional wisdom, it has been argued (Taylor, 1980) that unions as the fifth estate have too little rather than too much power; that unions in Western industrial societies have become so enmeshed in our emergent corporate states that their role has been reduced to that of mediators rather than workers' champions. And this development has affected all levels of industry. Union leadership, caught up in the centripetal force of corporatism, has become increasingly identified with government, either as protagonists or as involved supporters. This has removed it further from the shop floor, where the feeling has grown that union leadership no longer represents its interests. The local shop steward, on the other hand, has been drawn outward by the same centrifugal force which impels both breakaway businesses and nationalist movements: the desire for local autonomy. Often an important figure, the shop steward is now much more than previously the focus of local-level militancy. Despite recessions, union leaderships are aware that they are riding a tiger.

At the same time, employing organisations have also grown in size to become national and supranational in scale, while government has grown in influence to the extent that it can (and must) intervene to sustain these organisations. The rescue of Rolls-Royce and the bailing-out of Chrysler UK and British Leyland illustrate this interdependence. Add to this the rush to acquire new technologies which are so massively expensive that only governments can command the necessary resources – the National Enterprise Board's initiative to gain micro-chip know-how and government involvements in aero and space development – and it can be seen that policy at government, union and board-room level is becoming increasingly removed from what is happening on the shop floor. Change is a built-in constant and, as Bridger (1971) and others have shown, the key problem for all kinds of organisation is now to accommodate their boundaries to changes in the form of intrusions from outside.

At ground level the feeling grows, therefore, that decisions are being taken, and that change is increasingly being introduced, by outsiders. Government pay policies are always seen as outside pressure on a normally internal wage bargaining system. Wages councils in particular appear to be out of touch with true as opposed to paper levels of reward. The wages council for the hotel and catering industry, for example, in which basic rates are notoriously nominal and where for some workers money is made up by tips, perks and pilferage within a total reward system, is widely considered irrelevant and insensitive to the labour market at kitchen and dining-room level (Mitchell and Ashton, 1974). And the unions themselves, growing more bureaucratic through increases in size and amalgamations, and becoming ever more dependent on professional expertise, find themselves ever more divorced from their grassroots. Their officers turn into bureaucrats and live lives more akin to the managers they deal with than the workers they are supposed to represent. These are the reasons why they readily and naturally find themselves aligned with (sympathetic) government pay policies, or pursuing the same kinds of unrealistic reward negotiations as do the wages councils. And this is why they, too, are increasingly coming to be considered outsiders.

But surely, it can be argued, at the level of direct contact with workers the onus can be placed firmly upon the manager. Is it not, after all, his job to manage, and should not this include a knowledge both of his men and of what their work really involves?

Unfortunately there is a range of constraining pressures that increasingly force managers too into the role of outsider. The first is that they are likely to be outsiders in the physical sense, to be in post in a different place from where they were born and reared – unlike most of the people for whom they are responsible. The second is that they are likely to be outsiders in a social sense. Even if they still live in their 'native' area they are likely to have gone through the isolating process of higher education and to enjoy a different life-style from that of their workers – and so to be perceived as different. Thirdly, they are likely to be cultural outsiders – to possess a view of the world that is different from that of their workers and which is conditioned by the nature of their job. This world-view is more likely to be appropriate for hawks than for other job types.

This leads to the fourth and most powerful isolating factor – management's ethnocentrism – its inbuilt difficulty in appreciating the otherness of other cultures (Mars, 1981). As hawks, managers find it difficult to appreciate the concerns of donkeys, wolves, or vultures, and because competition is a central tenet with them they are likely to see equal and lesser hawks only in terms of their relative power positions.

Ethnocentricism is at its most extreme in management relationships with wolves and vultures. Despite a vaunted emphasis on the 'management team', the reality is that managers are and have to be individualists. They are concerned with their individual careers;

with individual perceived responsibility for their individual advancement. They find it difficult not to believe that everyone thinks as they do. Thus they impute individual motivation to leaders of collective action and find it difficult to accept that men often see their best interests in collective rather than individual terms. Or they impute individual motivation in designing systems of piecework payment for latent vulture groups who then collectivise. As well as under-rating the importance of group in workplace affairs, they are also prone to under-rate the intrusion of values from the local community (Gowler, 1970).

At one time there used to be at least the possibility of a bridge between management and men in the form of promotees who could often reconcile the two different sets of values. With the growth of complex organisations, however, and because of increasing technological complexity, there is now much less opportunity for the worker who is intelligent but lacking in formal education to occupy such managerial roles.

Outsiders, whether from government, the unions, or from management, are by definition unaware of (or officially unable to take account of) covert institutions. Whatever they do is therefore likely to disturb 'the way things are done' — and to do so in ways which have consequences that often cannot be foreseen. This frequently happens when, for example, management consultants are asked how to streamline the organisation of a business if this is deemed too difficult for the existing management to cope with. 'Streamline' here frequently means no more than to offer senior management legitimation for action to remove covert institutions. Not surprisingly, management consultants often uncover 'non-jobs'; Fleet Street's 'ghost squad' of between 2,000 and 3,000 printers who drew wages but never had to put in any hours for them is perhaps the most extreme example. But they occur frequently enough, though less flagrantly, in a wide range of industries. While management consultants at the behest of one level of management will attempt to rationalise structures, a lower level of management will often collude with employees to make them more complex. The 'deputy' and 'assistant' labels, for instance, can be used to get round pay restraint by promotion to a previously non-existent job. Or they can be a useful device for moving an employee sideways. Both distort logical management structures.

Change introduced by outsiders is always resented because it disrupts informal rules and tends to push workers upgrid when new rules formalise and replace existing informal 'rules'. For example, the introduction of a two-tier postal service by the UK Post Office guaranteed next-day delivery only to first-class mail. Second-class mail implicitly had an open-ended processing period, because it had to wait its turn. Consequently, some sacks of mail often waited up to a week to be sorted. Post Office designers then suggested introducing a labelling system, in which a different coloured label would signify which day of the week the mail had been received. Thereafter, there was no excuse for sacks of mail being 'overlooked'. Clearly there was also additional pressure on postal workers to clear the mail according to this externally derived criterion. Though this was a well-meant innovation, it *fundamentally* undermined the postal workers' *modus operandi*: it moved them upgrid where rule was increased and individual freedom to allocate time curtailed. Such a radical yet simple change in procedure came from designers who were 'outsiders' to the ground-level conception of who should control working practices (someone, an insider, with broadly the status and responsibilities of a foreman).

With those who should theoretically be 'insiders' (like the full-time officers of unions) becoming or appearing to become 'outsiders', the worker at ground level feels increasingly isolated and at bay. He is therefore prone to move defensively in the opposite direction, to informal *ad hoc* groupings (the stuff of action committees), to defend what he sees as his rights. Part of these rights are informal practices, of which fiddling is only one.

Covert institutions are precious to people at work because they provide the social and logistical framework for a whole range of unofficial action: from the destructive (industrial sabotage), through what one might call the 'redistributive' (occupational pilferage), to the 'regenerative' (moonlighting which may lead to the formation of new, less formal activity: which is how, indeed, many breakaway businesses set themselves up).

Change from outsiders is change from a source that may not even be aware that it threatens covert institutions. They are, in fact, unlikely even to be aware of their existence. Outsiders are increasingly those individuals who come from large organisations; they may be from 'head office', far removed from the action at local levels, or they may come from government departments. But because they are not locally rooted and because they are ethnocentric they will have a tendency to be insensitive to the pressures supporting an *ad hoc* style of management at ground level or to entrepreneurial activity that they do not countenance. These defects will affect most of their managerial actions. They will in particular make it unlikely for them to understand the bases of 'total rewards systems' by which — often through individual contracts — employees expect to top up a basic wage with tips, perks and pilferage.

Another source of external change derives from the private security industry, the role of which, as it applies to the hidden economy, is one carefully examined by Henry (1978). In the context of industrial relations, outside security is often introduced as the result of a need for economic belt-tightening which may convince an employer of his need to reduce fiddling. However, such outsiders, as we saw, are bound to run across the grain of covert institutions. They are misfits because their role is specifically designed to isolate them from normal social relationships with a firm's employees. Oliver and Wilson's (1974) standard security manual is perhaps the ultimate guide in how to construct an isolated, insulated, ultra-strong grid occupation. If they are successful in this, security men come to have a 'sterilised' view of losses, seeing them in purely legal and economic terms and ignoring their social role. Their disturbance of covert institutions is likely to be all the more crude (Henry, 1978, ch. 7). And if they are unsuccessful in absorbing such strong-grid values, they can become corrupt. Both responses imperil the development of good industrial relations.

A readiness to resist change, therefore, is not necessarily the perverse Luddism it sometimes appears. But neither is it to be understood in purely economic terms – whether such economic return is open or covert. On the contrary, it is often to be understood as an effort to hold on to initiative in the workplace; to retain flexibility; to ensure the continuance of valued work and social groups and of a freedom to transact that is often as much at stake as any fear of economic loss.

Resistance to change operates like a reflex to outside pressures if these threaten to push workers upgrid. From the viewpoint of the innovating middle and upper levels of bureaucracies, however, there is only seen to be one way of doing things and this only rarely takes account of the kind of grassroots reality we have been discussing.

It is the centripetal tendency of large organisations and the increasing distance of industrial policy-makers from the sources of action that encourage a 'do not disturb' attitude to innovative and regenerative behaviour. The opposing centrifugal tendency of the entrepreneur, the organisation rogue and the fixer constantly create new ways of doing things.

As large expansionist unions and big business corporations begin to retreat to the formal heights of high technology, the fittest of them to survive will be those that adapt. One way is for them to accommodate to their employed entrepreneurs – to give them a place in the organisation that allows and encourages their enterprise – and to charge them for the benefits. This specialised kind of subcontracting will be discussed in the following section.

Listening to the 'Music' of Fiddlers: Some Implications for Management and Unions

It should be clear now that management or unions who introduce or propose a change to the workplace without considering its covert institutions are operating blindfold. Even, and perhaps especially, broad-based schemes for the improvement of industrial relations such as the UK Bullock proposals for worker places on management boards are likely to founder if they take no account of the real nature of total rewards. And secrecy about these will still extend from the shop floor to the board-room, despite formal procedures to the contrary.

What should managements do? First, they should try to estimate honestly how much their workforce really earn, and how they earn it. They can assume that these earnings they have to guess at will be tax-free, and that therefore any change they introduce that cuts guesstimated gross earnings will affect total net earnings very seriously. It is no use officially paying a man an additional £50 a month that is taxable if this prevents him from unofficially earning a tax-free £50.

Secondly, managements should look carefully at the way fiddles produce their own sets of social relationships in the workplace, and gauge the effect that any planned change would have on them. The municipality as the dustmen's employer and their union negotiators would, for instance, need to *know* and account for the practice of totting and the effects this has on group relationships among dustcart gangs before they enter into negotiations. And they must be prepared to discuss freely both the presence and the implications of these practices and not shelter behind the false defence of moral outrage.

Managements and unions, in short, need to broaden their perception of the occupations they control or represent. They need to be able to look at jobs through a worker's eyes. A job considered low grade by management may be rated quite differently by workers. A 'promotion' may look nothing of the sort to a worker if it moves him out of a fiddle-prone job into a fiddle-proof one. The increase in salary is not likely to cover the loss in unofficial earnings. Workers who say that they do not want promotion because it removes them from the action, or from the camaraderie of the shop floor, are often only telling part of the truth. A reporter who is moved to the news desk loses the freedom to negotiate his own reward. He cannot claim the reporter's out-of-office expenses when he is now so visibly *in* the office.

But not all resistance to change is about money. The danger is that managements and unions, who are locked into the dynamics of market exchange and who use money as the main medium of the joint bargaining position, will overestimate money's importance to workers. They may feel that all they need to do, when introducing change, is to engineer things so that real wages are maintained or improved. Yet, as has repeatedly been shown, fiddles and the relationships they create are very likely to provide *social and psychological* benefits to workers which may be quite as important as, or more important than, financial benefits. Fiddles which operate through barter rather than money have a strong social element. Often payment in kind is nominal in relation to the value of the goods. 'It'll cost you a pint', as one of Henry's (1978) informants put it, suggests that the fiddle worked for another is worked as a favour. Payment is often more symbolic than real: the real coin of payment is to be understood as a continuing chain of obligations and reciprocities.

Covert institutions are alternatives; they are counter-institutions that mirror the more formalised ways that jobs are organised and restore to the worker the autonomy of which the organization has stripped him. Prisoners serving long sentences are advised by colleagues to 'do your time and don't let your time do you'; fiddling allows many workers to control their jobs rather than be controlled by them.

The existence of, and the reason behind, such covert institutions is cold comfort for unions. To the ordinary member a union can appear a source of control — especially if it enjoys a closed shop — that affects him no less rigidly than does management in its control over him. Its instructions not to work, even if arrived at by a mass vote, have to be obeyed by the individual in the same way as a contract of employment has to be obeyed. Why, then, should the worker not react to *both* forms of control by contriving fiddles? They can give him a real degree of worker's control.

A probation officer once remarked that skinhead gangs were made up of people who would be decorated in wartime rather than (as was happening) sent down in peacetime. In the same way, many fiddlers could well become the entrepreneurs of the future provided their jobs are designed in such a way that it strengthens their sense of individuality and develops as well as rewards their flair. It is a short-sighted and short-term aim merely to bring wages up to the level of total rewards. Something more radical is needed: a repositioning of the individual at the centre rather than at the periphery of things.

These are two models for this redesign. The first is the hawk fiddler's occupational style. As we saw in Chapter 2, he creates a radial pattern of relationships, with himself at the centre. In this position, he is able to subcontract. Different people get different pieces of his action. The hospital consultant is able to use the human and technical resources of a general practice, a Health Service hospital, a private nursing home and his own consultancy without becoming involved in the total performance of any one of them. The general practitioner, on the other hand, will be responsible for much of the actual running of his practice. He may be able to subcontract only secretarial duties, and then often to his wife.

Subcontracting allows the individual to concentrate on the exercise of his particular skills rather than dissipating his time and energy on the services which support those skills. Subcontracting works against the tendency of large organisations to create hierarchies of 'middle bureaucracies', which, because they are multi-levelled, fragment decision-making, frustrate quick action and, for the security of their incumbents, depend too much on the benefit from economies of scale.

A loose-limbed organisational design can be found in the slim-line publishing companies which have been set up over the last ten years. Many of these have been breakaways from large organisations (Granada begat Quartet, Penguin begat Wildwood House, and so on), and from both necessity and choice they have exchanged a horizontal system of operation for a vertical one. Printing, distribution and promotion, normally all handled by the publisher, have been hived off. New publishers 'plug in' to centralised distribution organisations when they need them, taking advantage of the benefits of scale without suffering, in organisational terms, the disadvantages.

Devolution of activities is a game large organisations can play, too. Sketching out ideas for the future, Macrae (1976) has suggested that big corporations could restructure themselves as 'confederations of entrepreneurs', setting up separate units within themselves to compete with each other in evolving new ideas, new ways of doing things. But this principle can be extended to take account of fiddle-prone occupations in general and those containing an element of entrepreneurial activity in particular.

Corporations could recognise the dynamics of 'covert institutions' by translating them into an official *modus operandi*. The fiddler 'borrows' an organisation's time and materials to further his own enterprise. Why should the organisation not allow him – even encourage him – to borrow its resources for a price, renting him time on its production equipment line or feeding his ideas into the corporation's computers? The micro-chip revolution might in this way be turned from a threat into a benefit to the individual. Micro-chips will automate those jobs which need not be done by individuals anyway. In *real* jobs the micro-chip provides the fastest way of translating individual ideas into action. It is a form of *technical* subcontracting, devolving all support activities to the micro-processor and allowing the individual to concentrate on real tasks.

In a similar way these principles can be applied to other occupations with the intention of enhancing the entrepreneuriality of their workers. As we saw in Chapter 2, the accountant Yoric Wintergreen fiddled his employer of time, office services and centralised information sources: he even skimmed off his firm's customers when he changed firms. It would be much more sensible to institutionalise the deviousness of Mr Wintergreen and of other professionals who work in our ever-growing and impersonal professional bureaucracies. As with some confederations of management consultants and barristers' chambers in the UK, there seems every advantage in arranging for confederations of lawyers and accountants to be the norm rather than the exception. In such a firm Mr Wintergreen would pay towards the office overheads and centralised intelligence services he uses and his enterprise and effort would be allowed a free rein.

But these practices, already to a limited degree established among some professionals, are eminently extendable to other fiddle-prone occupations and should be extended precisely *because* they are fiddle-prone. Repairmen involved in maintaining domestic consumer durables are an obvious case in point. They are certainly eligible to be federalised. Like minicab drivers, they and their customers would gain enormously from a centralised managerial core that would allow them to operate as tradesmen-entrepreneurs. In a similar way, there is every reason why a hotel's dispense bar – being a constant source of problems in control – should be leased out by the hotel. And if dispense bars, why not catering and chambermaid services? Delivery drivers, too, could act as their own men with their own vehicles who might competitively lease their rights to a route – perhaps for a year or two at a time. Perhaps the new progression of peripheral to core worker should be the move from journeyman to master; perhaps starting as an employee and after a period moving into sub-contracted self-employment. This, after all, is the well-accepted career progression of the owner cab driver who pays his share of a radio network overhead. It seems ludicrous that British Rail should have to charge extremely high prices for its mediocre food in order to maintain an extensive organising bureaucracy to control its stewards, when they can do the jobs of supply and of control more effectively than any bureaucracy – as recent fiddle revelations have shown (Moore, 1976). Their 'business within a business' fiddle is in any case well established, but it gives both the customer and the railway the worst of both worlds – high prices, bad service *and* fiddles.

What is being argued for here is a cross between subcontracting and franchising as a way of building upon the positive aspects of fiddle-proneness. It is leasing, but with an emphasis on rights in a job rather than rights to property or market access. Through leasing the centrifugal and centripetal forces at work in society need not be mutually self-defeating. The one can use the other: the individual and, where appropriate, the group using the benefits of scale provided by centralism, and the organisation benefiting from the entrepreneurial and innovative skills of its workers. But the organisation in this new type of operation will be a different shape; slimmer, with fewer middle managers to organise its lower-level workers who will be organising themselves, supervising themselves and using their initiative and intelligence to positive and legitimated ends.

This brings us to the second model for change, which applies particularly to donkey jobs and to jobs without an entrepreneurial element. Not all jobs are suitable for leasing and certainly not all workers would appreciate it, even if it were offered. Most donkey jobs are not convertible and probably most donkey workers would not welcome it if they were. In these cases emphasis should focus on removing the overstructured nature of such jobs. Autonomy can be increased and group relations can be encouraged by allowing people a greater say in what they do. And this means obtaining their consent, involvement and participation in designing and managing their own jobs.

The ways that people might design and manage their own jobs vary from one situation to another. However, certain features about jobs tend to come up repeatedly. For instance, a job that limits the chance of communicating with colleagues is usually less well liked and loses the opportunity of co-operation when it is necessary. Interdependence (and not just teamwork) is more highly valued than its absence. A job that gives a chance to learn new things is often valued above a more restricted or repetitive one. Allowing scope and discretion in dealing with queries is usually preferred to a more prescribed working to the book. These are simply *examples* of the kind of factors that people – *if given the opportunity* – can raise, think about and discuss. One of the essential jobs of a manager will increasingly be to give his staff – perhaps with the aid of specialist consultants – the chance to take part in such an experience and to have a real stake in the outcome. Managers can overcome their ethnocentrism, but only if they learn to listen to 'the music behind the words'.

Fiddles are too often dismissed as disruptive, the symptoms of the exploited exploiting the exploiters (Ditton, 1977b). Yet in the context of covert institutions they provide working models of the individualisation of contracts and a movement from overconstrained jobs. These positive aspects of fiddles will be needed if organisations are to provide incentives for their employees. Fiddles are therfore much more than an index of dissatisfaction with the sttus quo. They are tacit suggestions about ways the status quo can be changed.

9

Some Economic and Political Implications

Alternative Work: the Social and Black Economies in Context

In this chapter we move away from our central concern with the cheating of everyday work life to the wider implications of alternative work where the principal victim of cheating is the state. This takes us from Boxes 3 and 4 of Table 1 on page 8 to Boxes 5 and 6, and especially to the political and economic implications of the black economy.

We saw in the Introduction how well established are the black economies in Western industrial countries, though their particular manifestations vary. In Italy, for instance, even a casual tourist is soon struck by the gloom of the average hotel. This is partly because they seem only to be lit by 15-watt bulbs and partly because corridors often have press-button switches that cut off the electricity almost as soon as they are pressed in. This economising is necessary because electricity in Italy is extremely expensive, bearing a heavy tax. With an estimated third of the Italian economy now black, there is little opportunity for the tax authority to raise revenue from direct taxation. It therefore imposes its taxes where it can, and light and fuel offer a source of revenue not easily evaded.

This simple example illustrates the interaction of the alternative and formal economies. It shows how a developed alternative

212

economy not only runs in parallel to a formal economy, but presents problems for its policy-makers and indeed dictates some of their actions in areas such as taxation. But it also leads us to other areas. It leads us to consider the effects that an erosion of the tax base has on those who pay (or choose not to pay) taxes and on welfare recipients who benefit from transfer payments. And it leads us, too, to consider the difficulties that governments face when much of their economic intelligence is obscured, as is markedly the case, for instance, with data derived from small businesses. Before considering these questions, however, we must first place alternative work in context.

One of the most influential commentators on recent economic development is Daniel Bell, who popularised the phrase 'the post-industrial society' (1974). Bell saw industrial society becoming more efficient, with rising living standards being produced by a relatively smaller, more capital-intensive manufacturing sector, and with an associated increase in services. The USA entered the post-industrial phase several years ago and well over 50 per cent of its economy is now in services. A similar pattern is present or imminent in much of Europe.

Bell's argument, in brief, is this. As manufacturing becomes more capital-intensive and efficient, it needs fewer people to produce the same output. To prevent unemployment and maintain overall demand, resources must therefore be spent on services whose employees will then be able to purchase the surplus manufactured products. The result is a shift of people into a growing service sector. Though manufacturing has certainly become more capital-intensive and efficient, however, there is some evidence to suggest that it is now in decline as the notion of service expenditure becomes more problematic.

Bell's analysis has been refined and in some respects refuted by Gershuny (1978) in a form that goes even further to explain the growth of the alternative economy. His argument is that cheap mass-produced capital goods now allow much of traditional manufacturing to be undertaken in the home or at least out of the factory. The widespread use of electric power tools and their

213

attachments, for instance, not only diverts production to the home, but diverts it also from the formal to the social and black economies. People can make and do not only for themselves but for their neighbours as well.

A further factor spearheading this slide to the alternative economy, says Gershuny, is that relatively high wages in capital-intensive manufacturing set the pace for wages in the rest of the economym This makes the cost of labour-intensive services disproportionately expensive and it is this factor, linked to the availability of cheap, mass-produced power tools, that increasingly moves services out of the formal economy. We thus see a move not so much from formal manufacturing to formal services as Bell predicted, as from formal manufacturing to black manufacturing and black servicing. Such a move is likely to gather speed with the introduction of outputs that can enter the black economy from small factories using micro-technology. These will employ few people, can escape the need for official approval and bypass trade unions, have minimal bureaucratic involvement with employees, and require low inputs of capital. And their production can cover much of what is now mass-produced but with the benefit of quick adaptability to the changes and idiosyncrasies of the market.

The type of society that is emerging, therefore, reflects more than just an increase in manufacturing efficiency and a growth in the service sector. It encompasses a dualism – the formal economy on the one hand, and the alternative economy on the other – with the former moving to centralisation, growth in scale and the quest for efficiency, while the latter emphasises the local, the personal and the small scale; the one integrated with government and unions, the other attempting to stand aside from what it sees as external controls.

We need, therefore, to put 'service' into perspective to grasp what this post-industrial shift implies for relationships and for the economy. Centralisation, growth in scale and the quest for efficiency apply just as much to the service sector as to manufacturing. In this process, although the service sector as a whole grows, the actual level of *personal service* paradoxically declines.

This is well illustrated by changes that have occurred in banking, for example. The banks' *personal* services such as Saturday morning opening have been replaced by automated, unstaffed cashpoints: the personal service element in banking as elsewhere has, in fact, been depersonalised. At the level of face-to-face dealings, valued relationships which were implicit in traditional personal service (for example, the corner shop natter) have been displaced. There has been a shift from the formal economy back to what has always been the dominant mode of personal transaction – the informal and the face-to-face.

While the alternative economy is based on personal relationships, the formal economy is moving towards transactions that depend upon records, book-keeping and bureaucratic procedures. And it is these that lead to perhaps the most significant difference between the two: that while the alternative economy is dependent on cash as its principal medium of exchange (with barter its second), the formal economy moves steadily into dealings that exclude cash.

Cash and Cashlessness

Cash transactions are coming to have a special kind of significance. In the USA cash is becoming increasingly obsolete for legitimate transactions and people who offer cash instead of cheques or credit cards are looked at with suspicion. The use of cash has come to symbolise the unofficial nature of a transaction. It is part of an underground language, like back-slang among London's working class. The cockney employed back-slang to outwit the police, and in doing so reinforced his group's protection of itself against a hostile environment. Similarly the alternative economy employs cash both to exclude and to protect. The fiddler outwits his customer or the boss or the Revenue, and in so doing becomes intimately bound in a network of people operating in the same way. They may combine to outwit those in another business, as manufacturers and others working on contract in the fashion

215

industry, or they may comprise the body of physically shifting employers and tradesmen 'on the lump' in the building and construction industries. The point is that cash transactions of this kind imply different social relationships from those which occur in official transactions: they are personalised and are bonded through collusion, and this works against the guardians of the formal economy (Henry and Mars, 1978).

In contrast to the increasing use of cash in the alternative economy, official, formal transactions are symbolised by an increasing absence of cash, by cheques and by 'plastic' money, the cash card and the credit card. There are sound reasons why the 'formal' economy should move towards an absence of cash. At a superficial level it is apparent that the use of cash is expensive: the Bank of England, the Royal Mint, the Post Office, the police and the private security industry all invest resources in the use and movement of cash. And while the labour costs of cash-handling have been rising, the costs of *automatic* handling have fallen. Advances in computer-based systems and in communications between banks (and their customers) have meant that the electronic transfer of funds is going to become even cheaper.

Despite the formal move to cashlessness, the amount of currency in circulation – even accounting for inflation – continues to grow. The direct and obvious reason for this is to fund illegal transactions and to facilitate tax evasion. For example, Gutmann (1977) estimated that for the USA

> The amount of currency in circulation outside banks is incredibly, indeed suspiciously large – 380·68 dollars per capita in December 1976 or 1,522·72 for a family of four. Why do people need these amazing sums? The answer's not hard to find: this currency lubricates a vast amount of non-reported income and non-reported work and employment, a whole subterranean economy, untaxed and substantially ignored, whose GNP of almost 200 billion dollars exceeds the entire legal GNP in the middle of World War II.

The figures have been much disputed, most notably by Feige

(1979) who, using later figures, comes out with even higher totals. He points out that the really disproportionate increases have been in the higher-denomination notes, a trend also observed in the UK. It seems reasonable to assume that higher-denomination notes are the main medium of black economy exchange.

Economic Planning and Policy

With a sizeable segment of total transactions that remain concealed and with these concentrated in certain economic sectors, it follows that economic planners and policy-makers face a range of problems. Their difficulties arise because the figures available to them not only fail to reflect reality but distort it. Strategies based on such figures are therefore likely to be similarly distorted. Distortion is inevitable since to be able to plan, economic planners need accurate intelligence on a whole range of variables. Among these are details of real alterations to GNP, whether of growth or of decline, and accurate assessments of both current and projected rates of inflation which depend in part on knowing the number of transactions in a given period. And they need realistic figures on the levels and distribution of total earnings, as well as accurate breakdowns for each of these by industry, sector and region. Even with these data they will require an understanding, at least to some degree, of international comparability in the areas of their concern. Finally, assessments must be continuously updated as new and similarly accurate data come to hand.

It is evident that this kind of intelligence is only available for the formal economy and sometimes not even for that, and that even approximate figures on the concealed side of these variables are almost entirely absent. Nor can it be otherwise, since a characteristic of the social, black and hidden economies in general is that they control information. No matter how good a government system for gathering statistics, it can only provide sound information on one part of its subjects' activities: the formal part. The hotel waiter will still declare a nominal sum in his tax returns for the 'tips' that he has received and he may withhold information about most of his real rewards. By dealing in cash, the small businessman can similarly restrict the information that a cheque transaction would divulge. The information central government gains about current activity levels is likely, therefore, to be misleading. While on paper unemployment levels might appear high, wage levels depressed and economic growth low, in reality economic activity can be livelier and rewards a good deal more competitive than they appear from a government viewpoint. Since government cannot take an informed account of the economy, its efforts to manage it will at the very least be hindered.

Economic Planning and the Small Business Sector

One area of perennial government concern is with the small business sector and it is one to which government planners have given much attention. This is valid for good reasons. First, small businesses in all Western countries employ a greater proportion of workers than large businesses which increasingly tend to replace labour with capital. Secondly, the small businesses of today are seen as the large businesses of tomorrow. Thirdly, they provide a source of innovation. Fourthly, they provide, on the whole, a better standard of service than large businesses. And finally they are quickly adaptable to changes in demand.

Despite the advantages possessed by small businesses, government planners are concerned about their number and their 'health' and they have frequently related this to their lack of adequate capitalisation. Banks have often been criticised for not being more prepared to loan them finance at crucial stages of their development and government aids are periodically offered to overcome the difficulties they face in raising money on the open market. So we find that right-wing governments offer them tax cuts (as in the 1981 and 1982 UK budgets) and attempt to encourage banks to be more liberal in their lending, while centre/left governments offer state-supported loans funnelled through special agencies.

There are, however, two apparent reasons for the reluctance of banks to fund small businesses and these go some way to explain why it is that government support seems to founder. The first is that formally based, small service firms in particular find it difficult competing against black service firms. As one example, legitimate small builders and decorators who cater mostly for the domestic market have come increasingly to face such unfair competition – often from their own moonlighting workers. They have three choices: to grow big; to go black; or to go bust. The second reason is that funding from an external and especially a formal source such as a bank depends upon examination of the firm according to the formal rules of accounting: books need to be scrutinised, turnover assessed and costs and profits accounted for. This cannot be done when small businesses are submerged or even partly submerged within the black economy.

One result of this inability to expand through legitimate means has been a growth of private and illegitimate brokers and bankers who provide financial services to small business as noted in Chapter 2. These services, which mirror the functions of their official counterparts, are based on neighbourhood, kinship and ethnic networks. They use money derived from cash-based black economy activities (such as market stalls and restaurants), which are difficult to find out about and even more difficult to control. Such illegitimate financing leads to a firm's even deeper involvement in the black economy and to that economy's further growth.

Taxation Policies and Erosion of the Tax Base

A developed alternative economy raises problems both for tax-gatherers and for governments. This is because taxation straddles the official and the alternative economies. It is becoming recognised, for instance, that indirect taxes such as VAT, while simple in conception, are extremely easy to evade – there being a mutual interest between buyer and seller to avoid payment. This is particularly so in the market for services.

Since the alternative economy is a system for avoiding payment of tax, the stage is set for invidious comparisons and the discontent of those in the formal economy who pay, as they see it, an unfair share of general taxes. But not all those in the formal economy have to pay taxes – or at least to the full extent of their liability. They can not only avoid the full cost of services by negotiating with black economy tradesmen, they can also fudge their income tax liabilities. They, too, therefore straddle the official and the alternative economies.

Fudging income tax can be arranged in two ways. The individual can turn the tax system to his own advantage or he can turn his back on it. The two responses are seen most clearly in tax evasion and tax avoidance. Tax *evasion* is illegal tax-dodging. It may be 'evasion by commission', taking deliberate action to evade the payment of tax; for example, by claiming child allowance where there is no child. Or it may be 'evasion by omission'; that is, taking *no* action, not telling the Revenue, for instance, about tips or moonlighting payments. Tax *avoidance* is defined as any legal method of reducing one's tax bill. The more concessions and allowances within the system, the greater the scope for avoidance. In this sense a 'complex equitable' taxation system inevitably contains the seeds of its own destruction – not least because it is only the rich who can afford tax lawyers and accountants. Tax avoidance is so difficult to define, its definition shifting with moral viewpoints and legal changes, that some commentators have thought it more useful to describe it as 'erosion of the tax base' (Sandford, 1977).

As a result of such erosion we may expect increasingly to see a growth in indirect taxes with an unavoidable impact. These are found where demand for a product is relatively inelastic and where a tax on its purchase is easily collected. Fuel is a good source of revenue, as we have seen, because it possesses these qualities, and because it is consumed by a large sector of the population. Taxes raised from it, therefore, satisfy arguments for equity and, in addition, can be projected as having an ecological function in a world of finite resources. We can now understand why it should be that the British government is following the same path as the Italian. In 1981 its government-controlled gas industry was forced to raise prices by 25 per cent with a proposed real increase of 30 per cent to come over the following three years. A spokesman for the gas workers' union pertinently observed: 'The gas corporation is being used as a tax-collecting agency to raise money which the government has decided, for party political reasons, it cannot raise from income tax' (*The Times*, 20 February 1981).

In a period of rising unemployment in the official economy and with a growing move of services to the black economy, both serving to restrict tax yields, there is temptation for a government to exploit sales of fuel which are relatively inelastic. Taxes on it are more easily collected and less avoidable than value-added taxes and taxes on incomes. It was for these reasons that the British government took a further step along the Italian path in its 1981 budget. It outraged many of its own supporters by imposing a 15 per cent increase in petroleum tax and a windfall profit tax on banks that raised £400m. It did this while leaving both income tax and value-added taxes untouched.

Citizens' Perceptions of their Civic Role

What is striking about the alternative and hidden economies is that they are both active and reactive. They react against economic environments which are inflexible, or inefficient and no longer able to reward individual aspirations. But they also have an innovatory vigour and an impetus. What lies behind this dualism is the 'take it or leave it' attitude of individuals towards the organisations which manage their affairs.

Let us return to the different occupational cosmologies to illustrate this. If 'government' is substituted for 'management', it can be seen that the relationship between individuals and their civic ties has similarities with the ties of individuals to their jobs. Even if their jobs are in the strong-grid donkey category, they are still able to bend work environments to their own use. They

221

transform rules of impartial dealing into partial ones with associates, friends, or relatives. The supermarket cashier's till is a device for impartial distribution: the customer gets exactly what the till says she deserves. But if the cashier arranges for a friend to buy goods and yet be charged for only a fraction of them, then she is no longer impartial. Even a solitary fiddle, ringing up 'no sale' and pocketing the cash, redistributes in her own favour and negates the system and her role in it. In individualist hawk jobs, as we have seen, entrepreneurs do not merely bend the rules: they can rewrite them. But whatever quadrant people find themselves in, they can always corner *some* measure of independence. And from these activities they gain more than just economic resources and independence of action at work; they also gain an independence of viewpoint which expands well beyond their narrow work concerns.

As we have seen, ordinary people, particularly those in strong-grid occupations, appear to take very much the same view of their employers' concerns as they do of government concerns. The supermarket chain management's preoccupation with its financial health is not generally shared by its employees. The decline of British Leyland and of British shipbuilders might concern their managements and their more aware backers but their fates appear to have less impact on their own workers or on the paying public at large. Attitudes to work and attitudes to the state are not only similar – they are linked and derive from the same bases.

Richard Rose, in a study of the impact of inflation on 'ordinary' people, points out that 'the greatest concerns of individuals are insulated from the macro-institutions of society' (1977). Rose suggests that this explains the curious paradox of hard times: that even in a period of 'stagflation' people are content, because they do not relate their domestic state to the larger concerns of society: government, economic conditions, and law and order. In the perception of the 'ordinary person', the world of family, home and friends is insulated from the larger world of the corporate state.

What this potential insulation means for both government and managements is that, despite their apparent structural rigidity, the individual can take or leave them both at will. Individuals feel that what organisations do for them either advances or threatens their interests and they choose to act accordingly. When there is high employment and wage levels are copperbottomed by legislation, Rose suggests that workers do not need to put much *individual* effort into advancing their economic well-being. They are content to settle into the strong-grid environment of the union, the organisation and the state where 'in exchange for union dues, bureaucratic loyalty and an occasional vote, individuals can delegate responsibility for maintaining an acceptable living standard to others ... '. When conditions change and living standards are threatened, people fight to maintain them. If unions, employers and government all appear unable to cope, then some individuals take up the option they have always had – to negotiate their own rewards for themselves.

Individuals thus take corporatism when it protects their interests, but when it threatens them they often can and sometimes do leave it. They leave it by exploiting their occupational enivronment through perks, tax evasion, moonlighting, or pilferage. When people reward themselves in this way it represents both an erosion of civic authority, what Rose calls 'civil indifference', and a shift that threatens collective and formalised business dealing.

But perhaps the most significant shift is from 'faceless' dealing to face-to-face transactions. When an individual recoups his right to better himself, he fits it to the style of his insulated, domestic dealings. It is a style well suited to the four basic characteristics of the alternative economies:

(1) face-to-face dealings within *ad hoc* trading networks;
(2) control of information: spoken agreements dispense with the paperwork of conventional arm's-length transactions, which provide too much information and an unwanted record about what is being transacted;
(3) fast adaptability: ears close to the ground to discover what the market's changing needs are;

(4) control over and flexible use of time: moonlighting time is domestic time, with jobs being slotted in at evenings or weekends or at the particular convenience of the client.

What this adoption of a domestic style suggests, in terms of the occupational cosmologies dealt with in earlier chapters, is that the individual joins the hawks; he becomes something of an entrepreneur or at least he moves downgrid. When an individual takes the negotiation of his rewards into his own hands or when it is in the hands of a group small enough for face-to-face relationships, he is able to be fully stretched and his potential realised. In a stronger-grid environment, he will tend to keep something of himself in reserve.

This 'holding back' is frequent in the context of large and complex organisations, whether they deal with wage-earners or welfare recipients. not only have they of necessity to control the mass of their employees or clients within strong-grid bureaucratised constraints, but their rewards systems, too, are essentially formalised — whether they involve wages on the one hand or social welfare payments on the other. And formal rewards are particularly vulnerable to the overlap of progresive tax and regressive welfare legislation which penalise individual incentive in the interests of collective reward and bureaucratised administration.

Individuals can never separate themselves entirely from the structures of large organisations. But they can often put them in what they regard as their proper perspective: with individuals in the foreground and institutions in the background. Pahl (1980) has suggested that welfare capitalism, far from grinding down the workers as Marx predicted, may have handed back to some of them the means of production. The man who controls his tools — power drills, chain saws, welding equipment — controls his own time (the domestic/hawk/entrepreneurial style of occupation) and he does not need a formal job at all. The state is put out to field at long-stop, providing unemployment and sickness benefits for him to fall back on and to prevent him from starving. Rather than opting out of it, he *uses* the mixed economy welfare state to its

224

utmost. He is a figure that Samuel Smiles would instantly recognise.

One of the problems with Samuel Smiles's view of the world, however, is that his autonomy is often achieved only at the cost of control over others. These others are likely to include the most easily exploitable donkey job-holders who are the most difficult to protect, especially when their work is organised and their rewards are illegally derived from small units. These preclude both effective supervision of conditions of work and attempts at collective action.

What Should Be Done?

How, then, should a society regard its alternative economies? As economically disruptive – rewarding those who can best grab an unfair share and who shift the tax burden to others? As socially divisive and unjust, adding to him who hath? Or should it see them as a system which distributes its rewards across a wide spectrum of classes, ages and occupations? Again, there is the suggestion that in a fiddling society there is one law for the rich and another for the poor. Ditton has argued (1976) that we define, legislate against and police fiddles selectively. Fraudulent benefit claims amount on average to an estimated seventh of the tax evasion bill, yet newspapers have cast the social security 'scrounger' rather than the tax-dodger as the folk devil. Ditton suggests that the severity and provision of control is *inversely* related to the amounts of money lost. Certainly the ambiguity of society's attitude does vary with the nature of the fiddle. Hawk fiddles on the Khashoggi/Lockheed scale and the massive tax evasions that these inevitably involve invite an awed admiration; social security fiddles, however ingenious, do not.

This is understandable, and not only in terms of class or privilege. Though the target or victim of a fiddle is important in defining attitudes to it, so too is the occupational structure within which it occurs. The individual taxpayer is the victim both of

225

large-scale tax evasion and of small-scale social security 'scrounging'. Yet each type of offender is different. In very large-scale evasion the offender is so big that he rates as no sort of threat through personal comparison with the observer: he is demonstrably in a distant and a different league. Such evasion is seen as somehow bound up with an individual's skills, and is directly linked to his earning power: to evade such a sum, you have to be worth such a sum and to possess the characteristics — flair, audacity, enterprise — that are admired and set up as modes to aspire to. In a small-scale social welfare fiddle, on the other hand, the offender fits into a stronger grid and a more despised environment. He is, in fact, despised whether he fiddles or not. The fiddles that are possible inevitably lack flair, and since they offend rules that are numerous and rigid their infringement can easily be discovered. When this happens the revelation leaves no surprises since there is almost no room for manoeuvre. And there is no ambiguity in public attitudes because there is nothing to admire. The different levels of policing and enforcement clearly have to do with class bias and discrimination, but they also are concerned with the differing structural complexities of fiddle systems, the scale on which they operate and the way they are perceived.

However, some areas of evasion are simply harder to control than others. In 1972 the French introduced new legislation to counter 'moonlighting'. They discovered, unsurprisingly, that moonlighting was difficult to stamp out. Their main problem lay in an inability to uncover both the informal networks of workers and the workers' collusion with employers. They found that moonlighters are difficult to discover because they work outside normal hours (and investigation officials work only inside working hours); and that control is difficult in close communities, where the inspectors themselves may be reluctant to name names; and, finally, that domestic moonlighting — plumbing, carpentry and electrical work in private homes — was especially difficult to control. Thus the informal, domestic nature of the alternative economy is often its best defence. It can literally melt away if too much notice is taken of it, and everyone has an interest in restricting information and in keeping chains of activity and networks secret.

Should societies, then, bring in more repressive legislation to counter the alternative economy? The French approach is uncomplicated. Workers who do not register with the *Repertoire des métiers* (the job index) and therefore avoid paying tax can be fined or imprisoned. A wide range of officials are enlisted to keep their eyes and ears open for evidence of offences: policemen, tax and customs officials, inspectors of works and inspectors in social and agricultural departments. In addition, they suggest enlisting the help of those who deal with the unemployed. For the future, they advocate a novel form of sanction: people convicted of 'moonlighting' and thereby of evading tax should lose any tax benefits they have gained through house purchase loans.

This draconian approach tackles the reactive (escaping payment of tax) but not the active features of the alternative economy. Illegal or not, moonlighting represents personal initiative and enterprise, and considerable economic activity. Non-payment of tax represents an incentive which legislation would displace rather than replace with anything else.

An overhaul of tax and welfare legislation could do much to restore incentives. The informal style of work could provide the means. A study of the alternative economy in Detroit (Ferman and Berndt, 1981) concluded that it was a staging post to the formal economy: no one wanted to work permanently in this sector, yet for the time being it provided an opportunity of increasing take-home pay.

The danger of the changes facing us is that as a society we may continue to act only from the perspective of one occupational quadrant without appreciating the totality of concealed economic transactions and their place in a society subject to constant change. The alternative and hidden economies are too large to ignore, often too informal to detect, and too resilient to control. Inside and outside the workplace, fiddles often represent untapped potential. Managements already tend to see this activity as a 'management problem' rather than as theft of company time, money, or

227

property. And so it is. But some jobs are structured in such a way that 'informal' work within them could be better harnessed and formalised for real rewards. Others must be prepared to lose the informal initiatives of their employees to *ad hoc* enterprises outside. Even if government and management do not recognise and make use of such activity, workers will. Alternative economies, for the time being and for increasing numbers, make more sense than traditional economies.

Bibliography

Alden, J. (1981), 'Holding two jobs; an examination of "Moonlighting"', in Henry (ed.), 1981, pp. 43–57.

Arensberg, C. M., and Kimball, S. T. (1940), *Family and Community in Ireland* (Cambridge, Mass.: Harvard University Press).

Batstone, E., Boraston, I., and Frenkel, S. (1977), *Shop Stewards in Action* (Oxford: Blackwell).

Becker, H. S. (1963), *Outsiders* (Glencoe, Ill.: The Free Press).

Bell, D. (1974), *The Coming of Post-Industrial Society* (London: Heinemann).

Beynon, H. (1975), *Working for Ford* (Wakefield: E. P. Publishing).

Boulton, David (1978), 'The pirate of Saudi Arabia', *Guardian*, 19 October, p. 11.

Bridger, H. (1971), 'A viewpoint on organisational behaviour', in *Proceedings of CIBA Foundation Symposium on Teamwork for World Health*, ed. G. Wolstenholme and M. O'Conner (London: J. and A. Churchill, pp. 187–90.

Bridger, H., and Wilson, A. T. M. (1947), 'Group discussion', *Monthly Review of the British Council*, vol. 1 (October), pp. 139–43.

Cahn, E. (1955), 'Cheating on taxes', in his *The Moral Decision* (Bloomington, Ind.: Indiana University Press).

Chaucer, G. (1951), 'The Manciple's Prologue', in *The Canterbury Tales*, ed. N. Coghill (Harmondsworth: Penguin), pp. 499–502.

Chiaramonte, L. J. (1971), 'Craftsman-client contracts: interpersonal relations in a Newfoundland fishing community', Institute of Social and Economic Research, Memorial University, St John's, Newfoundland, Canada.

Chivers, T. S. (1973), 'The proletarianisation of a service worker', *Sociological Review*, n.s. 21, 633–56.

Clegg, H. A. (1972), *The System of Industrial Relations in Great Britain*, 2nd edn (Oxford: Blackwell).

Codere, H. (1950), *Fighting with Property* (New York: Augustin).

Colquhoun, P. (1800), *A Treatise on Commerce and Police Forces of the River Thames* (London: Joseph Mawman).

Cort, D. (1959), 'The embezzler', *The Nation*, 18 April, pp. 339–42.

Council for the European Communities (1980), 'Report and recommendations to the Council on part-time work', COM(80)(405), 17 July.

Cressey, S. (1953), *Other People's Money* (Glencoe, Ill.: The Free Press).

Dalton, M. (1964), *Men Who Manage* (New York: Wiley).

Davis, Fred (1959), 'The cabdriver and his fare: facets of a fleeting relationship', *American Journal of Sociology*, vol. 65, pp. 158–65.

Deaglio, Mario (1979), 'The "black" economy', *The Banker*, May, pp. 85–7.

Dennis, H., Henriques, F., and Slaughter, C., (1956), *Coal Is Our Life* (London: Tavistock).

Dilmot, A., and Morris, C. N. (1981), 'What do we know about the black economy?', *Fiscal Studies*, (Institute for Fiscal Studies) vol. 2, no. 1 (March), pp. 58–73.

Ditton, J. (1972), 'The problem of time: styles of time – management and schemes of time – manipulation amongst machine paced workers', Working Paper No. 2, Durham University Department of Sociology.

Ditton, J. (1976), 'The dual morality in the control of fiddles', mimeo, Outer Circle Policy Unit, London.

Ditton, J. (1977a), *Part-Time Crime: An Ethnography of Fiddling and Pilferage* (London: Macmillan).

Ditton, J. (1977b), 'Perks, pilferage and the fiddle: the historical structure of invisible wages', *Theory and Society*, vol. 4, pp. 39–71.

Ditton, J. (1979), *Contrology: Beyond the New Criminology* (London: Macmillan).

Douglas, M. (1970), *Natural Symbols* (London: Crescent Press).

Douglas, M. (1978), *Cultural Bias* (London: Royal Anthropological Institute).

Douglas, M. and Isherwood, B. (1978), *The World of Goods: Toward an Anthropology of Consumption* (Harmondsworth: Penguin).

Dubois, P. (1979), *Sabotage in Industry* (Harmondsworth: Penguin).

England, K. (1980), 'The persistence of the private retailer: a sociological investigation', MA thesis, University of Wales at Swansea.

Feige, E. L. (1979), 'How big is the irregular economy?', *Challenge*, November/December, pp. 5–13.

Ferman, L. A., and Berndt, L. E. (1981), 'The irregular economy', in Henry (ed.), 1981, pp. 26–42.

Ferrarotti, F. (1978), BBC Radio 4 *File on Four*, 5 July.

Fishlock, T. (1981), 'Delhi tries to raise "black money" from its underground economy', *The Times*, 4 February.

Forge, A. (1970), 'Learning to see in New Guinea', in *Socialisation: The Approach from Social Anthropology*, ed. P. Mayer (London: Tavistock, pp. 269–91.

Gershuny, J. I. (1977a), 'Post industrial society: the myth of the service economy', *Futures*, April, pp. 103–14.

Gershuny, J. I. (1977b), 'The self-service economy', *New Universities Quarterly*, Winter, pp. 50–66.

Gershuny, J. I. (1978), *After Industrial Society?* (London: Macmillan).

Gershuny, J. I., and Pahl, R. E. (1980), 'Britain in the decade of the three economies', *New Society*, 3 January, pp. 7–9.

Gilding, B. (1971), *The Journeyman Coopers of East London*, History Workshop Pamphlet No. 4 (Oxford: Ruskin College).

Gluckman, M. (1955), *The Judicial Process Among the Barotse of Northern Rhodesia* (Manchester: Manchester University Press).

Goffman, E. (1961a), 'Role distance', in his *Encounters* (Harmondsworth: Penguin), pp. 83–152.

Goffman, E. (1961b), *Asylums: Essays on the Social Situation of Mental Patients and Other Inmates* (Harmondsworth: Penguin).

Gouldner, A. W. (1954), *Wildcat Strike: A Study in Worker–Management Relationships* (New York: Harper & Row).

Gowler, D. (1970), 'Socio-cultural influences on the operation of a wage payment system: an exploratory case-study', in *Local Labour Markets and Wage Structures*, ed. D. Robinson (Farnborough: Gower Press), pp. 100–26.

Grapin, J. (1981), 'Moonlighting: an indication of hyper development', *The Times*, 3 March.

Grossman, G. (1977), 'The second economy of the USSR', *Problems of Communism*, September/October, pp. 25–40.

Gutmann, P. (1977), 'The subterranean economy', *Financial Analysts Journal*, November/December, pp. 20, 27, 34.

Henderson, J. P. (1965), *Labour Market Institutions and Wages in the Lodging Industry* (East Lansing, Mich.: Bureau of Business and Economic Research, Michigan State University).

Henry, S. (1978), *The Hidden Economy: The Context and Control of Borderline Crime* (Oxford: Martin Robertson).

Henry S, (ed.) (1981), *Can I Have It In Cash? A Study of Informal Institutions and Unorthodox Ways of Doing Things* (London: Astragal Books).

Henry, S., and Mars, G. (1978), 'Crime at work: the social construction of amateur property theft', *Sociology*, vol. 12, pp. 245–63.

Hill, J. M. M., and Trist, E. L. (1962), *Industrial Accidents, Sickness and Other Absences*, Tavistock Pamphlet No. 4 (London: Tavistock).

Hill, S. (1976), *The Dockers: Class and Tradition in London* (London: Heinemann).

Home Office (1973), *Shoplifting and Thefts by Shop Staff: A Report of a Home Office Working Party on Internal Shop Security* (London: HMSO).

Horning, D. M. (1970), 'Blue collar theft: conceptions of property and attitudes toward pilfering and work group norms in a modern plant', in Smigel and Ross, op. cit., pp. 46–64.

Inland Revenue (1981), *Report of Commissioners for Year Ending 31 March 1980* (London: HMSO).

Irwin, J. (1972), 'Participant observation of criminals', in *Research on Deviance*, ed. J. Douglas (New York: Random House), pp. 117–64.

Kaiser, R. (1976), *Russia: The People and The Power* (Harmondsworth: Penguin).

Kerr, C., and Siegel, A. (1954), 'The interindustry propensity to strike: an international comparison', in *Industrial Conflict*, ed. A. Kornhauser, R. Dubin and A. M. Ross (New York: McGraw-Hill), pp. 189–212.

Klein, L. (1964), *Multiproducts Ltd* (London: HMSO).

Laird, D. A. (1950), 'Psychology and the crooked employee', *Management Review*, vol. 39, pp. 210–15.

Law Society (1977–9), *Evidence to The Royal Commission on Legal Services* (London: The Law Society).

Leach, E. (1977), *Custom, Law and Terrorist Violence* (Edinburgh: Edinburgh University Press).

Liverpool University (1954), *The Dock Worker* (Liverpool: Liverpool University Press).

Macrae, N. (1976), 'Ten green bottles', *The Economist*, 25 December, pp. 41–65.

Mars, G. (1972), 'An anthropological study of longshoremen and of industrial relations in the port of St John's, Newfoundland, Canada', PhD thesis, University of London.

Mars, G. (1973), 'Hotel pilferage: a case study in occupational theft', in *The Sociology of the Work Place*, ed. M. Warner (London: Allen & Unwin), pp. 200–10.

Mars, G. (1974), 'Dock pilferage', in *Deviance and Control*, ed. P. Rock and M. McIntosh (London: Tavistock), pp. 109–28.

Mars, G. (1977), 'Some implications of fiddling at work', in *The Social Psychologist in Industry* (London: British Psychological Society), pp. 7–19.

Mars, G. (1979), 'The stigma cycle: values and politics in a dockland union', in *Social Anthropology of Work*, ed. S. Wallman (London: Academic Press), pp. 135–58.

Mars, G. (1981), 'The anthropology of managers', *Royal Anthropological Institute News*, no. 42 (February), pp. 4–6.

Mars, G., and Mitchell P. (1976), *Room for Reform? A Case Study of Industrial Relations in The Hotel Industry*, Unit 6, P881 (Milton Keynes: The Open University Press).

Mars, G., and Mitchell, P. (1977), 'Catering for the low paid: invisible earnings', *Low Pay Unit Bulletin*, No. 15 (London: LPU).

Mars, G., Mitchell, P., and Bryant, D. (1979), *Manpower Problems in Hotels and Restaurants* (Farnborough: Saxon House).

Mars, G., and Nicod, M. (1981), 'Hidden rewards at work: the implications from a study of British hotels', in Henry (ed.), 1981, pp. 58–72.

Marx, K. (1972), *Capital*, Vol. 1 (London: Dent).

Mitchell, P., and Ashton, R. K. (1974), 'Wages councils: do they matter?', *Journal of the Hotel and Catering Institute Management Association*, vol. 1, pp. 20–8.

Mead, M. (ed.) (1955), *Cultural Patterns and Technical Change* (New York: Mentor Books).

Montias, J. M., and Rose-Ackerman, S. (1980), *Corruption in a Soviet-Type Economy: Theoretical Considerations*, Kennan Institute Occasional Paper No. 110 (Washington, DC: Kennan Institute).

Moore, P. (1976), 'Exposed: the great train robbery by the buffet car fiddlers', *News of the World*, 29 August, p. 7.

Motoring Which, (1970–81), 'Reports on garage servicing' (London: The Consumers' Association), October 1970, October 1972, October 1973, October 1977, January 1981.

Nove, A. (1977), *The Soviet Economic System* (London: Allen & Unwin).

O'Brien, D. P. (1977), 'Why you may be dissatisfied with garage servicing', *Motor*, 10 September.

O'Higgins, M. (1980), *Measuring the Hidden Economy: A Review of Evidence and Methodologies* (London: Outer Circle Policy Unit).

Oliver, E., and Wilson, J. (1974), *Security Manual* (Epping: Gower Press).

Origo, I. (1963), *The Merchant of Prato* (Harmondsworth: Penguin).

Outer Circle Policy Unit (1978), *Policing The Hidden Economy: The Significance and Control of Fiddles* (London: Outer Circle Policy Unit).

Pahl, R. E. (1980), 'Employment, work and the domestic division of labour', *International Journal of Urban and Regional Research*, vol. 4, no. 1 (March), pp. 1–20.

Peet, T. E. (1924), 'A historical document of Ramesside age', *Journal of Egyptian Archeology*, vol. 10, pp. 116–26.

Phelps-Brown, H. (1977), *The Inequality of Pay* (Oxford: Oxford University Press).

Powis, D. (1977), *The Signs of Crime: A Field Manual for Police* (London: McGraw-Hill).

Quinn, P. (1977), 'The background to the first national strike of the Fire Brigades Union and some factors affecting industrial relations in the fire service', mimeo., Diploma in Industrial Relations and Trade Union Studies, Middlesex Polytechnic.

Rayner, S. F. (1979), 'The classification and dynamics of sectarian organisations: grid/group perspectives on the far-left in Britain', PhD thesis, Department of Anthropology, University of London.

Riis, R. W., and Patric, J. (1942), *Repairmen Will Get You If You Don't Watch Out* (Garden City, NY: Doubleday, Doran).

Rock, P. (1973), *Deviant Behaviour* (London: Hutchinson).

Rose, R. (1977), 'Ordinary people in extraordinary economic circumstances', mimeo., paper presented to European-American Symposium on Values in Everyday Life sponsored by the Fritz Thyssen Foundation, Jekyll Island, Georgia, September.

Roy, D. (1952), 'Quota restriction and goldbricking in a machine shop', *American Journal of Sociology*, vol. 57, no. 5 (March), pp. 427–42.

Sandford, C. T. (1977), 'Discussion paper on tax evasion and avoidance', mimeo., Outer Circle Policy Unit, London.

Scott, W. R. (1966), 'Professionals in bureaucracies – areas of conflict', in *Professionalization*, eds H. M. Vollmer and D. L. Mills (Englewood Cliffs, NJ: Prentice-Hall), pp. 264–75.

Smigel, E. O., and Ross, H. L. (1970), *Crimes Against Bureaucracy* (New York: Van Nostrand Reinhold).

Snizek, W. E. (1974), 'Deviant behaviour among blue-collar workers-employees: work-norm violation in the factory', in *Deviant Behaviour: Occupational and Organizational Bases*, ed. C. D. Bryant (Chicago: Rand McNally).

Stirling, A. P. (1968), 'Impersonality and personal morality', in *Contributions to Mediterranean Sociology*, ed. J. G. Peristiany (The Hague: Mouton), pp. 49–64.

Strodtbeck, F. L., and Sussman, M. B. (1955–6), 'Of time, the city and the "one-year guarantee": the relations between watch owners and repairers', *American Journal of Sociology*, vol. 61, pp. 602–9.

Taylor, R. (1980), *The Fifth Estate: Britain's Unions in the Modern World* (London: Pan).

Taylor, L., and Walton, P. (1971), 'Industrial sabotage: motives and meanings', in *Images of Deviance*, ed. S. Cohen (Harmondsworth: Penguin), pp. 219–45.

Terkel, S. (1975), *Working* (London: Wildwood House).

Thomas, M. (1969), *Government Social Survey. The Fire Service and Its Personnel: An Enquiry Undertaken for the Home Office* (London: HMSO).

Tunstall, J. (1962), *The Fishermen* (London: McGibbon & Kee).

US Department of the Treasury (1979), *Estimates of Income Unreported on Individual Tax Returns* (Washington, DC: Internal Revenue Service Publications).

Wiles, P. J. D. (1981), *Die Parallelwirtschaft* Sonderveroffentlichung des Bundesinstituts für Ostwissenschaftliche und Internationale Studien (Cologne: Bois).

Wright, K. G. (1971), *The Shopkeeper's Security Manual* (London: Tom Stacey).

Zeitlin, L. R. (1971), 'Stimulus/response: a little larceny can do a lot for employee morale', *Psychology Today*, vol. 5, pp. 22, 24, 26, 64.

Index